William MacDonald, Jaime Luciano Balmes, y Velez Alejandro dela Torre

Letters to a Sceptic on Religious Matters

William MacDonald, Jaime Luciano Balmes, y Velez Alejandro dela Torre

Letters to a Sceptic on Religious Matters

ISBN/EAN: 9783744704670

Printed in Europe, USA, Canada, Australia, Japan

Cover: Foto ©Thomas Meinert / pixelio.de

More available books at **www.hansebooks.com**

ON

RELIGIOUS MATTERS.

BY

REV. JAMES BALMES,

AUTHOR OF "FUNDAMENTAL PHILOSOPHY," "PROTESTANTISM COMPARED
WITH CATHOLICISM," "THE CRITERION," ETC. ETC.

Translated from the Spanish

BY

REV. WILLIAM M'DONALD, A.B., S.Th.L.

TRANSLATOR OF THE "ESSAYS" OF JOHN DONOSO CORTES,
MARQUIS OF VALDEGAMAS.

DUBLIN:
WILLIAM B. KELLY, 8 GRAFTON STREET.
LONDON: SIMPKIN, MARSHALL, & CO.
1875.

INTRODUCTION.

—◀◦—

THE name of Balmes is well-known in the Republic of
Letters. As philosopher, as polemic, as publicist, he
occupies a distinguished place among the writers of the
present century. Without counting numerous minor
works of his, we have only to mention his "Fundamental Philosophy," his "Protestantism Compared with
Catholicism," and his wonderful "Criterion," in proof
of our assertion. With these books, however, we have
nothing to do at present, as they do not come under
our observation just now. Our remarks will be wholly
confined to another production of his, called "Letters
to a Sceptic."

This volume is not a treatise on, nor an apology of,
religion; it is simply a collection of letters written to
a sceptic in religious matters. It consequently is not a
methodical compilation, nor a fundamental work, nor a

profound disquisition ; it is only, as I said, a number of letters addressed by the author to a friend, who was so unfortunate as not to believe. His intellect was full of errors and prejudice, his heart full of weakness, and his will, though anxious for the good, had not the fortitude necessary to say :—" I believe ; I submit."

It is not an apology, I repeat ; if it were, probably Balmes would not have written it. The sceptic with whom Balmes was dealing, knew the solutions the apologists give to the objections of infidels, but they did not satisfy him. He requires his opponent to go still farther to settle doubts, to remove prejudices, to strengthen the proofs, and shed additional light on the solutions. It is here we discover the difficulty of the undertaking, the keenness of the author's mind, and the merit and utility of the work.

It is easy for an apologist to trace out the plan of a work, laying down his principles, arranging his proofs in order, and making everything bear on the one end he has in view, which is to carry conviction to unprejudiced minds. When a general is besieging a fortress, he can make his preparations according to a fixed plan, and when all is ready, can choose the fittest hour for the assault. So also is it easy to lay down a series of propositions, skilfully disposed, and to refute whatever objections may turn up, in the proper manner, place and

time. An ordinary mind, possessing the requisite knowledge, is able to do all this, as an ordinary general is
capable of carrying a fortress, whose siege presents
no unusual difficulties. The genius is required when
you have to contend with an enemy who observes no
rules, who despises concerted plans, and attacks unex-
pectedly ; the genius is required when you have to deal
with a sceptic who has read everything to be found in
books, and is dissatisfied with it, who is acquainted with
the ordinary solutions, and is still as perplexed as ever,
and who expects you to fill up the void which exists in
his heart, and to dissipate the murky clouds the apologists have been unable to remove from his understanding. In the first case the contest is with ideas, in the
second it is with the man also : in the first it is enough
to bring scientific knowledge into play ; in the second,
you need, besides, a profound acquaintance with the
heart and its infinite folds. A delicacy of touch and
superior tact are indispensable to reach the error, without wounding the susceptibilities of the man, to press the
sceptic, without hurting the citizen, the friend, the man
of culture. You require a penetration of intellect, and
a sweetness of expression such that, yielding as far as
possible, recognising whatever is good and noble in your
adversary, you may softly bear him along to conviction
by quiet argument and persuasion, holding up before

him the truth with all its attractions. This was the task which Balmes had to undertake.

If, then, this work be not an apology, that is, a complete treatise of religion, it is more than that ; it is the complement of all apologies ; ˊit is a model of personal polemics with unbelievers. This sort of contest should be conducted with all possible courtesy, without neglecting the claims of charity, or the interests of religion.

Considered under this aspect, perhaps this is one of the best books which have issued from his prolific pen, for it has a merit very likely unknown to Balmes himself, as he did not aim at it—the merit of originality, and of standing alone in its class. From the dialogues of Plato, and Marcus Tullius, to those of Fénélon, many treatises on various subjects have appeared in the same form ; but their personages were creatures of the imagination, whom the author made say what he pleased. The sceptical opponent of Balmes, on the contrary, is a real man, and the struggle between them, a real struggle. From Cicero to Madame de Sévigné, familiar letters have been written, which might serve as models of this class of composition ; but no one up to Balmes' time had written a series of letters to a sceptic in religious matters.

It is true, the subject is often treated irregularly, and generally the matter of one letter has no connection with that of another. Well, we have already said that in

this book you need not look for a fundamental composition on the motives of credibility; that it is not an
apology of religion, but simply a discussion with a
sceptic. The incoherence of its matter, far from being
a blot on the work, constitutes the essence and the
peculiar form of this class of ecclesiastical literature : it
is not a defect; it is a merit. The fault, if there be any,
is not Balmes' ; it is the fault of the sceptic. The latter
is like a badly-mouthed steed, which chafes at the bits,
or takes them between his teeth, and rushes from side to
side, or, it may be, clears the fence, and dashes into the
fields : the former is like the horseman, who tries to
guide, or bring that steed under control; but he needs
all the strength of rein and arm which superior talent,
solidity of faith, universality of knowledge, and above
all, unlimited charity, can give him, to assert his mastery,
and bring the wanderer back to the broad level road of
discussion. Balmes several times complains of the ebb
and flow of his adversary's vacillations, which puts to the
proof his character for learning, his Christian patience,
and his priestly charity. But we should be thankful for
this trouble and annoyance of his, as they have opened
up for us the view of a new side of his character. In his
other works he had given ample proof of the extensive
range of his privileged intelligence ; here he shows
us the charms of his noble heart. In them he was the

man of learning, who contended with the power of argument, and the force of his intuitive genius; here he is, besides, the Christian who attracts with sweetness, the cultivated man who captivates with his superior manners, the priest who lavishly pours out the balm of charity. And so the "Letters," rather than a book or a treatise, are a mirror and an example : a mirror in which is reflected the weakness of the sceptic's proud reason; an example or proof of how far the humble reason of the believer can reach. In the former, all is doubt, confusion, want of connection; in the latter, all is consequence, firmness, light. The sceptic's arguments, devoid of reasons sufficient to defend a theory, which he has not, or to support a system, which he is incapable of founding, only serve to manifest the disgraceful treason his weak intelligence has committed against the cause of truth ; the apologist, on the contrary, penetrated with the importance of that cause, and ready to sacrifice his existence in it, enters the arena with conviction in his understanding and confidence in his heart, certain to find arguments teeming with reason and common sense, with which to crush his adversary. The sceptic regards not the truth when placed before him ; he regards only himself and his reputation with the world; the apologist forgets self, forgets everything but the eternal truth, whose depositary he is, and whose interests are confided to him ; he is ready to give freely what he has received freely, and his most anxious desire is to become the instrument of communication between an erring soul and the mercy of the Redeemer. Scepticism is not a system; it is a sickness, it is a plague ; Catholic faith is not only the grandest of all systems, but the specific for all intellectual plagues,* and moral diseases of the heart.

---

* The plague of scepticism exists even in Ireland. Catholics in our country seldom become theoretical sceptics ; but Protestants do. If a Catholic gives up the practice of religion, it is because he is buried in some vice. Breaches of the sixth commandment are usually the forerunners of the Catholic layman's indifference, of the Catholic priest's apostasy : the flesh is faith's most formidable enemy. The theoretical sceptics are *logical* Protestants.

I once met one of these in the train to Dublin. We were perfect strangers to each other, but we soon got into conversation, and in the course of it he told me he had been born and reared a Church of England Protestant ; that when he grew up he began to inquire into the grounds of his belief ; that he soon saw it was a great inconsistency to listen to any preacher, or learn religion from any minister, or accept any one's interpretation of the Bible, if he were to enjoy and exercise the right of private judgment, which meant, if it meant anything, that the individual himself was to be the judge in religious matters. He said he soon found it was not he was judging, but that another judged for him ; that the Protestant population saw with the eyes of the minister or its parents ; that the ministers must have imposed on themselves, if they were not impostors on others, for they gave the people the right of judging, but did not allow them to use it ; and that consequently Protestants generally continued to live on in the sect in which they were born, and profess the doctrines imposed on them in youth, without ever calling their truth into question. He met the same difficulty of comprehension in the Trinity and Incarnation, as he did in the Real Presence, and as he rejected the latter, in common

Such are the relations between our author and his adversary ; and if we have heretofore said that this work is not an apology but rather a book of living polemics, in strict conformity with the reality met with in the world, we may now go farther, and call it a type, the type of two distinct reasons. It is the lively image of the proud, and because proud, empty, silly reason of

with Protestants, because he did not comprehend it, he could not see why he should not reject the two former, for the same reason ; and he consequently did reject them.

He then more fully asserted his independence of thought and judgment, and went on from dogma to dogma, from mystery to mystery, expunging everything he could not comprehend, till he reached the bitter end, and called the existence of God, and of his own soul, into question. He assured me he was sorry to have to take this step ; that he would willingly believe if he could ; that he knew if the truth were anywhere, it must be in the Catholic Church ; and that if he saw it, he would accept it at once, and was prepared to sacrifice all considerations to embrace it. He was a young man of great intelligence, and he had read a good deal. I did what I could with him at the time, but apparently without success. We bid good-bye at the station. I was on my way to collect for a new church which was building in our parish, and in making my domiciliary visits I chanced to stumble again on my railway companion, in a house in Thomas Street, where he discovered the object of my journey to Dublin. On the following day I had occasion to return to the same house, and I then found, to my agreeable surprise, that he had left a subscription for me with the lady of the establishment, expressing a hope that he should meet me some time again, and hold further converse with me. Poor fellow ! I have prayed for him, and others more worthy than I have prayed for him also, and who knows whether God has not been moved by his charity of heart and sincerity of mind, to bestow on him the greatest of all His gifts —the gift of Faith ?—(TRANSLATOR).

the sceptic, and the animated reflection of the humble,
and because humble, prudent, powerful, creative reason
of the apologist of the Christian priest. And consequently, rather than a book of polemics of doubtful
result, it may be regarded as the victorious demonstration of the truth of our faith, and of the sanctity and
purity of our religion.

In achieving this victory, Balmes does not triumph
solely by his superiority of intellect, nor his great scientific knowledge; his triumph is secured by what he
himself appreciated much more by the solidity and
firmness communicated to him by the calm possession
of the truth. Learning, talent, clearness, contribute
largely; but the victory after all, is the victory of
faith, of humility, of charity.

On seeing the picture Racine drew of the interior man
struggling with himself, the carnal man with the spiritual,
Louis XIV. is said to have exclaimed : "Ah ! I know
those two men well ! " So, on beholding the noble figure
of Balmes struggling with the sceptic, every fair, rational
being should exclaim : " This man is more than learned,
he is an apostle of the Gospel, the propounder of a
grand theory, the professor of the truth." And if, fortunately, this book should fall into the hands of a
sceptic, when he sees the vivid portrait of the mists and
shadows of his reason, the weakness of his will, and all

his uncertain fluctuations, contained in it, he must say to himself :—" That agitated existence looks so like my unsettled spirit !—that sceptic am I ! "

ALEJANDRO DE LA TORRE VELEZ, D.D.,
*Canon of the Cathedral of Salamanca, and Professor
of Sacred Scripture, &c., &c.*

SALAMANCA, *May 1st,* 1875.

CONTENTS.

LETTERS TO A SCEPTIC.

I.

Scepticism, Religious and Philosophical.

MY ESTEEMED FRIEND,—You have marked out a
difficult task for me in your letter when you speak
about scepticism. This is the problem of the age—the
capital and absorbing question, which rises above all
others, like the lofty cypress among the lowly brush-
wood. What do I think of scepticism? what conception do I form of the actual state of the human mind,
infected as it is so deeply by this disease? what are the
probable results it must entail on the cause of religion?
All this you desire me to tell you; to these questions
you require a formal and satisfactory answer, and add,
"that perhaps the darkness of your intellect shall be
thus dissipated, and you disposed to enter anew under
the rule of faith."

You tell me you have an objection to my answers
being too dogmatical and decisive, and throw out a
charitable hint "that it is well for one to divest himself

A

for a moment of his own convictions, and endeavour to make philosophical discussion partake as little as possible of the immobility of religious doctrines." I could not help smiling when I read these words, and saw how mistaken you are as regards the true state of my mind ; for you thought you should find me as dogmatical in philosophy as in religion. I think, through sheer force of declamation against the slavery of the Catholics' intellect, infidels and Protestants have in a great measure attained their wicked object, which is to persuade the incautious that our submission to the authority of the Church in matters of faith, impedes exercise of mind, and so completely destroys liberty of examination, even in branches unconnected with religion, that we are incapable of embracing an elevated and independent philosophy. Thus we have generally the misfortune of being judged without being known, and condemned without being heard. The authority exercised by the Catholic Church over the intellect of the faithful by no means curtails the just and reasonable liberty expressed in those words of the Sacred Text—*He delivered up the world to the disputes of men.*

I will even venture to add, that Catholics, certain of the truth in the matter of most importance to them, can engage in purely philosophical questions with a more calm and tranquil mind than infidels and sceptics, as there exists between them the same difference as between an observer who contemplates the terrestrial and celestial phenomena from a position secure from all danger, and another who is compelled to make his observations from a fragile plank abandoned to the mercy of the waves. When will the enemies of religion comprehend that submission to legitimate authority has no servility in it, and that the homage paid to dogmas revealed by God is not a base slavery, but the most noble exercise we can make of our freedom ? We too examine ; we too doubt ; we too launch forth on the sea of investigation ; but we never lose sight of our faith, which is our compass by day and our polar star by night for the proper direction of our course.

You speak of the weakness of our mind, of the uncertainty of human knowledge, of the necessity of discussing with that modest reserve inspired by the feeling of one's own debility ; but what—really are not these reflections the most eloquent apology of our conduct? Is not this the very thing we are continually insisting on when we establish and prove that it is useful, prudent, discreet, nay indispensable, to live subject to a rule? Now, my esteemed friend, as the opportunity presents itself, and straightforwardness requires us to speak with all sincerity and frankness, I must tell you that, except in religious matters, I am inclined to believe you do not carry your scepticism as far as he whom you considered so dogmatical.

There was a time when the prestige of certain names, the hallucination produced by the aureola encircling their brows, my want of experience of the scientific world, and above all, the fire of youth, eager to devour any noble and seducing fuel, had given me a lively faith in Science, and made me anxiously look forward to the happy day

when I should be introduced into her temple, to be initiated in her profound secrets, even if only as the least of
her adepts.   Oh ! that was the most beautiful illusion the
human soul could labour under.   The life of the learned
appeared to me to be that of demi-gods on earth ; and
I recollect that more than once I fixed my eyes with
infantile envy on the roof which sheltered a man of
moderate talents, but whom I in my inexperience
regarded as a giant.   To penetrate the principles of
things, to lift the thick veil which covers the secrets of
nature, to ascend to superior regions, discovering new
worlds which escape the view of the profane, to breathe
in an atmosphere of purest light, where the spirit could
divest itself of the body, anticipating the enjoyment
of the delights of a new and glorious future—these I
believed to be the advantages to be reaped from science.
I looked on the learned as wading in this felicity ; the
applause and glory with which they were surrounded
coming in at the end to solace them during the fleeting
moments in which, descending from their celestial excur-
sions, they deigned to set foot on earth again.

Their investigations, I said to myself, about the
beautiful, the sublime, good taste, and the passions, will
supply them with infallible rules for producing in the
minds of their audience or readers the effect they desire ;
their studies in logic and ideology will give them a clear
knowledge of the operations of the mind, and of the
manner of combining and guiding them to come at the
truth in every class of subjects.   The mathematical and
physical sciences should rend asunder the veil which

covers the secrets of nature, and the entire creation, with all its mysteries and wonders, shall be displayed to the eyes of the learned, as a rare and precious picture is unfolded to the gaze of favoured spectators. Psychology will give them a complete idea of the human soul, of its nature, of its relations with the body, of how its action is exercised on it, and how it receives the various impressions from it. The moral, social, and political sciences will display to them in a vast picture the admirable harmony of the moral world, the laws of the progress and perfection of society, and supply them with infallible rules for governing well. In a word, I imagined science was a talisman that wrought marvels without number, and whoever was so fortunate as to possess it, was raised to an immense height above the vulgar herd of miserable humanity. Vain illusion, which only too soon began to fade, and in the end became divested of its charms, like a floweret dried up by the ardent rays of the sun.

The more golden my dreams had been, and consequently the more eager I was to know what reality they contained, the more bitter the lesson I received, and the sooner came the hour of discovering my mistake. Scarcely had I entered on those subjects in which some important questions are examined, when I began to feel an undefinable restlessness because I did not feel myself sufficiently enlightened for what I read or heard. I smothered in the depths of my soul these thoughts, which would incessantly rise, without my being able to prevent them ; and I endeavoured to silence my discontent by flattering myself with the hope that it was reserved for the future to have my desires fully satisfied. "It must be necessary," I said, "to see first the whole body of doctrine, of which you know but the first rudiments at present, and then, undoubtedly, you shall discover the light and certainty you feel the want of now."

With difficulty could I have been persuaded, at the time, that men whose lives were consumed in immense labours, and who offered to the world the fruit of their toil with such security, had learned, in the serious subjects on which they employed themselves, little more than the art of speaking with facility for or against an opinion, creating a great noise with hollow words and pompous discourses. I attributed all my difficulties, all my doubts, and all my scruples, to my dulness in comprehending the sense of what such respectable authors told me, and for this reason the desire of knowing the art of learning took possession of me. The ancient alchemists did not employ more pains in search of the philosopher's stone, nor modern politicians in the discovery of the equilibrium of power, than I in pursuit of that wonderful art ; and Aristotle, with his infinite sectaries, and Raymond Lullus, and Descartes, and Malabranche, and Locke, and Condillac, and I know not how many others, did not suffice to satisfy my ardour. One occupied and confounded me with a thousand rules about syllogisms ; another looked on *judgments* and *propositions* as of more importance; another preferred clearness and exactness of perception ; another overwhelmed me with precepts about method; another led me by the hand to the investigation of the origin of ideas, but was sure to leave me in greater darkness than ever ; in fine, I was not long in remarking that each one moved in his favourite path, and they would surely turn the head of whoever should persist in following them.

These gentlemen, I said, who call themselves the directors of the human intellect, do not understand each other. This is the tower of Babel, in which each one speaks his own tongue ; with this difference, that *there* pride entailed the confusion as a punishment, whilst here the very confusion serves to increase their pride ; each one proclaiming himself the only legitimate master, and that all the rest have but apocryphal titles to the right of teaching. I also remarked that nearly the same occurred in all the other branches of human learning ; and so I found it was absolutely necessary to banish for ever the beautiful illusion I had formed about the sciences. These disenchantments had prepared my mind for a real revolution ; and though vacillating at first, I decided in the end on declaring against my scientific rulers ; and raising a banner in my intellect, I inscribed on it—*Down with scientific authority.*

I had nothing wherewith to substitute the rule I was just after destroying, for if those respectable philosophers knew little about the deep questions whose solution I was in search of, I knew much less, for I knew nothing at all. You may imagine it was rather painful to me to consummate such a revolution ; and I sometimes even accused myself of ingratitude, when, carrying out the principle of destruction to its ultimate consequences, I was forced to exile such respectable parties as Plato, Aristotle, Descartes, Malebranche, Leibnitz, Locke, and Condillac. Anarchy was the necessary result of such a step ; but I willingly resigned myself to it, sooner than summon again to the government of my intellect those gentlemen who had deceived me so. Besides, having once experienced the pleasure of liberty, I had no intention of staining my triumph by passing through the Caudine forks.

My mind, pressed as it was by the thirst after truth, could not remain in a state of complete inactivity, and so I began to seek for truth with greater pains, as I could not believe that man, while in this world, is condemned to ignorance of it. Undoubtedly, you will believe that a universal scepticism was the immediate result of my revolution, and that, concentrating myself within my own interior, I doubted of the existence of the surrounding world, and even of my own body; and, fearing lest my whole being should escape from me, and I should, as it were by enchantment, find myself reduced to nothing, I grasped hastily at the reasoning of Descartes—*Ego cogito, ergo sum : I think, therefore I exist.* But nothing of the sort, my dear friend ; for though I had some inclination for his philosophy, I was not a fanatical admirer of the philosopher ; and, without much reflection, I became convinced that to doubt of everything was to deprive one's self of the most precious part of human reason, which is common sense. I had some knowledge of the axiom or enthymema of Descartes, and of other similar propositions or principles;

but I was always under the impression that I was just as certain that I existed as that I thought, and my conviction of the existence of motion, of my own body, of the impression of the senses, of the world which surrounded me, could not be stronger; and so, reserving to myself the right of feigning that doubt for a few moments when leisure and humour should permit, I remained in quiet possession of all my former convictions and beliefs, save the so-called philosophical ones. As regards these, I was then, I have been, and I shall be, inexorable. Philosophy unceasingly proclaims examination, evidence, demonstration: be it so; but let her know, at least, that as long as we are men, and nothing more, we shall regulate our convictions, as we ought, by following the inspirations of common sense; but in the moments in which we become philosophers, which in most men's cases are few and far between, we will incessantly claim the right of examination; we will require evidence; we will demand dry demonstration. Whoever reigns in the name of a principle must inevitably resign himself to suffer all the irreverence that springs from the consequences.

It is clear that, in this universal shipwreck of my philosophical convictions, my religious ones rode safely at anchor. I had acquired them by other means; they presented themselves to me with other titles, and above all, they tended to direct my conduct, to make me not wise, but good; and consequently my pyrrhonic susceptibility was not excited against them. Even more; far from feeling inclined to separate from the belief and

convictions with which I had been inspired in my
infancy, I became convinced of their necessity, and even
of the interest I had in preserving them; for I began
to regard them as the only plank of salvation in this
boisterous sea of human cavillations.   The desire of
clinging to the Catholic faith increased, when, occupying myself sometimes with a spirit of complete independence, in the examination of the transcendent
questions philosophy proposes for solution, I found
myself surrounded on all sides by dense darkness,
unable to discover more light than a few doubtful rays,
which, instead of illuminating my path, but served to
render visible the profundity of the abyss on whose
brink I was standing.

For this reason did I preserve the Catholic faith in
the depths of my soul, as a treasure of inestimable
value; for this reason, when tortured in sight of the
nothingness of the science of man, and when doubt
appeared to be taking possession of my whole mind,
causing the entire universe to disappear from before my
eyes, as fade from the view of the spectators the false
illusions with which a clever juggler might have entertained them for a few moments, would I cast a glance
at my faith, and the sole recollection of it was sufficient
to comfort and sustain me.

On running over the questions which, like unfathomable seas, surround the principles of morality; on examining the incomprehensible problems of ideology and
metaphysics; on casting a glance over the mysteries
of history, and the scruples of the art of criticism; on

contemplating humanity in its actual existence, and in
the dark secrets of its future, melancholy thoughts
would sometimes flit through my brain, like unknown
monsters, which poke out their heads and frighten
travellers on solitary shores ; but I had faith in Providence, and Providence saved me. Here is how I
reasoned to fortify myself, trusting to grace that my
weak efforts might not be sterile :—" If you cease to be
a Catholic, you will not certainly become a Protestant,
or Jew, or Mohammedan, or idolater ; you shall then be
into Deism in one spring. Then you shall find yourself
with one God, but you shall know nothing about your
origin or destiny ; nothing about the incomprehensible
mysteries you see and feel within yourself and all
humanity ; nothing about the existence of rewards and
punishments in the other world ; nothing about the
other life, or the immortality of the soul ; nothing about
the motives Providence could have had in condemning
His creatures to so many sufferings on earth, without
giving them any knowledge which might console them,
or any hope of a better fate ; you shall know nothing of
the great catastrophes the human lineage has suffered,
still suffers, and shall yet suffer ; in a word, you shall
nowhere find the action of Providence, and consequently
shall not find God, and so must doubt of His existence,
if you do not decidedly embrace Atheism. Without
the God of the universe, the world is the offspring of
chance, and chance is a word without meaning, and
nature is an enigma, and the human soul an illusion,
and moral relations nothing, and morality itself a lie.

Logical, necessary, inflexible consequence; fatal term, which man cannot contemplate without a shudder; dark and unfathomable abyss, which cannot be approached without horror and dread!"

In this way did I measure the road I should inevitably pursue, once separated from the Catholic faith, if I should attempt to continue in the philosophical examination, deducing consequences from the principles I would have established at the moment of my defection. I had no wish to reach such stupidity; I had no desire to commit suicide by destroying my intellectual and moral existence, and extinguishing at a blast the only lamp that could illumine me through the short course of life. Thus have I a great want of confidence in the science of man, but profound religious faith. You may call it pusillanimity, or by whatever name you please; but I do not believe I shall be sorry for my resolution when I shall find myself on the brink of the grave.

There are in the regions of science, as well as in the paths of practice, certain rules of judgment and prudence, from which a man should never wander. Everything that struggles with the cry of common sense and the voice of nature, for the purpose of indulging in vain cavillations, is foreign to the prudence, as it is contrary to the principles, of sound sense. On this account, a system of universal scepticism, even in purely philosophical matters, should be condemned, without it being necessary, for all that, to blindly embrace the opinions of this or that school. But where sobriety in the use of reason particularly suits is in religious matters;

for these being of a high order, and galling in many
points to the irregular inclinations of the heart, as soon
as reason begins to cavil and subtilize, a man finds himself in a labyrinth in which he pays dearly for his presumption and pride. The intellect falls into a weariness
and indescribable prostration the moment it rises up
against Heaven ; as history tells us of that arm which, on
the instant it was extended to a sacred object, was struck
with paralysis. And mark it well! religious scepticism
is found in the midst of earthly prosperity alone ; it
takes up its residence tranquilly in man only when full
of life and health ; when he regards as a distant eventu-
ality the supreme moment when it shall be imperative
on the spirit to divest itself of this mortal body, and pass
to another life. But the moment this existence is in
danger, when sickness comes, as the herald of death,
to announce to him that the terrible passage is not far
distant ; when an unforeseen risk warns us we are hanging
by a thread over the abyss of eternity, then scepticism
ceases to be at all satisfactory ; the false security it
produced a little before, turns into a cruel and torturing
uncertainty, full of remorse, horror, and dread. Then
scepticism ceases to be pleasant, and becomes terrible ;
and in this mortal prostration a man seeks the light,
and finds it not ; he calls on faith, and faith answers
not ; he invokes God, and God attends not to his tardy
invocations.

And to experience what a cruel torment of the soul
scepticism is, one does not require to wait for those formidable moments when man fixes his fearful gaze on

the darkness of an uncertain future. In the ordinary course of life, in the midst of the most common events, he feels the poison of the viper he is nourishing in his bosom, fall drop by drop on his afflicted heart. There are moments in which pleasures weary, the world disgusts, life becomes heavy, and existence trails along over a time that advances with sluggish step. A profound weariness takes possession of the soul, an indescribable ill-humour tortures and torments. It is not overpowering grief corroding the heart; it is not a sadness subduing the spirit and forcing from it painful sighs through means of torturing recollections. It is a passion which has nothing lively or sharp in it; it is a mortal langour and a disgust of everything that surrounds us; it is a painful stupidity of all the faculties, like that restless stupor which in certain ailments announces a dangerous crisis. For what purpose am I in the world, man says to himself. What advantages do I derive from having emerged from the state of nothingness? What can I lose by departing from the sight of a world parched up for me, of a sun which shines not for me? To-day is insipid as yesterday, and to-morrow will be more so than to-day. My soul seeks after enjoyment and enjoys not; it is avaricious of happiness and does not obtain it, exhausting itself like a lamp that dies out for want of sustenance. Have you not, my dear friend, often felt this torment of the fortunate ones of the world— this gnawing worm of those who pretend to be superior to all others? Did that movement of desperation which

presents itself to man as the only remedy for so insupportable an evil never raise its head in your breast?
Well, believe me, one of its sad causes is scepticism—
that vacuum of the soul which disturbs and torments
her—that dreadful absence of all faith, of all hope—
that uncertainty regarding God and nature, the origin
and end of man—a vacuum all the more sensible, as it
seizes on souls exercised in the art of reasoning through
the study of the sciences, excited in all their mental
faculties by a mad literature, which only aims at producing effect, though that effect be an electric shock or
a galvanic convulsion—souls that feel all their passions
kindled and sharpened by a crafty world, which speaks
to them in all languages, and with its infinity of resources excites them in a thousand ways.

There you have, my esteemed friend, what I think of
scepticism and its effects on the human mind. I regard
it as one of the characteristic plagues of the age, and
one of the most terrible chastisements God has inflicted
on the human race.

How can an evil of such magnitude be remedied? I
know not; but what I *will* presume to say is, that its
progress can be retarded; and I am inclined to believe
that this must be done, at least for the interests of
society, the order and well-being of the family, and the
repose and quiet of the individual. Scepticism has not
fallen on a sudden on the civilised world; it is a gan-
grene which has spread slowly; slowly too must it be
remedied; and it will be one of the most stupendous
prodigies of the right hand of the Omnipotent, if the

course of many generations be not necessary to effect its cure.

From this you may perceive, my esteemed friend, that I do not form illusions regarding the true state of things, and whilst I float in the midst of the waves on a plank that shall bear me to a port of safety, do not lose sight of the destruction that exists around me. I do not forget the dreadful catastrophe that has befallen the mind of man, through a fatal concurrence of circumstances during the last three centuries.

How is it, you say, that God permits humanity to fluctuate in the midst of so many errors regarding the very points which interest it most?

This difficulty is not limited to the divine permission with regard to the dissenting sects, but extends to all religions; and as these have been many and extravagant since the human race wandered from the purity of the primitive traditions, the objection embraces universal history, and to require its solution is nothing less than to demand the key to the explanation of the secrets found in such abundance in the history of the children of Adam.

This is not a subject which lends itself to a brief explanation, if the little which weak man can reach in so profound a mystery can be called an explanation. I shall, however, treat of it in another letter, now that the present has assumed greater proportions than were desirable.

You have now my opinion on religious scepticism, and the compatibility of Catholic faith with a prudent distrust in the systems of philosophers. Many, perhaps, will not be pleased with this way of regarding things; experience, however, shows the mind is perfectly at home in this state, and a certain degree of scientific scepticism renders religious faith more light and tolerable. If I were not detained in that faith by the authority of a Church which counts more than eighteen centuries of duration, in that faith which has, in confirmation of its divinity, its preservation through so many storms, the blood of innumerable martyrs, the fulfilment of the prophecies, infinite miracles, the sanctity of its doctrine, the sublimity of its dogmas, the purity of its morals, its admirable harmony with everything that is beautiful, and grand, and sublime, the ineffable benefits it has showered on the family and society, the fundamental change it has realised in favour of humanity wherever it has been established, and the degradation and debasement I find where it does not hold sway—if, I say, I had not this imposing collection of motives to preserve me addicted to my faith, I would yet make an effort to avoid separating from it, if only that I might not lose my peace of mind.

Cast a glance around, my esteemed friend, and you shall behold nothing on any side but horrid shoals, desert regions, and inhospitable shores. This is the only asylum for sad humanity; let whoever wishes surrender himself to the fury of the waves, I will not leave this blessed dry land on which Providence has placed me.

If some day or other, fatigued and wearied by contending with the tempest, you approach this fortunate shore, happy shall your humble servant be if he can be of any service to you by reaching you a friendly hand. Till then he has the pleasure of subscribing himself your attached friend,

J. B.

II.

Difficulty of the Multiplicity of Religions.

MY ESTEEMED FRIEND,—I am going to discharge the debt contracted in my last, by answering your difficulty about the divine permission regarding so many different religions as exist. This is one of the arguments the enemies of religion unceasingly bring forth, and are accustomed to propose with such an air of security and triumph, that one would think it alone was sufficient to destroy our religion entirely. Do not imagine I am try-ing to escape the difficulty by shrinking from looking it straight in the face, or to diminish its force by covering it with a veil to disguise it. Far from it; for, on the contrary, I think the best way to surmount it, is to present it in all its magnitude. I will add that I do not deny there is in this a profound mystery; nor do I flatter myself with being able to give entirely satis-factory reasons in answer to your difficulty; for I am intimately convinced this is one of the incomprehen-sible secrets of Providence, which it is not given to man to penetrate. However, I think it appears to many more knotty than it should ; and so far am I from believing it in any way destroys or weakens the Catholic religion, that, on the contrary, I think we can discover in its very force a new proof of the truth of our belief.

It is a fact that the existence of many religions is a grievous evil. This we Catholics acknowledge before all others, for it is we who hold there is but one true religion ; that faith in Jesus Christ is necessary for eternal salvation ; that it is an absurdity to say that all religions are equally pleasing to God ; in fine, it is we who give such importance to the unity of religious teaching, that we consider the alteration of any of our dogmas an immense calamity. From this you may see it is not my intention to attenuate in the least degree the force of the difficulty, by concealing the gravity of the evil on which it rests; and I consider this evil greater than you who raise the objection. No one surpasses, or even equals, the Catholic in confessing the immensity of that calamity of the human race ; because his creed compels him to regard it as the greatest of all. Those who consider all religions false; those who imagine that in any of them man can make himself agreeable to God, and gain eternal salvation; those who, while professing one religion, do not at the same time profess the principle of universal charity without distinction of race, can contemplate with less pain those aberrations of humanity ; but this cannot be done by Catholics, in whose belief there is no truth or salvation outside the Church, and who are obliged, besides, to regard all men as their brethren, and desire, from their inmost heart, that they may open their eyes to the light of faith, and enter on the road of eternal salvation. It is easy to see I do not shrink from the weight of the difficulty, but rather endeavour to paint it in lively colours. I am now going to examine its value in a point of view in which, unfortunately, it is not generally considered.

There is a principle of logic which says—*Quod nimis probat, nihil probat: what proves too much, proves nothing ;* which signifies, that when any argument leads not only to the conclusion we desire, but to some other evidently false, it is of no weight even in proof of what we intended. The reason on which this principle is founded is very clear : what leads to a false result must be false itself. Hence, no matter how specious an argument may be, no matter what apparent solidity it may have, from the very fact of leading to a false conclusion, it supplies us with an infallible sign that it either involves some false statement in the propositions of which it is composed, or some defect of reasoning in their connection, and consequently in the deduction to which it brings us. If, for example, I try to demonstrate that the sum of the angles of a triangle is greater than a right angle, and my demonstration proves it greater than two right angles, it will be worth nothing, because it proves too much, for it proves an impossibility; and this result will ever be an infallible sign that there is some defect in my demonstration, so that I can never employ it to prove anything.

Other examples : if, after examining an ancient manuscript, I reject it as apocryphal, and for so doing assign a rule of criticism from which it would result that others, whose authenticity admits of no doubt, should be involved in the condemnation, it is clear I should lay aside my argument, certain of its being ill-conceived; for it proves too much, and consequently proves nothing. If, on examining the veracity of a traveller's narrative, I assert we should credit his word, alleging in support of my assertion certain reasons from which it can be inferred we should also give credit to other narratives known to be false, my mode of reasoning would be defective, because it would prove too much.

Pardon me, my dear friend, if I have dwelt on the explanation of this principle, which serves in thousands of cases, and of which I intend to make use in the present question; and from this you may know I do not regard all rules for reasoning aright as useless, and my want of confidence in philosophers does not extend to everything to be found in philosophy.

Let us apply these principles. The multiplicity of religions is objected to us Catholics, as if the difficulty embarrassed us alone; as if all those who profess any religion, be it what it may, should not put up with all the annoyance that can result from it. In fact, if the multiplicity of religions prove anything against the faith of the Catholic, it proves it against that of all; so that, not only ours falls to the ground, but as many as exist or have existed. Besides, if the difficulty raised against the permission of this evil signifies anything, it is nothing less than a complete negation of all Providence, that

is, atheism, or a negation of God.   The reason is obvious.
The evil of the multiplicity of religions is undeniable;
it is before our eyes at the present time, and all history
bears irrefragable testimony that it has existed from a
very remote period ; if then, it be denied that Providence
can permit it, the existence of Providence, or God, must
also be denied.

You may infer from this, that the permission of a
multitude of religions is a difficulty which embarrasses
the Catholic and Protestant, the Mussulman and idolater,
the man who admits any religion whatever, as well as
him who professes none, provided he does not deny the
existence of God.   For example, if a Mohammedan comes
to me with his Koran and Prophet, pretending his religion is the true one, and has been revealed by God Himself, I can raise this objection to him :—" If your creed
be true, how is it God permits so many others?   If
those who live in a religion different from yours are
miserably deceived, why does God permit all the
countries in the world except yours to be deprived of
the light ? "   It is impossible for whoever does not deny
the existence of God not to admit His bounty and providence ; for a wicked God—a God who takes no care of
the work He Himself has created, is an absurdity which
can have no place in a well-organized head ; and I will
even make bold to say, it is less impossible to conceive
atheism in all its horror and blackness, than the opinion
which admits a blind, negligent, and wicked God.   Supposing, then, the existence of a God of bounty and
providence, the difficulty proposed above holds good ;

how does He permit the human race to err so sadly in that most serious and important affair—religion? If we be told that God is satisfied with the homage of the creature, no matter what belief he professes, or in what form he offers Him the tribute of the expression of his gratitude and respect, we will ask, how is it possible that, in the eyes of a Being of infinite truth, truth and error could be quite indifferent? How is it possible to conceive that, in the eyes of infinite sanctity, sanctity and abomination can be indifferent? How is it possible that a God infinitely wise, infinitely good, infinitely provident, should not have provided His creatures with some means of arriving at the truth, and knowing the manner most pleasing to Him of presenting their homage and supplications? If the various religions had only some slight differences between them, the absurdity of regarding them all as good would be less repugnant; but it must be recollected that almost all are diametrically opposed in most important points; that some admit one God, and others adore many; that some recognise free-will in man, and others reject it; that some establish the creation as a fundamental principle, and others are pleased with the eternity of matter. Bring to mind the enormous variety of their respective dogmas, of their codes of morals, of their forms of worship, and say if it be not the greatest absurdity to suppose that God could be satisfied with adorations so contradictory.

You see, my esteemed friend, how applicable to this question is the dialectic principle I mentioned above; and how a difficulty, which some persist in directing exclusively against Catholics, does not regard them alone, but all men who profess any sort of religion— even pure deists themselves. What should be done in such cases? How can difficulties so great be obviated? Here is the path which, in my opinion, a sensible and prudent man should pursue; here the manner in which he should argue conformably with reason :—" The evil exists, it is true; but that Providence also exists, is no less certain; apparently these are two things which cannot co-exist; but, as you know for certain they do exist, this apparent contradiction is not sufficient to make you deny their existence. What you should do, then, is to seek a means of removing this contradiction, and in case you cannot possibly discover one, attribute this impossibility to your own inability."

If we pay attention, we shall see that in the most ordinary affairs of life we make use of a like train of reasoning. We find ourselves in presence of two facts whose co-existence seems impossible, for in our judgment they exclude and repel each other; but for all that, do we obstinately deny that the two facts do exist, when we have motives sufficient to give us entire certainty of it? Certainly not. "This to me is a mystery," we say; "I do not understand it; it appears impossible it could be so, yet I see it is." We, then, if the matter be worth the trouble, seek for a reason to explain the mystery; but if we cannot succeed, we do not therefore believe ourselves justified in rejecting those facts, of the existence of which we cannot doubt, no matter how contradictory they may appear.

From this you may see, my esteemed friend, that an inconceivable blindness often prevents us from employing, in the examination of the most important religious truths, those prudential rules of which we avail ourselves in our most ordinary affairs ; and we reject as offensive to our independence and the dignity of our reason that line of conduct we do not hesitate to follow in the direction and arrangement of the most insignificant business.

So impressed on my mind are these principles, inspired by sound logic and prudence, that they serve me in many other difficulties, and do not suffer me to become disturbed at sight of the obscurity I discover in them, and which in my weakness I am unable to remove. What considerations more dreadful than those suggested by the terrible difficulty of reconciling human liberty with the dogmas of prescience and predestination ? If a man attend to nothing but the certainty and infallibility of the divine prescience, he becomes horror-stricken; he is affrighted at the bare consideration of the immutability of destiny ; the blood freezes in his veins at the thought that before he was born God knew what his destiny would be ; but as soon as he recovers from the terror and desperation which had seized him, and reflects for an instant, he finds sufficient motives for quieting himself: he here discovers a mystery, fearful it is true, but one which does not depress or dispirit him.

"Should this mystery," he says, "which I do not comprehend, alter my conduct in any way, and make me careless about doing good, or negligent in avoiding evil ? Is it prudent or logical to think that, let me do what I may, what God has foreseen shall ever take place, and consequently all my efforts to follow the path of virtue are in vain ? No; and why ? Because what proves too much, proves nothing ; for if this reasoning would hold good, it would follow I should not take care of my temporal affairs either ; for, after all, nothing can become of them but what God has foreseen. Hence it would follow I should not eat to support life, nor cover myself from the inclemency of the weather, nor walk with care when passing along the edge of a precipice, nor use medicine when I feel ill, nor get out of the way when a runaway horse is dashing right on top of me, nor try to escape from a house when tumbling down about me, and hundreds of things of this sort : that is, to follow such a rule would deprive me of common sense, and make me a complete madman. Hence the rule is false ; hence it is of no service to me; and what I have to do is to leave to God His incomprehensible mysteries, and conduct myself like a sensible, judicious, and prudent man."

To this are most of the difficulties raised against religion reduced. Viewed superficially, they present a formidable front ; examined closely, and touched with the wand of reason and common sense, they disappear like fleeting phantoms.

Let us now see if we can discover why God permits such a multitude of religions—such a shapeless mass of errors in a point of such interest to the human race. I am not able to discover the explanation of this mystery,

except in another mystery—in the Roman Catholic
dogma of the prevarication of Adam, and the conse-
quent degeneration of his posterity, sin and its conse-
quent punishment—*darkness in the intellect, corruption in
the will:* this is the formula for solving the problem.
Turn over history, consult philosophy; they will tell
you nothing to enlighten you, unless they appeal to this
fact, mysterious and obscure, but, as Paschal says, less
incomprehensible to man than man himself without it.

This is the only key to the enigma; by it alone can
we explain those lamentable aberrations of the greater
part of humanity; there is no other means of reaching
a plausible explanation of this immense calamity, and
many others which affect the unfortunate offspring of
the first prevaricators. The dogma is incomprehensible,
it is true; but dare to reject it, and the world becomes
a chaos; the history of humanity is nothing but a series
of catastrophes without reason or object, and the life
of the individual a chain of miseries; and you shall
nowhere discover anything but evil—evil without counterpoise or compensation; all ideas of order and justice
become confounded in your mind, and rejecting the
creation, you end by denying God.

On the contrary, establish this dogma as a corner-
stone, and the edifice rises spontaneously, and a vivid
light is cast on the pages of the history of the human
race. You discover profound reasons and adorable
designs where once you saw nothing but injustice or
chance, and the series of events from the creation to
our days is spread out before your eyes like a magni-

ficent painting, in which you find the works of an inflexible justice and an inexhaustible mercy combined and harmonised in the ineffable plan traced by the finger of Infinite Wisdom.

If, then, you ask me why so considerable a portion of humanity sits in the darkness and shadow of death, I will tell you that our first father wished to be as God, knowing good and evil; that his sin has been transmitted to all his posterity, and that, in just punishment of his pride, the human race is afflicted with blindness. This great calamity does not require we should point out any other source for it than the common one of all the others which afflict us. The terrible words which followed the calling of Adam, when God said to him, *Adam, where art thou?* vibrate sadly even yet, after so many centuries. And in all the events of history, in the whole course of life, the terrible flash of the sword of fire placed at the entrance of Paradise is to be seen. *The sweat of the brow* and *death* are apparent in every direction. Nowhere shall you find that things follow an even course ; the formidable standard of punishment and expiation shall ever meet your gaze.

The more one meditates on these truths, the more profound shall he find them. *In sudore vultus tui vesceris pane: you shall eat your bread in the sweat of your brow,* God said to our first father ; and in this sweat does his whole posterity eat it. Examine that penalty, and make the application to as many objects as you please, and you shall find none excepted from it. *Man does not live on bread alone, but on every word that proceedeth from*

the mouth of God; the terrible penalty, then, is not
verified solely with respect to the morsel of bread with
which we sustain ourselves, but in everything that con-
cerns our perfection. Man advances in nothing without
painful toil; he never reaches the point he desires without many wanderings, which fatigue him; in everything
is it realised that the earth, instead of fruit, gives him
briars and thistles. Has he to discover a truth? He
shall not come at it except after many extravagant
errors. Has he to bring an art to perfection? Hundreds
and hundreds of useless attempts will fatigue those who
occupy themselves with it, and it is fortunate if the
grandchildren reap the fruit of what their grandfathers
sowed. Has the social and political organisation of a
State to be improved? Bloody revolutions precede the
desired regeneration; and the unfortunate country, after
prolonged sufferings, is frequently left in a worse state
than it groaned in before. Has the civilisation and
culture of one people to be communicated to another?
The inoculation must be effected with fire and sword;
entire generations are sacrificed to obtain a result which
but very distant ones shall see. You shall not find
genius without great misfortunes, nor the glory of a
people without torrents of blood and tears, nor the
exercise of virtue without painful trials, nor heroism
without persecution: the beautiful, the grand, the sublime, is not attained without protracted toil, nor preserved without exhausting labour: the law of punishment and expiation is met with in some terrible form
in all directions. This is the history of man and

humanity—a history sad, indeed, but incontestable, authentic, and written in fatal letters wherever the children of Adam have imprinted their footsteps.

I know not why, my esteemed friend, this point of view has not attracted more attention, or why philosophers should be scandalised at the dogmas of religion, which are found in such harmony with what the annals of all times and daily experience continually proclaim. The prevarication and degeneration of the human race is the secret to deciphering the enigmas of life and the destiny of man ; and if to this be added the adorable mystery of the Reparation, purchased with the blood of the Son of God, there is formed the most admirable system imaginable—a system so sublime that at the very first glance it manifests its divine origin. A combination so astonishing could not spring from human head ; finite intelligence could not conceive a plan so vast and stupendous, in which one secret is so interlaced with another, that, from the depths of their awful obscurity, they send forth rays of vivid light to illustrate and solve all the questions constantly raised by philosophy about the origin and destiny of man.

This is the principal part of what I had to say about the difficulties you proposed. I know not whether you shall be entirely satisfied. Be that as it may, what I can assure you of, with all the sincerity and conviction of which I am capable, is, that in the works of all the philosophers, from Plato to Cousin, you shall find nothing on this subject with which a man of solid sense could be content, if it be not taken from religion. They know

it, and they themselves confess it. Once they begin to
doubt of the divinity of Christianity, they know not at
what to grasp. They accumulate system on top of system,
words on top of words ; if they be not of a lofty frame
of mind, they abandon the task of investigating, disgusted at not discerning in any quarter of the horizon a
ray of light, and sink into *positiveness*, or, in other words,
endeavour to take all they can out of life by enjoying
its conveniences and pleasures. If their soul has been
created for science—if, thirsting after truth, she consents
not to abandon the task of seeking it, no matter how
great the toil may be, and how evident the inutility of
her endeavours, they suffer during their whole life, and
end their days with doubt in their intellect and sorrow
in their heart.

At present, being an enthusiast of philosophy and
an admirer of certain names, you shall not easily comprehend all the truth and exactness of my words ; but
a day will come when you shall recollect them, ay,
even long before silvery hairs shall whiten your head.
You shall not require old age, loaded with lessons and
disenchantments, to come to open your eyes. I know
not if you may open them to see and embrace the true
religion, but you shall, at least, to perceive the futility of
all the philosophical systems with relation to the origin,
life, and destiny of man. What more ? Why, you shall
not even require to study them deeply, to become profoundly convinced of the impotence of the human mind
when abandoned to its own resources ; in the very
vestibule of the temple of philosophy you shall discover

doubt and scepticism; and penetrating into her sanctuary, you shall hear Pride disputing about matters of little worth, and find her occupied in playing on symbolical and unintelligible words, and endeavouring, as far as possible, to conceal her ignorance by eluding, with an affected preterition the questions which interest us most, such as those relative to God and man. Do not allow yourself to be dazzled by the various titles with which the different systems decorate themselves, nor abandon yourself to a superstitious credence with respect to the pretended mysteries of the German school, nor regard as profoundness of science what is only obscurity of language. Let us not forget that simplicity is the garment of truth, and that he who ventures not to present them to the light of day places little confidence in his discoveries. Those vaunted philosophers who live surrounded by darkness, like workmen engaged in rich mines in the bowels of the earth, why do they not show us the pure gold they have obtained? Some other day, if opportunity offers, we shall enter again on this discussion. In the meantime, I remain your affectionate friend,

J. B.

III.

Existence of Hell, or Eternity of Punishment.

MY ESTEEMED FRIEND,—I see from your last we are likely to have a serious dispute on matters of religion; but the assurance you give me that your extravagance has not reached the extreme of doubting of the existence of God, has filled me with indescribable consolation. This wonderfully smoothes the path to discussion, for it is impossible to advance a single step in it without agreeing on this fundamental truth. And it was not without motive I desired to be satisfied about the ideas you professed on this subject ; for I can never forget what happened me with another sceptic, whom I suspected of doubting even of the existence of God, or at least of forming a wrong conception of it. When I asked him in consequence a few questions, he gave me a most strange answer, which would be facetious if it were not sacrilegious. I remarked to him that before all discussion it was necessary to agree on this point, and he answered with the greatest nonchalance imaginable:—" I think we can go on ; for I believe it is of little importance to ascertain if God be something distinct from nature, or nature itself ! " To such a length does the confusion of ideas go, when disordered by impiety ! and this man was in other respects of more than ordinary education and had a clear intellect !

I beg a thousand pardons for presuming to indicate my misgiving on this head ; though I should scarcely repent my conduct, for it has produced at least one great good, it has made you explain yourself in such a way as to reveal much sound sense, and make me conceive great hopes that my efforts shall not be in vain. A thousand times have I read those judicious words of your letter, in which you explain the view you take of this important truth. Allow me to transcribe them and

C

warmly recommend you never to forget them. "I have never troubled my head much with seeking for proofs of the existence of God: history, physics, metaphysics, would supply me with everything I want for such a demonstration, but I ingenuously confess that for my own conviction I need not so much scientific apparatus. I pull out my watch, and on contemplating its curious mechanism, and its ordered movement, no one could persuade me that all was effected by chance, without the intelligence and labour of the artist: the universe, I think, shows a little more skill than my watch; some one then must have fabricated it. Atheists tell me of chance, of combinations of atoms, of nature, and I know not of what all; but with these gentlemen's pardon, all those words are void of sense." I have nothing to suggest to one who appreciates the value of the two systems with such equity. I esteem those words, simple as they are profound, more than a volume filled with reasons and proofs.

Coming to the point of which you speak in your letter, I will commence by telling you I was rather amused to find you open the discussion by attacking the dogma of the eternity of punishment. I did not expect you would make so early an attack on this flank; and between ourselves, this anomaly makes me think you have got some little fear of hell. The subject, however, is not out of place; it is serious and urgent; in a few years hence we shall know from experience all about it, and well may you say that for those "who are now deceived the price of that knowledge will be dear indeed."

I have no objection to enter on religious questions in this way ; but I must remark it is not the best method of rendering them as clear as were desirable. Catholic doctrines form a whole, in which there is such connection and reciprocal dependence that one cannot be rejected without rejecting all ; and on the contrary, if certain capital points are admitted, it is impossible to resist the admission of the rest. It often happens that the impugners of those doctrines select one of them for attack, completely isolating it, and crowding together difficulties, which, considering the weakness of human intellect, naturally enough suggest themselves. " This is inconceivable," they say, " the religion which teaches it, cannot be true ;" as if Catholics ever said the mysteries of their religion were within the reach of man; as if they were not constantly assuring us that there are many truths to the elevation of which our limited comprehension cannot rise.

When we read or hear of a phenomenon or any event whatever, we inform ourselves above all things of the intelligence and veracity of the narrator ; and if satisfied on this point, no matter how strange the thing may appear, we do not take the liberty of rejecting it. Before the circumnavigation of the globe, there were few who comprehended how a ship which sailed to the west could return by the east ; but would this justify disbelief in the assertion of Sebastian de Elcano, when he succeeded in carrying out the bold design of the unfortunate Magellan ? If one of our ancestors rose from the tomb, and heard of the wonders of industry in civilized countries, should he carefully examine the account of the details of this or that machine; of the agents which propel it, and the class of work it produces, and reject at once whatever should appear to him incomprehensible ? Certainly not ; what he should do, acting in conformity with reason and prudence, would be to assure himself of the veracity of the witnesses, and examine whether it were possible they could be deceived, or could have any interest in deceiving him ; but once convinced that none of these circumstances existed, he could not without rashness refuse credit to what he might be told, no matter how inconceivable or how far beyond the limits of possibility it might appear.

In like manner should one proceed when he comes to treat of religious questions. What we should examine is whether revelation really exists ; and whether the Church is the depositary of revealed truths. These two bases once firmly established, what matters it whether this or that dogma appear more or less plausible; whether reason be more or less humbled by its inability to comprehend them ? Does revelation exist ? Is the truth in question revealed ? Is there any competent judge to decide whether it is or not ? What does that judge say about it ? This is the logical order of ideas and the proper way to examine such matters; to act otherwise is to wander astray, and expose one's self to lose time in disputes which lead to nothing.

Far from me, however, the intention of avoiding by means of these observations, the body of the difficulty ; but they are not out of place, and we shall require to

keep them in mind. I am now going to take up the
difficulty. You say you find it very hard "to give
credit to what preachers tell us of the pains of hell, and
you often heard things so horrible that they became
almost ridiculous." I reserve for by-and-by what I have
to say about those horrors; for the present, not knowing what motives of complaint you may have on the
subject, I will content myself with remarking that the
Catholic dogma has nothing to do with this or that idea
which might have occurred to a preacher. What the
Church teaches is, *that those who die in a bad state, that
is, in mortal sin, shall suffer punishment without end.*
This is the dogma: whatever may be said about the site
of this place of punishment, or about the degree and
quality of its pains, is not of faith; and belongs to those
points on which it is lawful to hold different opinions
without wandering from Catholic belief. What we
do know, for the Scripture says so expressly, is,
that these pains are awful; and what more do we
require? Terrible pains without end! is this idea
alone not sufficient to deprive us of all curiosity regarding all other questions that might be started on the
subject?

" How is it possible," you say, " that a God, infinitely
merciful, could chastise with such rigour?" How is it
possible, I answer, that a God, infinitely just, should not
chastise with such rigour, after calling us in vain to the
way of salvation, through the many means with which
He supplied us during life? When man offends God,
the creature outrages the Creator, a finite the infinite

Being; this, then, demands a chastisement in some sense
infinite. In the order of human justice an attack is more
or less criminal, according to the class or rank of the
person offended.   With what horror a son who ill-treats
his parents is regarded! ʹ What circumstance more
aggravating than to offend a person in the very act of
bestowing a favour on us? Well, now, make application
of these ideas.   Recollect that in man's offence against
God, there is the rebellion of nothingness against an
infinite Being; there is the ingratitude of a son to his
father; there is the disrespect of a subject to his supreme
Lord ; of a weak insignificant creature to the Sovereign
of heaven and earth.   How many motives to intensify
the fault ! how many reasons to increase the severity of.
the punishment!   For a simple attempt against the life
or property of an individual, human law chastises the
guilty with the pain of death—the greatest of all earthly
pains—and exerts itself—does violence to itself—to inflict
an infinite chastisement, by depriving the victim of all
the goods of society *for ever.* Why, then, cannot the
Supreme Judge also chastise the guilty with punishments which shall last for ever ? And remember that
human justice is not satisfied with repentance: the crime
once consummated, the penalty follows, and it is not
enough that the criminal may have changed his mode
of life.   God asks for a contrite and humble heart ; He
does not desire the death of· the sinner, but that he be
converted and live; nor does He discharge the fatal
blow on the head of the delinquent without placing life
and death before him, and giving him the choice ; with-

out offering a friendly hand through the aid of which
he might escape from the edge of the precipice. Whom,
then, can man blame but himself ? Where is the repugnance or cruelty of these ideas ? It is easy to deceive
the incautious, by pronouncing emphatically *eternity of
pain* and *infinite mercy;* but examine the matter profoundly ; attend to all the circumstances connected with
it, and the difficulties which at first sight presented
themselves, disappear like smoke. The secret of the
most deceptive sophisms consists in the artifice of presenting to view one side of objects only, and approxi-
mating two ideas, which, if they appear contradictory,
it is because the intermediate ones that connect and
harmonise them, are left out. We all know that the
most celebrated authors amongst the enemies of Religion
often solve the gravest and most complicated questions
with an ingenious remark or a sentimental reflection.
As all things have so many different aspects, it is not
difficult for an acute genius to seize on two points, whose
contrast may sharply wound the reader's mind ; and if
to this be added something to interest the heart, it costs
little trouble to upset in the mind of the incautious the
best grounded system of doctrine.

Now that I have mentioned sentimentalism, I cannot
pass over the abuse made of this class of arguments, by
speaking to the heart in many cases in which the intellect alone should be addressed. Thus in the present
case, how could a sensitive heart resist the horrid spectacle of a poor wretch condemned to suffer for ever ? It
has been said that great thoughts come from the heart;

and in this, as in all propositions which are too general, there is one part true and another false. For if it be indubitable that in many things sentiment affords great assistance in comprehending certain truths, it is no less so that it should never be .taken as principal guide, or allowed to domineer over the eternal principles of reason. The rights and duties of parents and children ; of husband and wife, and all family relations, will not be comprehended, perhaps, so perfectly, if while analysed in the bare light of a dissecting philosophy, the inspirations of the heart are smothered ; but on the other hand, the sound principles of morality will be upset, and disorder introduced into the bosom of families, if we prescind from the severe dictates of reason, and obstinately persevere in regulating our conduct by the suggestions of our voluble affections.

I am greatly deceived if we do not find here one of the most fruitful sources of the errors of our age. If we pay attention we shall find that the human mind is traversing a period whose distinctive characteristic is the simultaneous expansion of all the faculties. These lose under certain aspects ; the one absorbing a great portion of the strength and energy, which in other circumstances would belong to another; but that which undoubtedly gains is sensibility, not in its generous and elevated part, but inasmuch as it is a pleasure and enjoyment of the soul. Thus we find that in literature it is not the imagination nor argumentation that prevails, but sensibility in its rarest and most extravagant colours, summoning to its assistance reason and fancy, not as friends but dependents. And consequently philosophy also suffers from the same defect; and the austere principles of eternal morality rarely come from her tribunal well balanced. Thus licentious sensibility labours hard to deify enjoyment; seeks an excuse for all perverse actions; qualifies crimes as slips; the most ignominious falls as weaknesses; transgressions as mistakes: it endeavours to exile from the world all severe ideas; it chokes remorse, and offers to the human heart one sole idol—pleasure; one sole rule—egotism.

You see, my dear friend, the existence of hell does not square well with so much indulgence; but man's error does not destroy the reality of things. If hell existed in our fathers' time, it also exists in ours; and the fact is in no way changed, either by the austerity of our ancestors' way of thinking, or by our indulgent delicacy. When the soul becomes separated from this mortal flesh, it shall find itself in presence of the Supreme Judge; and thither it will not bring the world for advocate. It shall be alone with its conscience displayed patently to the eyes of Him, to whose sight nothing is invisible, and from whom nothing can be concealed.

These reflections on the relation between the character of the expansion of the human mind in this century, and the ideas which have sprung up against the eternity of punishment, are susceptible of many applications to other analogous matters. Man has thought himself capable of changing and modifying the Divine laws as he does human legislation; and purposes introducing into the decrees of the Sovereign Judge the same suavity he has given to those of earthly magistrates. The whole system of criminal legislation clearly tends to diminish the penalties attached to guilt, by rendering them less afflictive ; by stripping them of their terrors, and econo- mising man's sufferings as much as possible. We who live in this age, are all more or less infected with this suavity. Capital punishment ; flogging ; everything that carries with it an afflicting idea, is insupportable to us ; and it requires all the efforts of philosophy and all the counsels of prudence to retain some rigorous punish- ments in our criminal codes. Far from me to oppose myself to this current ; and would that to-morrow were the day society did not require for its good order and government to make blood and tears flow ; but I also wish people would not abuse this exaggerated sentimentalism. We should remember that all is not philosophy that covers itself with her cloak, and humanity, well understood, is something more noble and elevated than that egotistical and feeble sensibility which will not allow us to see others suffer, because our weak organisation makes us participators of their pains. Such a one faints at sight of a destitute wretch, and yet has a heart hard enough to refuse him a little alms. What are sensibility and humanity in such a case ? The first, a weakness of the organization ; the second, pure egotism.

But God does not look at things with the eyes of man, nor are His immutable decrees subject to the caprices of our sickly reason ; and there can be no greater forget- fulness of the idea we should form of an eternal and

infinite Being, than to insist on His will's accommodating
itself to our foolish wishes. So accustomed is the present
age to excuse crime and interest itself in the criminal,
that it forgets the compassion which, on undoubtedly
more just titles, is due to the victim ; and gladly would
it leave the latter without reparation of any kind, if
it could spare the former the suffering he has deserved.
Accuse as you may the dogma of the eternity of punishment of severity and cruelty ; say that such a tremendous chastisement cannot be reconciled with Divine
mercy ; we shall answer, that neither can the want
of this chastisement be reconciled with Divine justice;
that the world would be surrendered to chance, and in
many of its events the most repugnant injustice would
be discovered, if there were not a terribly avenging God
waiting for the culprit on the other side of the tomb, to
demand from him an account of his perversity during
his sojourn on earth.

What ?—do we not at every step behold injustice
haughty and triumphant; mocking the abandoned
orphan; the destitute sick ; the ragged and hungry poor
and unprotected widow, and insulting with its luxury
and dissipation the misery and other calamities of those
unfortunate victims of its oppression and plunder ? Do
we not contemplate with horror heartless fathers, who,
by their dissipated conduct, fill with anguish the family
of which God has made them the head; hurrying to the
grave a virtuous consort ; plunging their children into
misery, and transmitting to them no other inheritance
but the sad recollection and the baneful results of a

scandalous life? Do we not sometimes find unnatural
sons, who cruelly insult the grey hairs of him who gave
them being; abandon him in misfortune or never speak
a word of consolation to him, and by their irregularity
and insolent petulance shorten the days of his afflicted
old age? Do we not find infamous seducers, who after
surprising the candour and staining the innocence of
youth, cruelly desert their victim, and surrender it to all
the horrors of ignominy and desperation? Ambition,
perfidy, treason, fraud, adultery, malediction, calumny,
and other vices that enjoy such immunity in this world,
where the action of justice is restricted, and there are so
many means of eluding and suborning it—have not all
these to meet with an avenging God, who will make them
feel the weight of His indignation? Must there not be
One in heaven to hear the moans of innocence demanding vengeance?

It is not true; no, it is not, that the culprit experiences
already in this life chastisement enough for his faults.
Gnawing remorse indeed torments him; the infirmities
produced by his irregularities grow on him, and the disastrous consequences of his perverse conduct weigh him
down; but neither is he wanting in means to blunt the
sharp sting of his conscience; neither is he devoid of
artifices to neutralise the evil effects of his revels, nor
short of resources to come clean out of the false positions
in which his excesses have involved him. And besides,
what are these sufferings of the wicked in comparison
with what the innocent suffer? Sickness presses them
down; poverty molests them; malediction and calumny

blacken them; injustice tramples on them; persecution leaves them no rest; tribulation of spirit is added too; and like their Divine Master, they suffer in this life the torments, the anguish, and the opprobrium of the cross. If his patience be great; if he knows how to resign himself like a true Christian, the just man renders his sufferings tolerable; but he does not, for all that, cease to feel them, and frequently more severe ones too than have fallen to the lot of the man stained with a thousand crimes. Without the punishments and rewards of the other life, where is justice?—where Providence?—where the stimulus for virtue and the curb for vice?

You ask me, my esteemed friend, if I comprehend what God's object can be in prolonging for all eternity the pains of the damned; and you answer in anticipation the reasons I might perhaps assign, viz., that thus Divine justice is satisfied, and men are kept from the ways of vice through fear of such terrible chastisement. As regards the first part of that answer you say you have never been able to conceive the reason of such rigour, and that though we can trace the relation there exists between the eternity of punishment, and the species of infinity of the offence for which it is imposed, there still remains some obscurity you cannot penetrate. You are far astray, my dear friend, if you imagine this is not the case with every one; for it is well known that the human intellect becomes cloudy as soon as it touches on the portals of infinity. For myself I will say that I cannot clearly conceive these truths either; and firm as is the certainty I have of them, I cannot flatter myself with the thought of their appearing to me with that evidence which those belonging to a finite and purely human order are capable of; but I was never discouraged by this mist arising from our weakness and from the sublimity of the objects themselves, and considered that if I should refuse assent from this motive, I could not retain many truths of which it was impossible for me to doubt, even though I made an effort. I am certain of the truth of creation, not only from what revealed religion teaches me, but also from what natural reason tells me; and yet when I meditate on it, and endeavour to form a clear and distinct idea of that sublime act, when God says:—*Let there be light, and light was made*, my weak intellect is unable to comprehend the transition from non-existence to existence. I am certain, and so are you, of the existence of God; of His infinity; His eternity; His immensity, and His other attributes; but are we able to form clear ideas of what is expressed by these names? Certainly not; and if you read all that has been written on the subject by the most renowned theologians and philosophers, you shall find they laboured more or less under the same inability as ourselves.

If I wished to give greater extension to these reflections, it would be easy to discover a thousand examples of this weakness of our understanding, even in physical and natural things; but this would involve me in long discussions about human sciences, and draw me away from my principal object; and besides, I have no doubt what I said will be sufficient to prevent this obscurity, in which certain objects are involved, from making an unfavourable impression on a man of your common sense. While we can acquire a sufficient certainty of them through a safe channel, we should not withhold our assent on account of certain difficulties more or less serious and embarrassing.

There are not many subjects in which more satisfactory reasons can be assigned in support of a truth than those indicated above in favour of the justice of the eternity of punishment. Whatever conception you may form of my reflections, at least you cannot say they are to be despised on account of the simple obstacle of a difficulty, which is founded in an exaggerated sentimentalism, rather than in solid and convincing reasoning. It therefore only remains for me to remind you that the question is not one of knowing whether our understanding comprehends or not with all clearness the dogma about hell, but of simply investigating whether this dogma is true ; and whether the foundations on which we build it have the characteristics of Divine revelation. What advantage would it be to comprehend it or not, if we had the misfortune of having to suffer it ?

With respect to the second point indicated in your letter, I do not agree with you that a punishment of limited duration would exercise on the minds of men, with regard to the regulation of their conduct, an equivalent impression of identical results. You hold that if it were accompanied with the circumstance of long duration, or terrible torture, it would be sufficient to curb unruly passions, and impose a limit on wicked desires ; and with this observation you think you upset the reason assigned by Catholics for the existence of hell, viz., that it is a safeguard of morality. But it appears to me you have not gone deeply enough into this subject; and you don't seem to remark that though it is true the idea of torment frightens and terrifies us, when it has to be suffered in this life, it makes but a very slight impression if it is reserved for the other. I shall give two proofs of this—one experimental, the other scientific.

The doctrine of purgatory involves a terrible idea; and books of devotion and preachers are constantly painting that place of expiation in frightful colours. The faithful believe it so; they hear it incessantly; they pray for their departed relatives and friends who may be detained in it; but frankly, is the fear people have of purgatory very great? Would it of itself be a strong enough dyke to oppose the impetuosity of the passions? Let each one answer from his own experience, and let those who have had occasion to observe it answer for others. We are told the pains endured there are terrible—it is true; their duration may be very long—certainly; the soul shall not escape without paying the last farthing— undoubtedly; but those pains shall have an end; we are sure they cannot last for ever; and placed between the risk of long sufferings in the other life, and the necessity of bearing slight annoyances in the present, we prefer a thousand times to run the risk than to endure the annoyances.

Reason points out the causes of what everyday experience places before our eyes; and to know them a very slight consideration of human nature is sufficient.

While we live on this earth, our soul is united to our
body, which unceasingly transmits the impressions it
receives from everything around it. It is true our soul
possesses some faculties, which, elevated by nature above
things corporeal and sensible, are directed by other principles; are employed on more lofty objects, and inhabit,
if we may say so, a region which of itself has no connection with anything of a material or earthly nature.
Without ignoring the dignity of these faculties, or the
sublimity of the region in which they dwell, we must
confess, such is the influence exercised on them by
others of an inferior order, that they often compel them
to descend from their elevation; and instead of obeying
them as their mistresses, reduce them to a state of
slavery. When things do not come to this extreme, at
least it frequently happens that the superior faculties
remain without performing their functions, as if they
were sleeping, so that the intellect scarcely descries in
obscure luxuriance the truths which form its principal
and most noble object, and the will does not tend towards
it except with great carelessness and sloth. There is a
hell to fear, a heaven to hope for; but all this is in the
other life and reserved for a distant period; they are
things which belong to an entirely distinct order in a new
world in which we firmly believe, but from which we derive no direct actual impressions; and hence we require
to make an effort of concentration and reflection to
impress on ourselves the immense interest they have for
us, incomparably beyond everything that surrounds us.
In the meantime some earthly object strikes our imagi-

D

nation or our senses; now impressing us with some fear, now soothing us with some pleasure; the other world disappears from our sight; the intellect falls back into its sluggishness, the will into its languor; and if either is excited anew it is to contribute to the greater expansion of the other faculties.

Man is almost always guided by the impressions of the moment; and when he weighs in the scale of his judgment the advantages and inconveniences an action can produce for him, the distance or proximity of their realisation is one of the circumstances that influence his action most. And why should not this occur with regard to the affairs of the other life, when it happens with respect to those of the present? Is not the number of those who sacrifice riches, honour, health, and life itself to a momentary pleasure infinite? And why is this? Because the object that seduces is present, and the evils distant; and man deludes himself with the hope of avoiding, or resigns himself to suffer them, like a person who casts himself down a precipice blindfolded.

From this we may infer it is not true, as you said, that the fear of a long punishment would be capable of producing an equal effect as the eternity of hell. It is not true; on the contrary, it may be asserted that from the moment the idea of eternity is separated from that of pain, it loses the greater part of its horror, and is reduced to the same class as that of purgatory. If the chastisements of the other life are to produce a fear capable of restraining us in our depraved inclinations, they must have a formidable character, the mere recollection of which, presenting itself to our mind now and then, may produce a salutary shudder, which will be felt in the midst of the dissipations and distractions of life, as the sound of sonorous metal vibrates long after the stroke is given.

I will not finish this letter without answering that other objection insinuated by you, and with which you apparently feel very satisfied, because, as you say, " though no more than a conjecture, it cannot be denied it is a very plausible and philosophical one, and perhaps not totally destitute of foundation." You then explain the system which has pleased you so much, and consists in considering the dogma of hell as a formula in which is expressed the idea of intolerance which presides in the doctrines and conduct of the Catholic Church. Allow me to transcribe your own words, as we shall thus avoid the danger of misunderstanding :—" The intellect and heart of man were to be subjected by binding them with a ring of iron : the means of accomplishing it were wanting in human things, and it was found necessary to make the justice of God intervene. Might it not be sus- pected that the ministers of the Catholic religion, more deceived, perhaps, than deceiving, have appealed to the common resource of poets, of clearing up a complicated situation by calling in the aid of some god, or, speaking in literary terms—by employing the machine ? I am greatly deceived if I cannot discover, in the pretended justice of an inexorable God, the Catholic priest with his inflexible obstinacy." You are rather severe, my esteemed friend, in the passage I am after transcribing, and no matter what surprise my words may cause you, I make bold to tell you that, far from finding you philosophical as usual, you are very inexact and very rash— inexact, because you suppose the dogma of the eternity of punishment belongs exclusively to Catholics, whereas Protestants also profess it; and rash, because you try to convert into an expression of the ruling thought of Christianity, a fact generally believed by the human race.

The prurience, so common in our day, even among first-class writers, of giving a philosophical reason founded on a new and sharp observation, has carried you away, and caused you to lose sight for an instant of what no historian is ignorant of. You wished to signify that this was an invention of the Christian priests, though respecting their good intention and candour, by supposing them victims of an illusion; but how could you have forgotten that centuries before the appearance of Christianity the belief in the existence of hell was widely extended and deeply rooted?

You are mildly satirical on "the good monks who delight in frightening children and women with the dreadful descriptions of torments forged in wild and rude imaginations, and which a man of sound sense and good taste can with difficulty hear without laughing or becoming disgusted." I can see you want to make the poor preachers pay dearly for the annoyance your good mother used to give you by bringing you to sermons, when you could be more agreeably employed at your play and diversions; but be it said, without any intention of giving offence, and solely in defence of the truth, you here make a sad stumble, in which your only consolation is your having, among those who lightly mock the dogmas and practices of our religion, many companions in misfortune.

You laugh at the *exaggerations of the monks*, which appear to you insupportable from their want of reason and their bad taste. Well, then, I challenge you to produce from among those you have heard from the mouth of a preacher, the description that may appear to you most extravagant, and I hereby oblige myself to quote for you another on this very subject which will not be behind it in frightfulness, extravagance, or horror. And do you know whose those descriptions shall be? Virgil's, Dante's, Tasso's, and Milton's. You never thought that behind the good Capuchin whom you attacked so furiously you would stumble on so respectable a reserve in matters of reason and good taste. Sometimes precipitation of judgment is more injurious to us than ignorance itself. It often happens that we despise an expression in hatred or contempt of the person who uses it—an expression which would appear to us admirable if we heard it from the mouth of another who commanded our respect. Hence Montaigne pleasantly said that he amused himself by scattering through his writings sentences from grave philosophers, without naming them, that his critics, believing they had to do with Montaigne alone, might insult Seneca and pull Plutarch's nose.

It is not easy to exactly describe the variety of the horrors of hell, but it is certain that Christians and

Gentiles have agreed in painting them in frightful colours. Virgil was neither monk, nor preacher, nor Christian, nor was he wanting in *good taste,* and yet it would be hard to bring together more horrors than he places before us, not only in hell, but even on the road :—

> " Just in the gate, and in the jaws of hell,
> Revengeful cares, and sullen sorrows dwell ;
> And pale diseases, and repining age ;
> Want, fear, and famine's unrestricted rage :
> Here toils, and death, and death's half-brother, sleep,
> Forms terrible to view, their sentry keep ;
> With anxious pleasures of a guilty mind,
> Deep frauds before, and open force behind : "

Before arriving at the fatal mansion we meet with *the tresses of vipers,* with *hydras that roar with a terrible noise,* with *monsters armed with fire,* together with *forbidden joys mala mentis gaudia,* weeping and revengeful remorse, *luctus et ultrices curæ.* But let us follow him still, and the horror increases till it becomes extreme :—

> " The Furies' iron beds, and strife that shakes
> Her hissing tresses, and unfolds her snakes.
>
> .   .   .   .   .   .
>
> Of various forms, unnumber'd spectres more ;
> Centaurs, and double shapes, besiege the door.
> Before the passage horrid hydra stands,
> And Briareus with all his hundred hands :
> Gorgons, Geryon with his triple frame,
> And vain Chimæra vomits empty flame.
>
> .   .   .   .   .   .
>
> Hence to deep Acheron they take their way,
> Whose troubled eddies, thick with ooze and clay,
> Are whirl'd aloft, and in Cocytus lost :
> There Charon stands, who rules the dreary coast ;
> A sordid god : down from his hoary chin
> A length of beard descends ; uncombed, unclean.

His eyes, like hollow furnaces on fire ;
A girdle, foul with grease, binds his obscene attire.

. . . . . .

The hero, looking on the left, espy'd
A lofty tower, and strong on every side,
With treble walls, which Phlegethon surrounds,
Whose fiery flood the burning empire bounds,
And press'd betwixt the rocks, the bellowing noise resounds.
Wide is the fronting gate, and raised on high
With adamantine columns, threats the sky.
Vain is the force of man, and heaven's as vain,
To crush the pillars which the pile sustain.
Sublime on these a tower of steel is reared,
And dire Tisiphone there keeps the ward.
Girt in her sanguine gown, by night and day,
Observant of the souls that pass the downward way.
From hence are heard the groans of ghosts, the pains
Of sounding lashes, and of dragging chains.

. . . . . .

These are the realms of unrelenting fate :
And awful Rhadamantus rules the state :
He hears and judges each committed crime ;
Inquires into the matter, place, and time.
The conscious wretch must all his acts reveal ;
Loth to confess, unable to conceal :
From the first moment of his vital breath,
To his last hour of unrepenting death.
Straight, o'er the guilty ghost, the Fury shakes
The sounding whip, and brandishes her snakes :
And the pale sinner, with her sisters, takes.
Then of itself unfolds the eternal door :
With dreadful sounds the brazen hinges roar.
You see, before the gate, what stalking ghost
Commands the guard, what sentries keep the post.
More formidable hydra stands within ;
Whose jaws with iron teeth severely grin.

. . . . . .

There Tityus was to see, who took his birth
From heav'n ; his nursing from the foodful earth.
Here his gigantic limbs, with large embrace,
Infold nine acres of infernal space.

A rav'nous vulture in his open'd side,
Her crooked beak and cruel talons try'd ;
Still for the growing liver digg'd his breast ;
The growing liver still supplied the feast.
Still are his entrails fruitful to their pains :
Th' immortal hunger lasts, th' immortal food remains.
Ixion and Pirithoüs I could name ;
And more Thessalian chiefs of mighty fame.
High o'er their heads a mould'ring rock is placed,
 That promises a fall, and shakes at every blast.
They lie below, on golden beds display'd
And genial feasts, with regal pomp, are made.
The queen of furies by their sides is set,
And snatches from their mouths th' untasted meat.
Which if they touch, her hissing snakes she rears :
Tossing her torch, and thund'ring in their ears.
Then they, who brothers' better claim disown,
Expel their parents, and usurp the throne ;
Defraud their clients, and to lucre sold,
Sit brooding on unprofitable gold ;
Who dare not give, and ev'n refuse to lend
To their poor kindred, or a wanting friend ;
Vast is the throng of these ; nor less the train
Of lustful youths, for foul adult'ry slain.
Hosts of deserters, who their honour sold,
And basely broke their faith for bribes of gold :
All these within the dungeon's depth remain,
Despairing pardon, and expecting pain.
Ask not what pains ; nor farther seek to know
Their process, or the forms of law below.
Some roll a mighty stone ; some, laid along,
And, bound with burning wires, on spokes of wheels are
    hung.
Unhappy Thiseus, doomed for ever there,
Is fixed by fate on his eternal chair :
And wretched Phlegias warns the world with cries
(Could warning make the world more just or wise)
Learn righteousness, and dread th' avenging deities.
To tyrants others have their country sold,
Imposing foreign lords, for foreign gold :

Some have old laws repealed, new statutes made ;
Not as the people pleas'd, but as they paid.
With incest some their daughter's bed profaned.
All dared the worst of ills, and what they dared, attained."
Dryden's Translation of Virgil.

Triple walls, bathed with a river of fire, groans, noise of lashes, clanking of chains, serpents, and the hydra with a hundred mouths, a vulture pecking the liver, and other things similar : behold what the poet represents in the mansion, as he himself says, of *defrauders, adulterers, those who are cruel towards their parents, the incestuous, traitors to their country,* and those guilty of other crimes. I doubt very much whether you have heard things more horrible. And as if the frightful picture he was after painting with inimitable pencil were not enough, he exclaims :—

" Had I a *hundred mouths,* a *hundred tongues,*
And *throats of brass,* inspir'd with iron lungs,
I could not half those horrid crimes repeat,
Nor half the punishments those crimes have met."

Be it as it may : within half a century the question of hell shall be practically solved for us both. I pray heaven it may be happily so ; but if you have the rashness to run chance for what may happen, I will bewail your fatal blindness, beseeching the Lord to deign to enlighten you before the day of wrath arrives, on which, in the presence of the Supreme Judge, your guardian angel will cover his face, not knowing what to allege on your behalf, to free you from the tremendous sentence. Your humble servant,

J. B.

IV.

Philosophy of the Future.

MY ESTEEMED FRIEND,—I am very glad you have afforded me an opportunity of giving my opinion of that philosophy which you call of the *future*; for though . you criticise so far as even to ridicule it, it is still evident it has made an impression on you, particularly in what it says of the *destinies* of Catholicism. You call it *philosophy of the future;* and, in fact, there is no other name better suited for qualifying that extravagant science which, without solving anything, without explaining anything, is solely engaged in destroying and pulverising, responding emphatically to all questions, to all difficulties, to all exigencies, with the word *future.* In the judgment of this philosophy, humanity has always erred, errs even at present; this philosophy knows it, and apparently it alone knows it; so serious and magisterial is the tone with which it announces it. Ask it where is the truth, when will man be able to discover it? —in *the future.* As, in its supposition, all religions are false, all are the work of men, a snare to deceive the masses, a laughingstock to the wise, and particularly to the professors of that *elevated philosophy*, who alone deserve the name; where in that case is the true religion?—when will men be able to profess it?—in the *future.* No philosopher has succeeded in deciphering the enigma of the universe, of God, and of man; will a fortunate day come on which the long-sought key shall

be found?—in the *future*. The social and political
organisation of the world must be radically changed.
No one knows what shall be substituted for the present
state of things. Who shall teach us how to solve this
thorny problem?—the *future*. The masses of the people
suffer fearfully in the most civilized countries; their
nakedness, their poverty, their shocking misery, stand
in scandalous contrast with the luxuries and enjoyments
of the powerful, and the *vita bona* of the philosophers:
whence shall come the remedy for such a miserable state
of things?—from the *future*. The future for history, the
future for religion, the future for literature, the future for
science, the future for politics, the future for society, the
future for misery, the future for self, the future for the
present, the future for the past, the future for everything.
The panacea of all ailings, the satisfaction of all desires,
the fulfilment of all hopes, the realisation of all dreams;
the golden age, whose radiant dawnings, hidden to the
eyes of the profane, are revealed to some spirits only,
who have obtained the ineffable privilege of reading the
history of the *future*, inscribed in divine letters. Hence
they salute it with joy; hence they run towards it like
a child to the arms of a mother who caresses it; hence
they pass with ironical smile through the midst of this
age that *does not comprehend them;* hence they would
live with pleasure the life of the disinterested philosophers of Greece; and they would retire from the world
like anchorites, if their presence were not necessary for
announcing the truth, if they dared shrink from the
mission they have received on earth. Poor men! victims

of an unhappy destiny, they cannot concede to their
intellect all the flight their *prophetic inspiration* would
demand, they cannot unburthen their breast as freely as
they desire, and they have no other consolation left, than
to solace themselves a few moments, by *singing* of the
coming time which their mind descries and their heart
augurs.

> " Saturnian times
> Roll round again, and mighty years begun
> From their first orb in radiant circles run.
>
> .   .   .   .
>
> The serpent's brood shall die ; the sacred ground
> Shall weeds and poisonous plants refuse to bear ;
> Each common bush shall Syrian roses wear.
>
> .   .   .   .
>
> Unlaboured harvests shall the fields adorn.
> And clustered grapes shall blush on every thorn,
> And knotted oaks shall flowers of honey weep ;
>
> .   .   .   .   .   .
>
> The labouring hind his oxen shall disjoin,
> No plough shall hurt the glebe, no pruning hook the vine,
> Nor wool shall in dissembled colours shine ;
> But the luxurious father of the fold,
> With native purple, or unborrowed gold,
> Beneath his pompous fleece shall proudly sweat,
> And under Tyrian robes the lamb shall bleat ;
> The Fates, when they this happy web have spun,
> Shall bless the sacred clue, and bid it smoothly run."

Do not ask them, my esteemed friend, how they have
discovered so many prodigies; who has revealed to them
such wonderful secrets: above all, do not demand from
them proofs for what they lay down as certain, nor
require them, as if they were vulgar thinkers, to demonstrate what they assert.   These are things of which one
has a *presentiment* rather than a *knowledge ;* they have

about them something poetical, something aerial ; they
are previsions involved in symbolic figures ; and whoever is not satisfied with this is unworthy of philosophy ;
the flame of genius has not touched his brow, creative
inspiration has budded not in his mind. Besides, who
does not already behold some signs of that marvellous
transformation ? All are not capable of foreseeing it as
clearly as those to whom it has been revealed in mysterious apparitions ; but the infallible symptoms which
announce a proximate and universal change can escape
no one.

> " Behold the mighty convex mass of earth,
> The land, the sea, with high heaven's wide scope ;
> All, all rejoice in hope of coming change."

It must be confessed the expedient adopted by these
philosophers is by no means a stupid one, and besides
it has the indescribable advantage of being very convenient. There is no possible gain to be derived from
presently regulating the world ; the point is, to defer all
to the future, and everything is settled. Socrates with
his torn garment, and afterwards with his hemlock ;
Diogenes with his tub, and his burning lamp ; Heraclitus
with his tears ; and Democritus with his laughter, did
not understand a word of philosophy. To mock the
past, to enjoy the present, and to deceive the world with
the hope of a brilliant future, this is the most suitable
formula that could ever be discovered to avoid annoyance and come out clear from all classes of engagements.
And if the future correspond not with their prognostics ?
some scrupulous individuals may object. We should

be pretty fellows if we were to trouble ourselves about
what may happen : the matter allows of delay ; the
period we mark is not short, or rather, to risk nothing,
we leave it indefinite ; we shall always have it in our
power to solicit a fresh postponement ; and if any of us
go so far as to be definite, fear not he will be so thought-
less as to forget the lines :—

> " My head is sick, his lordship sighed ;
> Fear not, my lord, the quack replied,
> For ten years more none of the four shall die,
> The king, his ass, my lord, or I."

Having done due justice to the philosophy of the
future, it remains to me to discuss the *nutantem pondere
mundum.* I mean, I have to examine the grave complication of the problems that weigh on society, and
see how far the philosophers have reason to talk to us
of the transcendent changes which future generations
are destined to witness. It is idle to say that many of
them consider it certain these changes will not take place
under the influence of religion ; that, on the contrary,
they think the latter is losing ground, and that one of
the principal conditions of the renovation of the world,
must be the substitution of philosophy for religion. As
in the opinion of some, religions, and particularly Christianity, are nothing else but "a spontaneous offshoot
from the ideas of the masses, forcing a passage for itself ;
and growing into form as these ideas ripen in the popular
imagination, under the excitement and hallucination
caused by the revelations that are proclaimed by it ;" *

* Jouffroy, " Lecture on the Destiny of Man."

a giant step will be gained in the race of social perfection, when the masses are sufficiently enlightened to
contemplate the truth in all its purity, face to face,
without the necessity of symbols and coverings, which
are only suited to the weakness of limited understandings. It is useless to say I do not agree with M. Jouffroy
in his strange definition, and consequently cannot admit
the deductions it leads to. I do not believe the masses
can ever be well directed (and in the word masses, I
include all society) without the influence of religion ;
and it appears to me as absurd to think philosophy can
ever fill up the vacuum by occupying the place of religion, as that the latter is the spontaneous production
of the ideas of the masses.

In this age of philosophico-historical analysis, the
demonstration professing to set forth the authentic data
showing that Christianity was the spontaneous production of the masses, would be very curious. From what
masses did the Gospel come ?—was it from the Jewish,
or from the pagan masses ? If from the former, how is
it that the warmest defenders of the law of Moses were
the capital enemies of Jesus Christ ? Where is there a
single fact, a single word, a single insinuation to show
that Jesus learned His sublime teaching from the Jews ?
Is it not, on the contrary, patent that the words of the
Divine Master were received as entirely new, and that
they filled those who heard Him with astonishment and
amazement, scandalising some by their novelty, and
accepted by others with transports of admiration and
with enthusiastic veneration ? Blind men ! If you have

read the Sermon on the Mount, if you have ever meditated on that spring of wisdom and love, which flows from the lips of a man who had never received any education, tell us — Whence came the doctrines expressed in it ? They were scattered, you will say, in the midst of the people ; but leaving aside the convincing remark, on what grounds do you lay down such a strange paradox ? Will you really go so far as to ground your assertion on the philosophy of the epoch ?—but, are you alone acquainted with it ?—do you believe scientific contemporaneous history has been lost to the world ? Besides, you do not even allow religion the honour of being born of philosophy ; you make it spring from the head of the masses ! Be it remembered then, and never forgotten, that the religion most admired by its very enemies, for the wisdom and sanctity with which it abounds, was the spontaneous production of the ideas of the masses of the time of Tiberius and Herod ! The ridiculous here vies with the sacrilegious.

Until now it was believed that the masses were involved in ignorance; that the presumption with respect to great thoughts, was in favour of certain privileged minds who should shed over the masses the light they needed. Now we shall know in future that this light pre-exists in them ; and not faintly, but prepared to produce its effects, as a ripe fruit; and that when an extraordinary man rises up among the multitude, he is indebted to that multitude for all he thinks and all he does. Undoubtedly, not even in the eyes of its enemies can Christianity appear less admirable than the most elevated philosophical system ; and hence we can infer that these must have the same origin.   In fact, religion in this case is nothing more than a philosophy masked in symbols and enigmas ; so that the invention of the former has one particular difficulty over the latter, which consists in successfully selecting the veils with which to cover itself. We can then affirm, without fear of mistake, that the philosophy of Socrates, of Plato, of Aristotle, of Bacon, of Descartes, of Malebranche, of Leibnitz, was nothing else but the spontaneous production of the masses ; and stranger still ! the same fate must befall that of Kant, Hegel, Cousin, and Jouffroy himself, lauded as it is.

It is well to have some one to supply us with such discoveries : some one to reveal with such stupendous sagacity the road which must be followed to arrive at the most lofty wisdom.   Oh ! how Descartes erred when he condemned himself to such long meditations, commencing from his very college life, when he obtained a dispensation from rising early, that thus he might foment, with genial heat, the contemplation to which he abandoned himself !   What a fool Malebranche was to pass his days in the greatest retirement, buried in his study, with the windows closed that the light might not distract him !   These poor philosophers, and their foolish masters and disciples, had got it into their heads that *the number of fools is infinite,* and that whoever desired to be wise, or less foolish, should take care not to allow himself to be too much contaminated by the atmosphere of the vulgar ; and even regarded as vulgar the many who try to free themselves from this epithet, no matter

E

how legitimate their titles may be to be ranked in that class. These good men were ignorant that, whether to conceive a system of philosophy, or to invent a religion, it is necessary to mingle with the masses, not precisely for the purpose of observing them in their wanderings, in their errors, in their passions, in their caprices, and studying thus the springs of the human mind, and learning to direct it, for we knew this of old; but with the view of observing the ideas that germinate in them, of following them in their growth and expansion, and on discovering they are ripe, taking advantage of the critical moment, giving them form, causing them to become *incarnate*, and then presenting the result to the astonished masses themselves, saying, "Behold a present from heaven."

Poor masses! They know not that they adore an idol fabricated by themselves; that they eat, as manna descended from heaven, the very fruit that has sprung from themselves; and moreover, that for the purpose of presenting it to them, the impostor has scarcely had any more trouble than to collect it when it was *ripe*.

If we Catholics should indulge in such monstrous paradoxes, if we had made bold enough to make such assertions, contrary to sound philosophy, in opposition with history, repugnant to common sense, without proofs of any kind, without the slightest reason, without the most remote foundation to support our conjecture; if, dissatisfied with the ordinary language, we had laid hold of symbolic expressions, making ideas become *incarnate*, and with the strange whim of applying to

them the metaphor *ripe*, thus presenting to view an extravagant contrast, all the dictionaries of satire would
not be able to supply appellations enough to cover with
ridicule such an attempt against philosophy and good
taste. Judge, my esteemed friend, between our adversaries and us; and let all men of sound sense judge
with you.

I infer from what I have just said, that the prophecy
of some philosophers of our age, that Christianity is
destined to die, and the philosophy of which they all
speak, without telling us in what it consists, to step into
its inheritance, is a pure chimera. On this head, the
conduct of M. Cousin, founded on the motives which M.
Peter Leroux has revealed to us in a number of the
Independent Review, appears to me astute and even
more convenient than astute. The passage is curious,
and is worth the trouble of copying : " Many years
ago," says M. Leroux, " when conversing with M. Cousin
on his apology, not of Socrates, but of the judges of
Socrates—a strange paradox, written it would appear
for the purpose of making wry faces at Plato and
Xenophon, we upbraided him with this irrational act,
which we regarded as a crime of *læsæ philosophiæ*. M.
Cousin interrupted his answer to ask us :—What length
of life do you think remains to the religion of our
country? That is not the question, I said to him ; we
are treating of philosophy, of truth ; never would philosophers have done anything good, if, in view of the
reality, they had interrogated themselves in this way for
the purpose of knowing what they should do. I, replied

M. Cousin, believe Catholicity has elements of life in her for three hundred years yet (en a encore pour trois cents ans dans le ventre), in consequence, I humbly raise my hat in her presence, and I continue at philosophy."

There was a time in which the mania of announcing the fall of Catholicity spread amongst Protestants, and they were accustomed to fix the time with as much precision as astronomers calculate an eclipse, or the passage of a comet. Certain of the prediction, they proclaimed it with great clamour; but the calculations must have been badly made, for the fatal epoch was accustomed to arrive, and the prognostics remained unfulfilled. Those prophets were sometimes very indiscreet : for they presumed to mark a short period, the course of which was not long enough to allow the announcement to be forgotten. M. Cousin, who must, undoubtedly, have recollected these prophetic mishaps, and like a good conservative, desiring to avoid extremes on the one hand, and on the other the ridicule he would be exposed to if his assertion proved untrue, selected a middle term, between the *secula seculorum of Catholics*, and the short space of the Protestant prophets, and granted to Catholicity a period of three hundred years. In this way, when any one in this or the succeeding age may wonder that Catholicity still continues to exist, the satisfactory answer, " M. Cousin prognosticated this long ago," will be ready at hand ; and when at the end of the three hundred years, on the expiration of the fatal period, it is seen that Catholicity does not die through inanition, but still retains elements of life — then no one will recollect M. Cousin, and much less his prophecy.

In the moral, as well as in the physical order, the first symptom of approaching death is want of growth and unproductiveness ; the near extinction of life is always known by the want of expansion and action. The leaves in trees dry up, the blossoms wither, the fruit does not come forth ; in animals heat departs, faculties act sluggishly, action is languid, fecundity ceases. Observe the intellectual and moral world, and you will remark the same phenomena. When a philosophical system falls into disuse, it loses its propagandist action, the number of its proselytes far from increasing, diminishes ; there is no new application made of its doctrines, those that have been made are neglected, everything is prepared for its sinking into contempt, and soon after into oblivion. A legislation about to perish is frequently disobeyed, its very upholders do not dare to make use of it ; it does not extend itself to other peoples, it is already a lifeless corpse to which the honours of the tomb alone are wanting. The same happens with institutions, be they of whatever order they may, and no matter what their importance may have been. The death which threatens them at hand, is manifested by infallible symptoms. Cast a glance over history, fix your gaze on all the social and political institutions, which from one cause or another have laboured under a mortal disease, and you will find that in the last periods of their existence, they resembled

those tottering edifices from which the inhabitants fly
in haste lest they be buried in their ruins.

Nothing of the kind is verified with regard to Catholicity. Rooted in Spain, Portugal, Italy, France, Belgium,
Austria, in various countries of Germany, in Poland, in
Ireland, with wide dominions in America, progressing
in England and in the United States, displaying lively
activity in the missions of East and West, diffusing anew
religious institutions in distant regions, vigorously sustaining her rights, now with energetic protests, now by
enduring persecution, defending her doctrines with great
learning and eloquence in the principal centres of intelligence of the civilized world, numbering amongst her
disciples illustrious individuals, who are not behind
those of any sect whatever,—where are the symptoms
of a proximate death?—where the signs that indicate
dissolution?

I now see, my esteemed friend, the difficulty you are
going to raise; and lest it might not occur to you, I
myself will take care to present it without diminishing
any of its force. If such be the life existing in Catholicity, if the signs with which she displays herself be so
clear and evident, why do you lament the evils that
afflict the Church in the present century?—why recall
at every step the glories she acquired in other more
favourable ages? To this I will answer, in the first
place, that I did not say Catholicity has not suffered
great shocks; I have only sustained that in her actual
state no harbingers of death can be discovered. These
two assertions are very different; the one has nothing

in common with the other. This answer is sufficient, and more than sufficient, to remove the above-mentioned difficulty ; but I will, moreover, presume to add, that there is often some exaggeration in speaking of the actual ills of the Church, in comparison with those she suffered in other ages. The decline of faith and morals is often dwelt on too much, not only by the enemies of the Church, but even by her most beloved children. These through zeal and holy sorrow ; those from a spirit of calumny, and through a secret pleasure of announcing the decay of what they desire to see ruined; all contribute to render loud the sobs in which the evils of the age are lamented, and to make ignorant or careless men imagine the Catholicity of to-day, compared with that of former times, from a pacific, rich, powerful, and flourishing kingdom, has become a miserable province, surrendered to a small number of inhabitants, the victims of degradation and anarchy.

With the pardon of those who think thus, and for the consolation of those who would desire to see a more pleasing picture in the Church, I must say this is not what history teaches us, and that if the evils of our times are lamented so bitterly, it is simply because the present sickness is always the worst.

Whoever would understand in some measure the history of Christianity, and not be scandalised at every step by the adverse events it presents in such abundance, should never forget that the religion of Jesus Christ is one of sufferings, of contradictions, of persecutions—a religion of sacrifice inaugurated on earth by the immolation of the Lamb without spot. Everything that appertains to it bears this seal: the Baptist, the precursor, is decapitated, and his head serves in a revel to quench a horrible vengeance with blood; the Apostles suffer martyrdom in different parts of the world; and after them comes a multitude which no one can number, of all tongues, tribes, nations, conditions, ages, sexes, who suffer torments and death for the faith, and wash their stoles in the blood of the Lamb. Are you disheartened by the apostasies you witness, the errors that spring up, the straying away of so many who, through interest, shame, or some other passion, deny your Divine Master?—but do you forget, then, the treason of Judas, and the denial of St Peter?

We see, it is true, a multitude of separated sects, we see how the arrows of sophistry and calumny are pointed against the Church, but is this anything but the repetition of what has occurred in all ages since her foundation? In the first, the immoral heresies of Simon, Cerinthus, Menander, Ebion, Saturnius, Basilides, and Nicholaus, spring up like unclean insects. In the second appear the Gnostics, the Valentinians, the Orphites, the Archontici, the Marcionists, the Montanists and others. In the third we meet with the sectaries of Praxeas, of Sabellius, of Paul of Samosata, of Novatus, of Manes; so that whilst the Church had opposed to her the rack, the torture, the knife, the fire, and all kinds of horrid torments, she saw ungrateful children creep out of her own bosom to gnaw her vitals by corrupting the purity of morals and doctrine, by raising chair against chair, and by spreading, as doctrines emanating from heaven, the dreams of illusion and imposture.

And what shall we say of the succeeding centuries? The peace of Constantine is talked of, the advantages that from it resulted to the Church are dwelt on; it is all certain and true: but it is not less so, that that peace was often interrupted, frequently embittered, and that her Divine Spouse did not allow her to forget for a moment she was in a land of peregrination, was militant, and was not to enjoy here below the peace and felicity reserved for her, when the Jerusalem of this world shall be absorbed in the celestial one. In the very century in which the cross was planted over the throne of the Cæsars, the Church experienced such trials that the rigours of persecution could hardly cause greater. Who is ignorant of the disturbance and disasters produced by the schisms of the Donatists, the Melecionites, and the Luciferians? The churches of Africa, of Egypt, of Asia, beheld altar erected against altar, the faithful scandalously divided, and the seamless tunic of Jesus Christ torn into shreds. And what would it be if we should call to mind the many heresies that sprung up at the time, and particularly those of Arius and Macedonius? Oppressing indeed is the toil of those whom the Holy Ghost has appointed to govern the Church of God in our age; but oppressive also was that of the bishops who formed the Councils of Nice and Constantinople. Nor were there wanting Emperors who afflicted the Church, by overstepping their faculties, and mixing themselves up in purely ecclesiastical affairs;

and there was a Julian the Apostate, who took pleasure in lowering and humbling her, and there were also venomous writers who spread on all sides their destructive doctrines; and the apologists of religion found themselves compelled to labour without ceasing, and to multiply themselves, if we may say so, in order to attend to the many points that demanded the aid of their learning and eloquence in defence of truth. The names of St Athanasius, St Cyril, St Basil, the two Gregories, St Epiphanius, St Ambrose, St Augustin, St Jerome, St John Chrysostom, and other stars of that age, remind us of the hard combats that truth at the time sustained against error—hard, I call them, since to obtain the immortal victory so many giants had to enter the arena.

Then follows the irruption of the Barbarians; and the Church, far from enjoying the period of rest she would seem to require, finds herself in the midst of the ferocity of the invaders, the devastations which Arianism had made among them, the blind and captious prurience of the Emperors of the East, and the spirit of resistance to authority which spreads in different heresies. How many Councils! how many decisions of Popes! How many writings of men eminent for their sanctity and wisdom! How many disturbances in the nations subjected to the Church! How much wavering in the faith! Where is that peace which some people regret —that undisputed sway, that enviable calm which they suppose surrounded the bark of Peter, while it sailed over a still and tranquil sea? In this way, with various

but ever agitated fortune, she comes to the tenth century. In it there were no heresies, but in exchange
there was a profound ignorance, the mother of corruption, which also in its turn engenders the most detestable errors :—"æternam metuere sæcula noctem." The
violences of princes just escaped from barbarism then
took body ; feudalism was enthroned ; the contest of
the people with the lords, and of these among themselves, and with the kings, followed; and from this
chaos sprang up new heresies, of a character more
practical, more invasive, more threatening than the old
ones. I do not require to remind you, my esteemed
friend, of the names of those who now with arms, now
with the pen, now from the pulpit were let loose against
the Church ; the history of these errors and contests is
inseparable from that of Europe ; I shall only say that
the apparition of Protestantism, though a catastrophe
of awful consequences, was not however an entirely new
fact, but one which assumed a peculiar character on
account of the age in which it appeared.

Great ills indeed has the Church to bewail at present,
but I doubt very much whether they be equal to those
of the sixteenth and following centuries ; it appears to
me that neither in errors nor in disasters was anything
left to the genius of evil to desire. As regards the last
century, it is too near us to require to be even mentioned ;
it is enough to recollect it was opened with the disputes
and obstinacy of Jansenism, and worthily closed with
the Constitution of the Clergy, and the persecutions of
the Convention.

I have not intended to draw even a slight outline of the contradictions which the Church in all ages has suffered, that they might be compared with those she endures at present : my sole object was to give a touch here and there, which might call up to recollection at least the principal events, which render her history so painful and at the same time so glorious. With this I would desire that the faithful who contemplate with excessive affliction the evils of our times should console themselves by reflecting it is not so certain as they imagine, that this is the time in which God has permitted the power of the prince of darkness to act with most audacity. At least I for my part entertain strong doubts on this head, which will strike any one who reads the ecclesiastical annals with attention.

Considering what has happened during the past and present centuries, I may be told the faith has lost much in France, and be reminded that this has also happened in Portugal, Spain, and Italy, but I shall answer it has increased in Ireland, and gained great ground in England and Scotland ; and without discussing the exactness of the compensation, I shall observe that the Church has acquired the immense advantage in our time, that among the most civilized and advanced States there is none that looks on her with persecuting hostility. And let not the example of Russia be cited to the contrary, nor a passing fit of the Government of Prussia, nor the anomalies of other countries : the cause of religion is all the more lovely when it is bound up with the recollections of the nationality of an unfortunate people ; and

the Church looks more beautiful and fresh when she
has for persecutors pettiness in politics, and nullity in
philosophy.

Some infidels measure the decay of faith, by what
they observe in the persons of their acquaintance ; and
as these generally entertain the same ideas as themselves,
deduce from it that incredulity is the normal state of
men's minds. The same occurs here as in morals. The
immoral man discovers immorality in all parts; for
him there is no honest man, no modest woman, no
straightforward magistrate, no honourable merchant ;
perfidy, corruption, bribery hold sway in all hearts ;
and if you mark well his mode of reasoning, his own
vices are nothing but the result of his profound conviction that the exercise of virtue is completely impossible.
He is not wanting in an excellent disposition, good
desires, nor the force of mind necessary for doing good ;
but what would he gain by constituting himself the only
exception on earth ? The victim of the evil practices
and passions of others, he would be a sterile holocaust
offered on the altars of virtue, that goddess who abandoned so long ago her sublunary mansions never to
return to them again. Is it not true, my esteemed friend,
it is thus immoral men speak, who have sufficient
knowledge to reflect a little on their state, creating thus
a species of antidote against the gnawings of their conscience ? Apply what I have just said to incredulity,
and you shall discover a perfect analogy. The infidel
speaks with men who share his errors : they cast a glance
over the state of belief, and as each of them recollects

having met with others of the same opinion as himself—
at least his masters or disciples—they all add their
contingent of incredulity observed in distinct places,
and infer without hesitation that the induction is complete, that all votes are taken, that the faith has not a
single partisan, is finally 'condemned, and exiled for
ever from the earth.   Such a one, they say, pretends to
believe, but it is hypocrisy; another feigns it for interest,
some other in order not to grieve a devout mother or
wife ; in fine, every man that thinks agrees on the point
—the fact is so certain it is beyond all discussion.

I have heard a person make such remarks in the
coolest way possible ; but I could not forget what I
had seen with my own eyes.   I, who also had not been
careless in observing and collecting facts on the same
head, could not resign myself to abdicate my opinions,
and to suppose all my calculations false. Besides, I discovered an additional motive for not giving much importance to the inductions of my adversary.   Without
appearing to contradict him, I gave the conversation a
turn which might indicate to me from what springs he
had drunk in that profound knowledge of the world,
the theatre in which he had made his observations on
the actual state of belief. I saw at once that the persons
and circles he spoke of did not abound in faith ; and
even though he had not told me, I would have immediately suspected it, if what he was revealing were not
already known to me.   I then spoke to him of another
society, as we say ; of other circles ; of other men ; he
had no acquaintance with them, they were not of his set.

I brought the conversation to the religious movement of this or that country; I pronounced the name of a distinguished author; I reminded him of an interesting passage of a select-work; he had not dedicated himself much to this class of literature; from self-love, he affected to have some knowledge of it at least, with the modesty however of not manifesting it; but I said to myself that man was speaking of what he knew nothing; in his calculations he deduced universals from particulars, and all his show of observation on the state of belief, was reduced to what no person of any education is ignorant of.

Society, my esteemed friend, is not all in the capitals; nor are the capitals formed exclusively of a certain number of circles, no matter how presumptuous and arrogant these may be. We must extend the view somewhat farther, when we desire to form a judgment on the state of belief. What happens in political or mercantile movement does not hold here. It is commonly limited to very narrow circles; and to judge of its situation and tendencies, it is generally enough to take one's stand in some of the centres around which they revolve. In matters of religion it is very different; its ramifications are immense, its roots penetrate the vitals of society; the proud capital, no more than the miserable village, is exempt from its influence; and so one runs great risk in judging of it from what he has remarked in contracted circles.

But this letter is already growing too long; and so I will sum up by saying that what you so justly call the philosophy of the future, is one of the many chimeras of which the human mind dreams; that it solves no problem, tells us nothing about the transcendent questions it proposes to discuss, its prognostics cannot be fulfilled, and Catholicity presents no signs of death or decay. As regards the profound changes which, in the opinion of those philosophers, must be wrought in society, I agree with them; but I do not believe they will be effected in the way they imagine. I have no hesitation in acknowledging we are in a state of *transition;* but I am inclined to believe that, far from this transition being characteristic of our age, it is in a certain sense common to the whole history of humanity; because it is evident the human race is continually *passing* from one state to another. The indefinite perfectibility of which the *philosophers of the future* are incessantly talking, is a subject on which I entertain my doubts; as also on what they consider certain, and beyond all question, viz.: that humanity, even here on earth, is continually advancing towards perfection, and making new conquests every day. The *philosophic* scepticism with which, as I told you in a former letter, I am somewhat infected, prevents me, on hearing any very general proposition announced, from being blinded, either by the celebrity or the magisterial tone of the person who announces it; and causes me, in right of my independence, to examine whether the celebrated master could have been deceived. This has happened to me in the present *transition,* and in the continual *march* of society, and in the changes prognosticated for the future. On all these points I will give

you my opinions in another letter I intend to write to
you some other day. At present I cannot do so ; as
well because it would lengthen the present too much, as
because " non tantum est otii."—I remain, your most
affectionate friend,   J. B.

V.

The Blood of the Martyrs.

I SEE, my esteemed friend, it will be very difficult for
me to realise the intention I had formed in the beginning, of giving a certain order to the religious discussion
on which we were about to enter, by confining it to a
channel from which it could not escape ; but at the
same time directing it through charming prospects, and
allowing it capricious windings, which might take from
it the appearance of scholastic regularity, and give the
subject an agreeable and entertaining aspect. All my
efforts to make you enter into this plan are in vain ; for
you appear to prefer to treat of unconnected points, and
wander like the bee from flower to flower. Although I
know very well the inconveniences of this method, and
if I recollect well I have indicated them in one of my
former letters, yet I am compelled to follow you in the
road you are pleased to take, in order that you may not
get it into your head that I want to shun delicate questions, and by involving my opponent in a cloud of
authorities and theological arguments, endeavour to
hide weak points and avoid the danger of an attack on

F

them. However this necessity would be more disagreeable to me, if you had not been good enough to tell me that you are acquainted with the best works that have been written in defence of religion, and that, deferring the study of them until you shall have more time and patience, your only object at present is to clear up by way of recreation some difficult points, as a person who removes the obstacles that block up the entrance to a broad and spacious road.

To tell the truth, I am not displeased you have brought the discussion to bear on the point of *the Blood of the Martyrs*, for it is a subject on which a great deal can be said, and on which sooner or later we should have entered, if the controversy had taken the course I desired. This *blood* is undoubtedly one of the strongest arguments in support of the truth of our religion, and so, in examining the reasons Christians can allege in defence of the faith, I should not have forgotten to draw your attention to this prodigy, in which persons of all ages, sexes, and conditions, die with heroic fortitude, sooner than profane themselves by a single act that was not in conformity with the faith of the Crucified.

But before I begin I wish you to speak; and so to avoid confusion in the ideas, and in order that neither you nor I may forget the true state of the question, and consequently that my answer may be rendered as full and complete as possible, I will transcribe what you say in your letter. " I respect as much as any one fortitude of mind wherever I meet it, and I frankly own that the heroism of suffering appears in my eyes much more sublime than the heroism of the combat. With this I will save you no little trouble, for you will at once perceive you have no need to dwell on the number of the martyrs, nor on their atrocious torments, nor on their invincible constancy, nor to excite my enthusiasm by pointing to feeble old men, weak women, and tender children, marching fearlessly to die for the faith. I doubt very much that you exceed me here in senti- ments of respect and admiration; neither have you to take it amiss that my scepticism goes so far as to raise doubts about the immense number of these martyrs, for it does not. I will not rack my brain to deny a fact of such known truth. My impotent negations could not certainly blot out the pages of history. But leaving aside, and expressly confessing the truth of the fact, I cannot agree in the consequences you wish to draw from it ; because it is well known that enthusiasm for an idea can produce like results; and as regards the propagation of the Christian doctrines which resulted from the perse- cution, you well know that the secret of a cause's pros- perity is its persecution and contradiction, and its power to present its defenders to the world with honourable wounds which betoken their profound convictions, and invincible constancy in sustaining them." I did not wish to lop off a single particle of your argument, nor to depreciate in the slightest degree the force of the difficulty; but you must also permit me to enter into its solution at large, as the importance of the subject requires it.

First of all, I willingly accept the confession that the

number of our martyrs is astonishing, as are also the circumstances of their martyrdom, whether we regard the torments, or the persons who suffer. And when I accept it with pleasure, it is solely from the complacency I feel, on finding you do not obstinately combat the known truth ; but not because it is a confession which I could not oblige my adversary to make : to effect this, I have nothing more to do than to open the pages of history ; and as you sensibly observe, those pages are not to be blotted out by *impotent negations.* The Acts of the martyrs are not devout stories, invented to nourish piety in the faithful : they are documents which have passed the crucible of the most severe criticism. Ruinart, Mabillon, Natalis Alexander, Fleury, Tillemont, Papebroche, Holsten, and other critics by no means suspected of excessive credulity, and whose immense erudition and refined discernment make them competent authorities, would have come to my aid, if you had not had the prudent precaution to abstain from entering on a contest, in which you should not have come off best, in spite of the brilliancy of your talents : what do arguments avail against facts clearer than the light of day ? The city of Rome alone is an invincible argument in confirmation of the truth of the immense number of martyrs. It has been said that the catacombs of the eternal city are a great sepulchre—worthy footstool of the Chair of St Peter ! "We saw in the city of Romulus, says Prudentius, innumerable ashes of saints : if you ask, O Valerian, for the inscriptions of the tombs and the names of the victims, it is difficult to answer you :

so great is the number of the just sacrificed by the impious fury of idolatrous Rome! On many of the sepulchres there are letters which indicate the name of the martyr, or contain a short panygeric; but there are mute marbles which enclose a silent multitude, and signify the number alone. What heaps of corpses without a name! I recollect that in one single place I saw the relics of sixty, whose names Christ alone is aware of."

> Innumeros cineres sanctorum Romula in urbe
> Vidimus, O Christo Valeriane sacer !
> Incisos tumulis titulos, et singula quæris
> Nomina? Difficile est, ut replicare queam,
> Tantos justorum populos furor impius hausit
> Quum coleret patrios Troja Roma Deos.
> Plurima litterulis signata sepulcra loquuntur
> Martyris aut nomen, aut epigramma aliquod ;
> Sunt et muta tamen tacitas claudentia turbas
> Marmora, quæ solum significant numerum.
> Quanta virum jaceant congestis corpora acervis
> Nosse licet, quorum nomina nulla legas,
> Sexaginta illic defossas mole sub una
> Reliquias memini me didicisse hominum,
> Quorum solus habet comperta vocabula Christus.

Thus spoke this celebrated Spaniard in the fourth century ; from which we can see that even in those times the catacombs of Rome caused the same profound and religious wonder they produce in travellers of our day. The Church counts ten persecutions under the heathen emperors, which are those of Nero, Domitian, Trajan, Antoninus Verus, Severus, Maximin, Decius, Valerian, Aurelian and Diocletian ; in all, horrid atrocities were committed : and we must keep in mind that the persecution was not limited to a few places, but extended over the whole of the empire. It causes one horror to read in contemporary authors of the dreadful scenes which the cruelty of the persecutors, struggling with the firmness of the martyrs, enacted at every step : never was religion subjected to so hard a trial, never was humanity seen more evidently elevated to a height immensely above its reach.

Enthusiasm for an idea, you say, can produce like results; this difficulty requires a lengthened answer. We shall not deny there are cases when a person may become excited by an idea, affection or interest, to such a degree as to be capable of sacrificing his existence : it were not difficult to discover examples in the history of past times, nor is there a lack of them even in our own. But we do not want to know how far the moral force and energy of this or that individual, powerfully affected by an object, can go ; we do not intend to dispute the possibility of his giving his life for it with pleasure, and even of his suffering atrocious torments : the force of our argument does not consist in any such assertions, belied by reason and history. What we say is, that considering human weakness, it is not possible without particular assistance from heaven, that for three centuries, in all parts of the known world, persons of all ages, sexes, and conditions, could be found in such prodigious numbers, to joyfully sacrifice their property, their honour in the eyes of the world, and finally end their life amid the most cruel torments, solely because they did not wish to abandon the faith of the Crucified :

this is what we say, and we shall require whoever con-
tradicts us to show us in the annals of humanity a like
example; not content with this or that isolated case, we
will demand of him millions of millions such as we can
show: and convinced that he cannot do this, we shall
continue to believe our right to assert that our religion
has a character of which others are destitute.

You tell me "that every country has had its martyrs,
for martyrs those can be called who die for the independence of their fatherland, generously sacrificing their
existence to the well-being of their fellow-citizens; and
nevertheless it has never been believed a special grace
from heaven was necessary for such actions." This
observation, my esteemed friend, makes me suspect
you have not meditated much on the human heart, in
its relations with sacrifices, you confound ideas so, and
distinguish not what sacrifices are most costly to us.
Have you never meditated on the distance between
valour and fortitude, between bravely confronting a
danger and awaiting it with calmness, between running
a passing risk, and tolerating with resignation a long
chain of troubles and torments? The number of those
who are capable of the former is very great, but those
who attain to the latter are very few. Reason proves it,
history and experience bear testimony to it.

It is well known that one of the principal springs of
man's movements, when he acts in the purely natural
order, is his passions; without them, the heart is cold;
reason may plan, but the arm does not execute.
And when I speak of passions, I do not refer to evil

inclinations solely, nor to movements of the mind excited to such a point, that it loses sight of the principles of sound reason, and the suggestions of prudence. Under the name of passions, I include also all legitimate and generous sentiments, all the affections of the soul, even the more tranquil and temperate ; so that they appertain not to the order of pure reason, or to the acts of the will that emanate solely from it. I include all spontaneous impulses that carry us, as if instinctively, towards an object without the direction of the intellect ; in a word— and to express myself in language less exact, but clearer and perhaps more accommodated to the generality of understandings—by passions I mean everything that is commonly called a movement of the heart.

We know from our own and others' experience, that when these movements exist, we find ourselves more disposed to act in the direction in which they impel us; and when they are wanting, no matter how profound our convictions, and firm and decided our will may be, we are infected with a debility, with an indolence, to remove which we have to make an effort, if the action in question is in any way opposed to our natural inclinations. Let us suppose two men equally persuaded of the merit of beneficence, with equal means of performing it, with identical opportunities of practising it; but the one gifted with a compassionate and tender heart, whilst the other is naturally cold. The superior part of the soul, reason and the will, is in the same state in the first as in the second, and yet who does not see that to the former the alms with which he succours the misfortune of his brethren, will be a real pleasure, and to the latter a sacrifice? The one will have a passion, a sentiment, a movement of the heart, or whatever you wish to call it, which impels him to beneficence; he will suffer if he does not good; the misery of his neighbour has communicated itself to him in a certain sense, because by leaving his fortune and his health intact, it makes him partake of the sufferings he witnesses; when he dispenses aid he will experience an alleviation, he will recover his lost ease, tranquillity will spring up again in his soul, and his trouble will be dissipated; he will enjoy the sweet satisfaction of having performed a duty, which he felt as a necessity in the depth of his soul. Nothing of the kind takes place in the man of cold heart, no matter how sound his reason may be, no matter how well adjusted to it is his will. If he succours the needy, he will be acting in conformity with the dictates of his conscience, but in obeying its precepts he will not feel that expansion, that tenderness which inundates with joy and pleasure a compassionate heart; on the contrary, he will feel himself compelled to struggle with the difficulty, which the depriving one's self of one's own to give it to another, always brings with it.

This example makes the powerful influence which the inclinations of our heart exercise on our acts sensible, and if I may say so, palpable. From this I infer that when we find ourselves in situations, in which any passion whatever is excited and active, it is not strange, that preponderating over the rest, and even over the natural instinct of self-preservation, it hurries us on to

difficult undertakings, and even to run the greatest
dangers. Thus, it should not be wondered at, that a
soldier in the field of battle, where his companions in
arms are witnesses of his valour or cowardice; thirsting
with vengeance against an enemy who is decimating on
right and left his friends and comrades; excited by the
pomp of war, the sound of martial music, of the fife and
drum, should with brave impetuousness rush to a glorious
death; the more because he entertains some hope of
avoiding it, and of winning by his valour the respect and
admiration of all that behold him.   Then we see develop-
ing themselves love of country, love of glory, ambition
roused by hope of reward, all acting at once on a mind
excited by critical circumstances, by the presence of an
imminent danger, the body being besides in the most
favourable disposition for maintaining the passions in
lively activity and effervescence, from the agitation and
heat of the contest.   In such cases there is a real struggle
of inclinations against inclinations; and it is very natural
that those should prevail, which being in more harmony
with the situation, are more suited to be put in motion,
to influence the will, to stifle all others that tend to stop
or moderate their impulse.

These observations show how it comes to pass that
many men despise death in defence of a cause; and let
it not be thought that to arrive at this point it is necessary that the mind should be excited in the way I have
described; circumstances may arise in which, without
its being so sensible, the phenomenon can take place in
a more or less similar manner.   Thus, a young man,

who finds himself involved in one of those risks of *honour*, as they are called, is not in the same case as a soldier in the field of battle; nevertheless, though the former situation appear ever so distinct from the latter, it is not so in reality, if we examine it in its relations with the causes that impel one to despise life. A deplorable prejudice, but one which for all that is deeply rooted in many minds, makes him believe, that if he does not accept the duel to which he is challenged, or if in his turn he does not challenge his adversary, according to circumstances, he will be covered with ignominy and shame, and cannot present himself in society without the dishonourable epithet of coward. In a man placed in this alternative, we do not certainly see so well at a glance the motives which impel him to run the danger, as we do in the soldier; the agitation of the mind fluctuating between hope and fear, between the love of life and that of honour, is not quite so patent; but for all that, the struggle exists, and exists perhaps as fully as in the field of battle. No matter what emptiness be concealed in the word *honour*, it cannot be denied that it exercises on our minds an influence so lively, so magical, that neither health nor fortune produces so strong and instantaneous an effect. Leaving aside the examination of the causes, I merely mention the fact to show that even in the case supposed there is a real excitement of the mind, a strong passion that subdues the rest, bringing them under its tyrannical rule, and hurrying along the conquered heart, even to the deplorable extremity of looking on life as a trifle.

I think, my esteemed friend, the observations I am
after making, are sufficient to distinguish valour from
fortitude, and to show how different it is to run fearlessly a risk, no matter how imminent, and to suffer the
greatest torments with unalterable calmness, marching
serenely to a death, which is sure, inevitable, surrounded
with the most atrocious sufferings. In the first case, we
see one passion opposed to another, we see the mind
sustained by a thousand motives which impel it forward,
and at the same time distract its attention from all that
might draw it back. In the first case, there are no
sufferings, or very brief, or if any there be, they are
counterbalanced by the alternatives or hopes of recreation, pleasure, glory. In the second case, we behold
reason and the will struggling with all the passions; we
behold the superior man opposed to the inferior; the
former armed with the idea of duty, with the hope of a
great object; the latter with all the attractions, with all
the threats, with all the fears, with all the vicissitudes of
feeling that ever restlessly heave in that tempestuous
region, which for want of a better name we call the
heart.

I do not mean to say by this, that in the purely
natural order there cannot be found an astonishing disinterestedness, or that supernatural grace must be supposed
to enter into all the acts which we denominate heroic;
such an assistance the Gentiles certainly had not, or the
many heroes belonging to false sects; nevertheless we
find in them surprising actions that fill us with wonder
and awaken our enthusiasm. Regulus returning to Car-

thage after giving a counsel that must cost him his life,
Scaevola with his hand in the fire; these and other in-
stances recorded in ancient history, are truly evident
proofs of what man abandoned to his natural strength is
capable of doing; but they do not destroy the argument
which we draw from our martyrs. The heroes of whom
we are speaking are very few, ours are innumerable; the
heroes were generally men of full age; hardened with
the toils of war; with minds enlarged by mingling in
public affairs; greedy of glory; placed in critical circumstances, in which their country's danger gave wings
to their enthusiasm and energy to their bravery; amongst
the martyrs we find old men, women, children; men of
the most humble conditions, who had never occupied
distinguished posts, and who consequently had never
acquired that fierce pride, which, as it is one of the
most powerful passions of our heart, sometimes communicates to us a firmness of which we are incapable
without it.

To form an idea of the merit of the martyrs, let us
approach one of these illustrious prisoners, so unfortunate in the eyes of the world, so happy in Jesus Christ.
His name is unknown, his position is obscure; why is
he in chains?—because he believes that a Man who died
as a criminal in Palestine is the Son of God and true
God, who took on Himself our nature, to satisfy the
justice of His eternal Father for our debts. What do we
see around him?—the disdain, compassion, or hatred of
all who behold him; some look on him as a madman,
others regard him as a fanatic; these call him a deluded

wretch, those accuse him of foul crimes. Not a ray of worldly glory is his, not a consolation has he on earth. In vain do you look for something in his situation that can strengthen him, by making his nature work by reaction against the evils that oppress him. All his passions are subdued by the low state and prostration to which his body is reduced ; and if pride should raise its head, it would find nothing around it to flatter or sustain it. What similarity is there between the hero of religion and those of the world ?

I may be told that the hope of a better life rendered their sufferings tolerable and death agreeable to them ; this is true, and Christians do not deny it ; but it is precisely in this very resolution of sacrificing the present to the future ; of rising above all natural inclinations ; of despising everything that surrounds them, and even their very existence ; it is in this resolution, I repeat, that the supernatural action of divine grace is visible ; for human weakness abandoned to itself could never effect it. In one of my former letters I remarked that man naturally inclines to allow himself to be carried away by the impressions of the moment, and everything he sees at a distance, be it evil or be it good, is of little interest to him. We unfortunately see this clearly in a great number of Christians, who, though believing the terrible truths of our religion, yet live as forgetful of them as Gentiles could. For this reason, on seeing that so astonishing a number of persons of all ages, sexes, and conditions, rise superior to this weakness of our nature, contradicting its inclinations with decision so heroic, we must necessarily acknowledge there is something here far above this natural region, something in which the Omnipotent is pleased to show forth the power of weakness when His almighty arm makes it strong.

I do not know, my esteemed friend, whether these reflections may have fully convinced you; but considering your good sense, I will venture to hope they have. I cannot persuade myself that your clear understanding does not see the immense difference between our martyrs and the heroes of the world, be they of what order they may. You are not unacquainted with their history; bring to mind all you have read, and you shall discover nothing that can be compared with this prodigy. What natural causes can your imagination suggest in explanation of it? Enthusiasm! But how is it possible for so fleeting a sentiment to last for three centuries? How could it be propagated through the whole known world? Human glory! But how can it be said that the man who perished without leaving even a name died for glory? And what sort of glory must that be which equally attracts the fiery youth and the feeble old man; the matron and the virgin; the adult and the child; the wise and the ignorant; the rich and the poor; the lord and the beggar? Let us be sincere, and we must necessarily acknowledge that no matter how powerful the influence of glory may be over our hearts, it never yet was able to produce an effect so great, so universal, in persons and situations so different; let us be sincere, and we shall here discover the finger of God.

If the Christians had been few, and had all dwelt in

the same neighbourhood, living subject to the same influences, and with a religion of short existence, then it would not be so contrary to reason to say, that a certain excitement of the mind was introduced among them, and was communicated from one to another. But throughout the whole world, and for the space of three centuries, and always the same constancy! Reflect, my esteemed friend, on this last observation, for it alone is sufficient to dispel all difficulties.

I come now to the other point indicated in your letter, concerning the weight of the argument founded on the rapid propagation of Christianity, in spite of the horrible persecution to which it was subjected for so long a time. You say it is well known the best means of making a cause prosper, and of diffusing a doctrine, is to employ violence against it; for from the moment its defenders bear on their brows the aureola of martyrdom, they excite the admiration and enthusiasm of all who behold them, and draw to them a great number of proselytes. More than once have I meditated on what you and others assert of the power of diffusion communicated by persecution; and I candidly confess that, whether I listened to the dictates of philosophy, or attended to the lessons of history, I have never been able to persuade myself that a good means of supporting a cause is to persecute it with fire and sword.

On this head there is great confusion of ideas and facts, which it is necessary to remove. In order to effect it, I shall separately propose some questions, on the solution of which depends our forming a right judg-

ment on the subject in hand. Is it true that the sight
of persecution excites enthusiasm or interest in favour
of the persecuted ? This question cannot be answered
without a distinction. Either the persecuted are considered innocent, or they are regarded as guilty; in the
first case we will answer affirmatively; in the second,
negatively, for then, all that they can inspire is compassion; but this has nothing to do with the enthusiasm,
or the interest of which we are speaking. There can be
no doubt of this; and from it I infer that to assert in
general that persecution honours, that it renders illustrious, that it excites sympathy, is true only in the case
of one who is regarded as innocent, and only with
respect to those who consider him such ; in the eyes of
these alone is the person truly persecuted ; in the eyes
of others, he has not this character, he is not a victim of
persecution, but an object of public justice. Hence it
follows that when a persecution is excited in a country
against a cause or a doctrine, if it be considered just and
holy, those who suffer for it will be respected and
admired, but if it be reputed false, unjust, contrary to
the common good, then the punishment of the criminal,
far from exciting any such admiration and respect, will
inspire at most sentiments of sterile compassion for the
deluded wretches, as they are supposed to be.

The Christian Martyrs were not at all favourably
circumstanced in any sense. Professing a religion
diametrically opposed to all those received by the
generality of nations ; preaching that the worship paid
to the reigning gods was nothing less than criminal

G

idolatry; avoiding the diversions of the Gentiles as accursed abominations, they were looked on with aversion, with hatred, with detestation—they were loaded with calumnies, they were regarded as enemies of the rest of men, as disturbers of society; and to make them drain the dregs of the chalice of affliction, they were accused of committing horrible crimes in the celebration of their mysteries. No one can be ignorant of the frenzy with which the blood of the confessors of Jesus Christ was sought: *The Christians to the wild beasts, the Christians to the fire;* this was the cry raised in all corners of the world. Covered with insults and mockery while expiring amid the most atrocious torments, it was considered a great happiness if some brethren could come out of their hiding-places in the night to give sepulture to their mutilated bodies that were left to be devoured by the beasts. Now that we see them on our altars; now that we hear hymns intoned in their praise; now that we know they bear on their brows in heaven the imperishable crown whose rays are reflected in the reverence paid them on earth, we find it difficult to conceive all the horror of the situation in which they were placed in the dread moments of their torments and death. No, they did not behold around them that respect, that admiration which we now offer them; they beheld instead the hatred, the insults, the calumny, and what perhaps is more grievous to the human heart, the mockery and contempt with which they were treated; God alone was their consolation; God alone was their hope; God alone was their stay in those terrible moments, in which, struggling with the world and with themselves, they fearlessly braved death in confession of the Faith of the Crucified. For such prodigies human causes are not sufficient, nor are the efforts of weak humanity. To whoever is not content with these reasons we will propose the famous dilemma : they were either miraculously sustained by Heaven, or they were not ; if the first be true, then you agree with us ; if the second, we then tell you it is the greatest of miracles to perform things so miraculous without a miracle.

We may infer from this that the constancy of the martyrs could not be sustained by the pleasure of exciting admiration and enthusiasm : and thus is refuted the assertion that the honours of persecution, by rendering the victims illustrious, contribute to the destruction of the object the persecutor has in view.

Is it true that the persecution of a doctrine is a good means of propagating it ? The question appears somewhat strange at first sight ; and yet the affirmative is hourly sustained in open contradiction of philosophy and history. If we were told that truth forces a passage for itself through persecution, the assertion would be very different; but to pretend that persecution itself is a vehicle of truth, is an absurdity ; unless we suppose that the infinite wisdom of the Almighty avails itself of this vehicle for its lofty ends.

Man naturally loves his well-being, he has a strong attachment to life, a great horror of death ; therefore torments and the scaffold are powerful engines to sepa-

rate him from a cause which exposes him to the risk of
suffering them. You tell me, my esteemed friend, of
" the beauty of suffering, of the brilliant aureola which
invests the brows of the victim who marches calmly to
offer himself in holocaust." All this is true; but I am
very much afraid it is not well calculated to influence the
generality of men ; I am very much afraid that in practice it would not appear so enchanting and attractive as
it does in books. And do not upbraid me with having
an insensible heart ; with not comprehending all the
sublimity of heroic actions; I feel it and comprehend
it very well ; but coming to examine reality, and not
fictions, I am compelled to adhere to what I see in the
pages of history, and to what the lessons of experience
teach me. How many men are there so generous as
to sacrifice their well-being, their fortune and their life,
in the cause of truth and justice ? They are now, and
always were, very few; and the very admiration with
which they inspire us is an evident proof that such
heroic fortitude is not the common patrimony of humanity. Do you desire to have partisans ? Distribute
honours; be prodigal of riches; scatter pleasures
around ; for if you have nothing but the palm of martyrdom, very soon shall you see your proselytes and
friends disappear ; very soon shall you be without rivals
to dispute with you the aureola of a life of sufferings, and
of a dreadful death.

To tell the truth, I did not believe I should be compelled to remind you of these truths, which, though sad
ones, do not for all that cease to be truths ; I imagined

that being a sceptic, you should be somewhat more *positive ;* and living in an age of vicissitudes, you would have learned to know men better, and to form more exact ideas on the inclinations of our heart.

The good sense of humanity has always rejected the philosophical discovery concerning the advantages of persecution ; tyrants have sometimes deceived themselves by outrageously abusing severity ; but in the midst of their excesses they were guided by a true idea, which is, that to destroy a cause or suffocate a doctrine, an excellent means is to fill them with dangers and ills for all those who might desire to follow them. I go about seeking in history the good effects of persecution in favour of the cause persecuted, and I do not find them. I meet with an exception in Christianity ; but this carries me on to think the cause of the exception is in the omnipotence of God. The stoning of St Stephen inaugurated an era of triumphs, by opening the glorious catalogue of Christian Martyrs ; but I do not find that the hemlock of Socrates inspired philosophers with the desire of dying : *prudence* gained ground ; when Plato announces certain delicate truths he takes care to cover them with a hundred veils.

Coming to later times I find the same phenomenon ; thus for example, I see that the sect of the Priscilianists against which much rigour was employed, was stopped in its progress and even totally extinguished. One of the religions that extended themselves most, was undoubtedly that of Mahomet ; and certainly its progress was not due to persecution, but to the arms by which it routed its adversaries, and to the allurements by which it drew after it a great number of proselytes. Neither do I see that at the time of the religious wars of the South of France against the Albigenses, these sectaries prospered by opposition ;⸱ on the contrary they were diminishing daily, till they fell into a state of prostration and of almost total annihilation.

You will tell me that Protestantism spread and took root in spite of the opposition it had to suffer ; and as the so-called Reformation extended notwithstanding persecution, it is not improbable the same might have happened with respect to Christianity. I do not know where you have found this tremendous opposition and these persecutions suffered by the unfortunate Reformation ; one would think we were speaking of the ages of hieroglyphics, facts are so upturned and such false comparisons made.

Let us cast a glance on the first days of Protestantism, and we shall see it was very far from owing its progress to the persecutions you make so much of. In Germany, from the moment it appeared, it had on its side many and very powerful patrons : amongst them some princes who openly manifested that patronage, now by protecting the diffusion and establishment of the new doctrines by various means ; now by appealing to arms, when they considered the time for violence had arrived. What happened in Germany, also occurred in the other countries of the Continent, more or less infested with Protestantism ; without excepting France, where, as is well known, besides the patrons it met with in the upper

classes, it was able to count, for a long time, on one who
was equal to them all—Henry IV. It is not necessary
to go over the history of Henry VIII. of England;
no one is ignorant of what means this violent monarch
employed to propagate and root deeply the schism to
which his blind passion hurried him ; and this persecutor's system continued in the following reigns, with
equal if not with greater violence.

A short time after the birth of Protestantism it had
already in its favour great armies ; powerful princes ;
entire nations ; what point of comparison is there then
between the propagation of the so-called Reformation
and that of the Christian religion? Again ; if there
were not wanting some who sacrificed themselves for
it, recollect that this is what happens in all civil disturbances : ever on one side and the other are there fiery
partisans found, who either die fighting in the field of
battle, or have nerve enough to mount the scaffold.

Let us imagine that for the space of three centuries
it had to struggle with the horrible persecutions of
which Christianity was the victim: where would it be
at present? Do you wish to know? Observe what
happened in the countries where it was repressed with
a strong hand. In France, it had different alternatives
of indulgence and rigour; but as soon as severe measures
were employed against it with some perseverance, it became debilitated and almost disappeared. To what
was it reduced some time after the revocation of the
Edict of Nantes? Never has it been able to recover
from the blow inflicted on it by Louis XIV.; and it is

worthy of note that even at present, after so many years of tolerance, it is yet very insignificant. In that country the immense majority is divided between Catholicity and infidelity.

What happened in Spain may give us an idea of the fortitude of Protestantism in making head against persecution. It is well known that in the middle of the sixteenth century it had made many proselytes, all the more dangerous, as they belonged to distinguished classes. The Inquisition, sustained and fomented by Philip II., employed against them that rigour of which we hear so much: at the end of a little time the partisans of the new doctrines had disappeared. Was this the conduct of the first Christians? Did they abandon so easily the ground where they had achieved some conquests? Let the whole world answer; let Spain itself in particular, watered and fertilized with the blood of so many martyrs, answer. It is no use to allege the rigour of the Inquisition; this rigour could not certainly be compared with that of the pro-consuls of the Empire; no matter in what colours the pains applied to heretics may be painted, they will never equal those which St Vincent suffered.

What has been said of Spain may be applied to Portugal and Italy, so that Protestantism was not able to hold its own in any of the countries in which it found itself compelled to suffer a well-sustained opposition. Wherever men seriously determined to extirpate it, it was extirpated; presenting in this a notable contrast with Catholicity, which even in the countries where it suffered the greatest shocks, has always been preserved, without its persecutors being able to effect its total extinction. In confirmation of this truth recollect what has happened in Great Britain.

I do not know, my esteemed friend, what answer can be made to the reasons I have adduced. I think that after reading them, the argument founded on *the blood of the martyrs*, must appear to you somewhat stronger than before. Examine with attention and impartiality this grand fact, that renders the first pages of the history of the Church at once horror-striking and sublime ; and I doubt not that you will find in it something miraculous, which it is impossible to explain by natural causes. I think I have removed the difficulties which prevented you from giving to our argument all the importance it deserves. Be that as it may, I am certain you cannot accuse me of having avoided treating the question under all its aspects, or of diminishing in the least tittle the force of the difficulty, that I might not be compelled to meet it. If I have not been able to agree with ideas which you looked on as received, neither have I taken the liberty of rejecting them, without adducing the reasons that lead me to do so. When one deals with sceptics, he too should not be over-credulous ; and consequently he should not accept anything without examining it, even though it be necessary to contradict philosophical authorities which pass as respectable. I would much wish we could continue the discussion on the motives of credibility ; but considering the course it is taking, I am not sure but

that after having passed through hell and then mounted
the scaffold of the martyrs, I shall next find you, at a
bound, among the choirs of the cherubim. In the meantime, believe me, ever yours, &c.,   J. B.

VI.

Social Transition.

MY DEAR FRIEND,—If I had no other proofs of the
truth of the Catholic doctrine, *that faith is a gift of God*,
what I have experienced in you and others who have
had the misfortune to wander from the faith of their
forefathers, would incline me in no small degree to regard
it as certain. They dispute, they listen, apparently
with docility—they make one conceive the greatest
hopes that they are about surrendering themselves to
the evidence of the arguments with which they are
pressed ; but in the end they come out with a cold,
"*but, what do I know,*" which freezes the blood, and
dissipates at one fell swoop all the illusions of the
believer, who was thirsting for the moment when he
might see the stray sheep return to the fold. This is
what you have done in your last ; you have nothing to
object to what I said about the *blood of the martyrs*,
you confess that no religion can bring forth such an
argument, you show yourself satisfied with the contents
of my former letters with respect to the various points
that formed the object of your doubts ; and when my
heart leaped with joy, thinking you were going to deter-

mine, I will not say on entering again into the number
of believers, but at least on diving deeper and deeper
into the discussion, with the desire of definitely finding
out the truth, I meet with this desolating clause that has
filled me with profound sadness: "What do we know,"
you say, with a prostration of spirit that penetrates my
heart, "what do we know? Man is of so little worth!
—let us cast a glance around us and we discover nothing
but darkness. Who knows where the truth lies ?—who
knows what in time will become of that faith, of that
Church which you believe shall last to the consummation
of ages ? I do not despise religion, I see that Catholicity
is a grand fact which I am unable to explain by ordinary
causes ; you appeal to history, you press me to cite
anything similar ; I have already told you on other
occasions I am not the one to intrench myself behind
impotent negations ; that I am not the one to resist the
evidence of facts, but for all that, *I cannot believe*. I
am contemplating present society, and I think its
restlessness is a sign that the world is on the eve of
colossal events ; the new era should undoubtedly be
inaugurated with an intellectual and moral revolution,
and then perhaps that dark horizon, where nothing is discovered but error and uncertainty, may in some measure
brighten up. Let us allow that period of transition to
pass, and perhaps new times will decipher the enigma."

Do not believe, my esteemed friend, that in my
affliction I wonder at such language ; you are not the
first from whom I have heard it ; but allow me at least
to tell you that with your words nothing is answered,

nothing is proved, nothing is affirmed, nothing is denied;
you do no more than relieve yourself vainly by painting
the true state of your mind.   You have the truth before
you, and you have not courage enough to embrace it;
you incline towards it for a moment, but soon allowing
yourself to fall fainting, you say—*I cannot*.   Then you
speak of that future at which you yourself laughed in
one of your former letters ; you speak of that *transition*
of which you know not in what it consists ; you doubt ;
you fluctuate ; you put off your resolution for a little
longer ; you postpone it to future times, to those times,
alas ! in which you shall have ceased to exist !   Sad
consolation !—deceitful hope !

But if you faint, my dear friend, I should not do so ;
God has commenced the work, and He will finish it ; I
have the sweet presentiment you shall not die in the
arms of scepticism.   You say you heartily desire to
discover the truth ; persevere in your determination ;
I have confidence that He who shed His blood for
you on the summit of Calvary will not fail to bring you
to it.

I know well you are not in a disposition to receive
an answer treating principally of purely religious subjects ; the scepticism of the age has recovered its ascen-
dancy over you in a sad way ; and jumping from the
discussion you have run into the regions of *socialism*
and of the *future*, talking about *transitions, critical*
epochs, and I know not what of the same kind.   I have
already said I will follow you wherever you wish ; if
you do not like to treat of dogmas to-day, we will leave

them aside ; and as you talk of *transition*, of transition will I talk too.

I told you in one of my former letters I did not believe transition was characteristic of our age, but was common to all ; because I cannot agree that under this conception, anything is taking place now which did not more or less take place always. But when I assert this, I speak principally of countries which move, not of those which, frozen in the midst of their career, remain fixed as statues during the course of ages. If we except these, and direct our view to the others, we shall see, in the first place, that the Greeks and Romans lived in perpetual transition. The age of Draco has no similarity with that of Solon, nor the latter's with that of Alcibiades ; nor do that of Alexander and that of Demetrius resemble one another. And yet these ages were very near one another, which indicates that Grecian society incessantly passed from one state to another very different. The time between Brutus who expelled Tarquin, and Brutus, Cæsar's assassin, is not very long ; but see what various phases the social and political state of the Romans presents in that space. Analogous observations could be made with respect to other ancient peoples; and even as regards those which we call stationary, it should not be forgotten that they are little known to us, that their internal history, which would portray their religious ideas, their domestic customs, their social organisation, their legislation, has remained for the greater part hidden from our view, and buried in the ruins of time, without our being able to acquire but a

very slight and superficial knowledge of them except
through the medium of foreign historians. Modern
science is making an effort to supply this defect;
but how difficult it is to discover the truth at such a
distance of time, in the case of languages so unlike; of
ideas and customs so dissimilar! Be this as it may, it
may yet be affirmed that these nations were far from
being in a state of immobility; and besides what the
little knowledge we possess regarding them manifests
to us, a simple reflection on the nature of things is sufficient to induce us to conjecture that their changes and
modifications have been more numerous than we are
aware of, and of greater importance than we are accustomed to think; and consequently they, too, have been
in a state of *transition.*

But leaving the ancient and comparatively unknown
peoples, and coming to modern ones, beginning from the
appearance of Christianity, the changes and modifications they have incessantly experienced are innumerable;
so that it is not possible to prognosticate any change in
society of the present day which had not its equivalent
or superior in former times. Though we should grant
that the most exaggerated predictions of some socialists
should be verified, and their wildest plans put in execution, the new social state would not be more different
from the present, than the various ones through which
Christian nations have passed.

If the men who lived when slavery was general and
was considered as an indispensable condition in all well-
organised society, had heard of a state similar to that

which European nations enjoy at present, they would not have been able to conceive how public order could be maintained ; nor labour distributed ; nor conveniences and pleasures supplied to the richer classes ; in a word, they would believe it impossible for societies so numerous to subsist when deprived of the basis, which was so necessary in their eyes. Tell a feudal lord entrenched in his fortress, that a day shall come when all his titles will be despised ; when his name and that of all those of his class will sink into oblivion ; when his descendants will be confounded with those of his poor and unfortunate vassals whom he regards with proud disdain, as they pass submissive and humble at the foot of his turrets ; tell him that that same people shall rise against him ; and struggle for a long time ; and triumph ; and become rich, powerful, influential, eclipsing all the splendour of their lords, and filling the world with the fame of their deeds ; tell him so, and he will hear you with astonishment ; and he will imagine you are relating fairy tales, or speak in jest, or have lost your wits. What more ? It is not necessary that you consider the social metamorphoses at such a distance in order that they may appear incredible ; announce to those nobles of the time of Charles VI. and Francis I., to those descendants of the ancients lords, who are transforming the independence of their ancestors into heroic fidelity to their kings ; who are translating their residence from the country to the capital, and hastening to become converted from warriors into courtiers ; that in the space of three centuries it will not be they who shall occupy the lofty posts in

the state ; who shall lead the armies to victory ; who
shall exercise the functions of the magistracy ; and that
their vote on great subjects will not be considered of
more value than that of the descendants of those ple-
beians who water the earth with their sweat ; who fill
the most lowly offices, and who, gathered in small groups,
appear to be content with the social position that fell to
their lot after the war of their ancestors—the Commons ;
and one may well venture to say that those nobles will
not comprehend you ; that they will not believe a particle of your prognostics ; and no matter how much you
labour to show them the signs which clearly appear · at
no great distance, they will think you take the illusions
of your imagination for reality.

Transfer yourself to the Europe of the eleventh and
twelfth centuries—to the Europe of Suger and St Bernard
—and tell the men of that age that the rich monasteries,
the opulent abbacies that compete in splendour and
magnificence with the castles of the feudal lords, will
disappear in time ; and that at a time not very remote nothing shall remain of them but some ruins, the object of
the curiosity of archæologists ; that the clergy whose influence in everything is immense, and whose power and
riches do not yield to those of any other class whatever,
shall find itself limited to the precincts of the temples,
despoiled of its privileges ; deprived of its property ;
curtailed in its right to teach, whilst the minister of
religion is placed in the category of the humblest citizen,
if he be not sunk below this level by being denied what
is granted to all ; tell them, I repeat, of this change, and

you will see how they will look on it as impossible, unless they conceive its realisation by supposing that a Saracenic invasion had subdued the Christian power ; or that new hordes of unknown peoples had been scattered over Europe and changed its face. They will not be able to conceive how, without irruptions of barbarous peoples ; without the conquest of the Saracens, but on the contrary, after their complete overthrow, the simple course of ideas and events could produce in society changes so profound.

All the revolutions that can take place, can in the end lead to no other result than to alter the position and relations of individuals and classes. Let what changes you will be supposed—scarcely can one be imagined with respect to property, organisation of labour, distribution of products, domestic condition, social rank, or political influence, of more importance or magnitude than those verified in preceding times. *Transition* has always existed as it exists at present ; European nations have incessantly passed through different states, either completely abandoning that which they had, or modifying it in a thousand ways, till they transformed it into another nowise resembling the former.

Make, my esteemed friend, what suppositions you wish, even the most arbitrary and capricious, and compare them with the historical facts of which no one is ignorant, and I am sure you will be convinced of the truth of what I am after saying. Do you wish to suppose the needy classes shall escape from the dejected state they hold at present, and approach the middle and

even the higher ones? See whether the labourers of
to-day are at a greater distance from their employers
than slaves from their masters, and vassals from their
lords. Certainly not: and nevertheless, not even a
trace of ancient slavery remains in Europe, and but
slight vestiges of vassalage are preserved, and the descendants of those who lived subject to these conditions,
hold the same rank as the grandchildren of those who
one day saw themselves placed at an immense distance
above them, as well in point of riches as of honours,
respect, and all kinds of distinctions and power. Do
you wish to suppose that property shall suffer great
modifications; that its distribution shall be subject to
laws very different from those that hold at present?
Compare the Middle Ages with ours, the France of Charlemagne, for example, with the France of Napoleon, that
of St Louis with that of Louis Philippe. Do you wish
to imagine a new organisation of labour, subjecting the
workman and the capitalist to other rules, notably altering their relations, and varying the present bases of the
partition of products? Compare the tenant of the present day with the vassal of the feudal lord; the workman of our time with the slave of old. Are industry
and commerce to be subject for the future to new laws,
which shall alter the internal organisation of nations and
their foreign relations? Open our commercial codes;
cast a glance at our habits and customs in this regard,
and compare them with what existed among our ancestors. No matter on how vast a scale these branches of
trade be extended; no matter how great the strength

and vigour they may acquire; will they differ more from
their present state than it differs from that in which they
found themselves, when the Church in her councils attended paternally to the protection of the newly-born
mercantile traffic? Do you not think the powerful commercial companies of France, of Belgium, of Germany,
of England, of the United States, differ somewhat from
those caravans of merchants whose safety on the road
the excommunications of the Church could with difficulty secure? Do you not think that in this there has
been no small *transition?*

'And what might we not say, if we attended to the
social and political changes—to the diversity of position
the different classes have respectively lost or won? We
are separated from our ancestors by an abyss so profound that if they should rise from the tomb, they would
understand nothing of the present state of affairs. Where
is the power of feudalism; of the nobility; of the clergy?
What became of the prerogatives, the privileges, the
honours, they enjoyed? In what do the thrones of the
present day resemble those of old? What similarity
exists between our forms of government and ancient
ones—between our administration—between our finan-
cial systems—between our wars and our diplomacy, and
those of other days? We think differently; we feel
differently; we act differently; we live differently; both
our private and public condition has changed so completely that to comprehend what it was, we have to
make an effort of imagination, which withal is able to
supply us only with very imperfect and discoloured pic-

tures. Why do those times appear to us so poetical, my esteemed friend ? Why do they cut such a figure in our literature ?—because they are at an immense distance from the reality before us.

I would infer from this, that when great changes in the organisation of peoples are announced, we should not refuse to believe them, simply because they may appear strange to us ; for on close observation, present society does not differ less from what preceded it, than the future one, in all the combinations that can be made and conceived would from ours. Instability is one of the distinctive characters of human things; and whoever prognosticates a long duration for what of itself is so weak and changeable, must have reflected very little on the nature of man ; must have derived very little fruit from the lessons of history and experience. Let society be under whatever power it may, revolutionary or conservative ; let them endeavour to impel it or detain it as they will, it always varies, it passes without ceasing from one state to another, whether that other be better or worse.

This alternation between better and worse, brings me, my dear friend, to another question, of which as far as I can understand you are fond, as you could not be otherwise, considering the spirit of our age. It is said every moment that progress is the law of society ; that it never disobeys it, and that in the midst of the most terrible revolutions and catastrophes humanity tends to a destiny, which, as the speakers know not what it is, they cautiously cover with a golden veil. I shall not be the one to dishearten the movement of humanity, by dissipating flattering hopes ; though neither can I allow a proposition which as it stands is in contradiction with philosophy, history, and experience, to be laid down with too much generality, and without the necessary explanation.

It is very usual to speak of perfection, of perfectibility, of the law of progress, without distinguishing anything ; without expressing whether societies taken in particular or in general are treated of ; that is, without determining whether the law, the existence of which is asserted, holds in all society, or is peculiar to the human race solely, considered with abstraction from this or that one of its parts.   I will make bold to ask those who say that progress towards perfection is the constant law of all society, what progress can be discovered in the north of Africa or the coasts of Asia, comparing the present state with that which they enjoyed when they produced such men as Tertullian, St Cyprian, St Augustin, Philo, Josephus, Origen, St Clement, and many others whom it would be too long to enumerate ?

This does not admit of reply, as, on the other hand, it proves nothing against those who say that though this or that society decays, humanity progresses ; that civilization migrates ; that one nation acquires what another loses, and that in this way there exists a real compensation.   Thus, for example, in the present case, humanity has been indemnified for its losses in Africa and Asia with the immense expansion it has attained in Europe and America ; for if the millions of men who live at present under civilized rule were counted, the number would be incomparably greater than it was then ; and if we add to this the advantages modern civilization has over the ancient, not only in its bringing with it a greater and more perfect intellectual and moral expansion, but also in its supplying a greater amount of material comforts, and greatly diminishing the evils that afflict the poor human race, the difference between them will be so great and so palpable, that it will be impossible to establish a rational comparison between them.

I confess, my esteemed friend, that these reflections are of great weight, and in my opinion decide the question, from the historical point of view, considering humanity in mass, and taking into account the compensations indicated above; so that I hold it as demonstrated that humanity has always progressed, that its state was better in the Middle Ages than during the ancient civilization, and that at present it has many advantages over what it had in all former times.

How, you will say, is it possible to forget the confusion and calamities of the time of the irruption of the barbarians, and the dark ignorance and sickening corruption that followed it ? Can we say humanity, at the time of Attila, was comparable with that of the age of Augustus ? I believe nevertheless that this, so false and absurd at first sight, is rigorously true, and besides susceptible of a demonstration so conclusive that it leaves no room for doubt. The diffusion of true ideas about God ; man ; society, and the relations existing between them ;

the propagation of civilization to a great number of peoples who lived previously in the most abject barbarity ; the abolition of slavery ; the extension to the generality of men of the enjoyment of the rights of man ; this was being realised at the time we are speaking of, and nothing of this was known in the age of Augustus ; with the leave, then, of the manes of Virgil and Horace, I prefer, without hesitation the so-called barbarous times.

Do you smile at the paradox, my esteemed friend ? Do you imagine I myself do not believe what I say ? Well, be sure I speak in all truth, and my words are the expression of profound convictions. I have already told you in one of my former letters, that in certain matters perhaps you did not carry the spirit of examination so far as I, and that I was moderately infected with scepticism : this prevents me from being dazzled with names or *received opinions;* and no matter with what certainly I hear anything asserted, I whisper to myself, a *who knows ?*—which renders me distrustful and meditative. In spite of all this, I think you will with difficulty forgive me the blasphemy I have uttered against the age of Augustus ; and so it is incumbent on me to make my excuses. Listen to them without prejudice, for in the end I should not wonder if you would agree with my mode of thinking.

And in truth, dazzling are the rays of science ; bewitching the enchantments of poetry ; seducing the brilliancy of the arts ; but if nothing of all this contributes to the good of humanity ; if it be limited to realise

splendour only, and to increase and quicken the pleasures
of a few who dwell in opulent palaces, living on the
sweat of the people ; dissipating the treasures wrung
from the provinces with the greatest cruelty, what does
the human race gain by it ? Is this civilization anything
more than a beautiful lie ? There is peace, but this
peace is the silence of the oppressed ; there are enjoyments, but they are the enjoyments of the few, and the
misery of the many ; there are sciences ; fine arts ; but
prostrate at the feet of the powerful, they do not fulfil
their mission, which is to improve the intellectual, moral,
and material condition of man ; all is vice ; prostitution ;
flattery ; perish then all, one would say who could extend his glance to future times ; let there be war, but a
regenerating war which will change the face of the world,
calling to Christian civilization hundreds of barbarous
nations ; dethroning the oppressor of the world, and
giving birth to great nations that will astonish us with
their advancement and power ; let there be public calamities, for at least they will not be so much felt or as
offensive as that slavery, which weighs heavily on the
greater number of the individuals who form ancient
society, and in the course of time will come the happy
era, in which to enjoy the rights of a citizen it will be
enough to be a man ; let the sciences and fine arts
perish, since for future ages are reserved prodigious
geniuses, as Tasso, Milton, Chateaubriand, Michael
Angelo, and Raphael, Descartes, Bossuet, and Leibnitz ;
let that false civilization, that ricketty refinement which
sanctions the monopoly of social advantages be torn

in shreds, and yield its place to another civilization and refinement more extensive, more splendid, and above all, more just and equitable ; that shall call to partici- pate in them a greater number of individuals, opening the gates that all may enjoy the advantages they bring with them, as far as the nature of man and of the objects on which he exercises his activity admits.

After the irruption and subsequent upheavings of the barbarous hordes came feudalism ; a social and political system against which you may say whatever you wish ; but it was undoubtedly a real progress, because by erecting, if we may say so, territorial property into sovereignty, a principle was established which, modified and corrected in the course of time, might aid much in the organization of modern societies. There were dis- orders ; oppression ; vexations ; evils without number, it is true ; but at least a system began to be established, a position was given to the conquering tribes, love of husbandry and respect for property were sown, the domestic spirit increased ; and the inclinations of the heart meeting with objects more stable and peaceable became of necessity less turbulent, and began to be calmed down and sweetened. Bad as the twelfth and thirteenth centuries were, who would not prefer them to those which immediately followed the dissolution of the empire of Charlemagne ?

No one can deny that up to the beginning of the sixteenth century European society was rapidly improv- ing ; so that as no notable decadence took place in any other part of the world, since the other nations it might

be said remained stationary, we can still confess that
the human race was progressing.   The great discoveries
that took place in the fifteenth century excited hopes
that in the sixteenth a new era of prosperity and felicity
should commence, which, overflowing from Europe,
might be extended through all the regions of the earth.
Unfortunately Luther's schism came to destroy, in a
great measure, those flattering hopes, and the calamities
that have befallen Europe during the last three centuries might make us doubt of the proposition we have
established.

Be this as it may, even taking into account the evils
brought on by the religious schisms, and the incredulity
and indifferentism which have been the consequence,
I do not think it can be denied that humanity has been
compensated as we said above.   Taking things from the
root—that is from the time Luther and his followers
divided in two the great European family—it should
be considered that the successive conquests Catholicism
has gone on making in the East and West Indies cover,
and perhaps more than cover, the losses the unity of
faith has suffered in Europe.   If to this we add that
wherever the Catholic religion has not been established,
there have been at least a few lights of Christianity
scattered by means of one or other of the dissenting
sects, which, whatever it be, is always preferable to the
idolatry and debasement in which these countries were
buried; if we attend to the progress, the intellectual,
moral, and material development of the individual and
of society has made even there, it results that even

painting the history of the last three centuries in Europe in the blackest colours, humanity has not lost, but on the contrary has been recompensed with usury.

Nor is it true either that Providence has chastised European pride in such a way as not to shower on us at the same time a torrent of inestimable benefits. The country where men so eminent in all the branches of learning were born; which boasts of astonishing geniuses in all regions, and which under the religious and moral aspect can present us with a St Ignatius of Loyola, a St Francis of Sales, a St Vincent de Paul, and hundreds of others of heroic virtues, who realised the life of angels on earth, cannot complain of Providence being unfavourable to it ; cannot lament in the midst of its material and moral revolutions, that a greater portion of misfortunes than usually befalls unhappy humanity has fallen to its lot.

This last consideration, my esteemed friend, brings me to examine what is the cause of this uneasiness which continually torments us Europeans, and all those who have participated in our civilization. To hear us complain of our lot, and bemoan our present situation, and paint the future in sombre colours, one would say we bear a greater amount of evils than any other people of the earth ; and even comparing us with our ancestors, it would appear they were much more fortunate. They never talked so much of *transition, of the necessity of new organizations, of the insufficiency of everything that exists,* they never announced, as we do, that epoch which is to realise the golden age, under pain of the world's sinking into chaos, after an astounding conflagration.

Every age has suffered its evils, and has had profound changes more or less; every age has had necessities either wholly unattended ,to, or hardly satisfied; every age has carried in its bosom a germ of death for something in it, which should yield to what the future involved. I will add, that I doubt much if the present time is at all behind the past, considering civilized nations in general, and not counting the exceptions, which of necessity must be transitory; and I am inclined to believe, that our evils are not greater, but appear greater for two reasons—1st, because we reflect too much on them; like the sick man who sharpens his pains by making them the continual object of his thoughts and words—2nd, because we have greater liberty to complain, as well *viva voce* as in writing, adding moreover that the Press, and not always with a right intention, exaggerates everything.

For instance, pauperism is spoken of. I admit it is a painful sore, and deserves to attract the attention of all lovers of humanity; but what I would wish to know is what result we should have, if we examined it with relation to the times that have preceded us. What greater and more painful pauperism than ancient slavery? —is that state to be compared with that of the inferior classes of our day, either in the number of the wretched or the degree of wretchedness? I know that some have gone so far as to say that the lot of the negro slaves is preferable to that of our labourers. I will not deny that if no more than some exceptional extremes be considered, as well in good as in evil ; if we take a black slave, whose lot has been cast with a rational, prudent, compassionate master, guided by the inspirations of sound reason and Christian charity, and compare him with some of our more unfortunate labourers, the comparison perhaps can be sustained ; but speaking in general, and placing on one side the mass of negro slaves, and on the other that of European labourers, is the lot of the former preferable to that of the latter ? Can it even be compared with it ? I do not believe it can ; and even though it were not possible to point out positive facts, which certainly are not wanting, the simple consideration of the nature of things would be enough to remove any indecision of judgment.

When slavery was abolished in Europe, and feudalism succeeded it, continuing with more or less pretensions for long ages, I do not believe the poorer class enjoyed a better state than it does at present. Read the history of those times, and you will not entertain a doubt of this. Let us imagine for a moment that the innumerable legions of pamphleteers, newspaper men, and writers of works that inundate civilized countries at present, had suddenly appeared in the midst of feudalism, that they had been able to examine the castle of the proud lord, scrutinizing its commodious apartments, its luxurious furniture ; that they had seen him go to the hunt, with his fiery horses, his bold attendants, his innumerable dogs, all insulting with the richness of their trappings the misery and nakedness of his vassals ;

that they had witnessed the unjust demands, the arbitrariness, the cruelty with which he harasses his subjects; and let us suppose, for a moment, that in the small towns that here and there were established, and which so laboriously won their liberty, the presses of Paris and London should appear by enchantment, and the people suddenly learning to read, should find infinite articles in which the violences, the injustices, the immoderate luxury of the lords, and the oppression, the misery, the calamities of the vassals, should be narrated and painted with the colours you may guess—do you not think the picture would come out black, that a general clamour would be raised in the four quarters of the earth, demanding vengeance?—do you not think the whole world would agree that never were the evils of humanity greater, that the application of a remedy was never more indispensable, that a profound change in the social organisation was never more necessary, never more imminent?

Let us turn the medal and look at the reverse; let us imagine that in the present age the Press and the orators held their peace; that public attention is distracted from politics; that no one thinks about questions of social organization; that masters occupy themselves with their business solely, and workmen with their labour; that no one takes the trouble to count how many poor there are in England, in France, and other countries; that descriptions of the sufferings of the needy classes are not circulated with a calculation of the ounces of bread or potatoes that fall to the lot of the wretched labourer and

his children, and with a picture of the poor and filthy
dwelling in which he hides himself, and that withal the
movement of industry should continue as now, and the
same hands be employed, and the same wages given,
and the price of food and clothing remain the same; is
it not very clear our social state would not appear in
such black colours, nor the future be regarded as so
threatening?

See here, my esteemed friend, with how much reason
I said our evils were greater because we thought more
on them; because there are a thousand means and
motives for recollecting them; for exaggerating them;
and because the present state of civilization necessarily
brings with it the reflective act of occupying itself with
itself. And do not believe that I am not for giving the
necessary publicity to the sufferings of the poor, or that
I desire silence should be imposed on the class that
suffers in order to avoid giving annoyance and molesta-
tion to the class that enjoys; I have merely wished to
indicate one character of our age, pointing out the reason
why it appears to have certain peculiarities, that are
attributed to it as such, notwithstanding their being
common to those that have preceded it. In sympathy
for the needy, I yield to none; and though respecting,
as I should, the property and other legitimate advantages
of the higher classes, I am not ignorant of the want of
reason and the injustice that often tarnish and injure
them.

I am inclined to believe that if you have not adopted
my opinions in all their parts, you will at least agree

they are not to be despised, supposing the truth of the arguments on which they are founded ; and I am certain that in future you will consider better the true meaning of the word *transition*, and will not give it so much importance as heretofore. Certainly I cannot conceive how so much noise has been produced by this and other expressions like it when, on being analysed, they are found to signify nothing more than the instability of human things ; an instability the knowledge of which does not surely date from modern times.

Neither can I conceive how some people venture to prognosticate the death of Catholicity, because, as they say, the new state into which society is going to pass, cannot admit of the dogmas nor the forms of this divine religion ; as if the world had endured for eighteen centuries without any kind of change ; as if the faith and the august institutions which Jesus Christ left us stood in need of the works of man for their preservation.

Was not the social organization of the first age of Christianity very different from that of the time of Theodosius the Great ? Did the Europe of the Barbarians resemble in the least the Europe of the Empire ? Was the period of feudalism at all like the confusion of the irruption of the northern hordes, or the preponderance of the barons similar to the power of the monarchy ? Was the age of Francis I. the age of Louis XIV., or his that of Louis Philippe ? In that space of eighteen centuries colossal revolutions took place ; innumerable vicissitudes passed over European society ; the public and private life of nations was modified and changed in a thousand ways ; and nevertheless, religion ever remaining the same, without submitting to any of those transactions that would destroy her very foundation, was able and knew how to accommodate herself to what the diversity of times and circumstances demanded ; without betraying the truth, she has not lost sight of the march of ideas; without sacrificing the sanctity of her morals, she took into account the changes of habits and customs ; without altering her internal organisation in what it has of unalterable and eternal, she has created an infinite variety of institutions accommodated to the necessities of the peoples subjected to the faith.

Are you ignorant of these facts, my esteemed friend ? —is there anything in them you can object to or dispute ? Then leave aside those vain words which signify nothing, and only serve to nourish with vague generalities that fatal state of doubt and scepticism which is the real agony of the mind. You well know I do not abhor the progress of society ; that I regard it as a favour of Providence ; that I am not a pessimist, and that I do not take pleasure in condemning everything that exists at present and everything that can be descried in the future ; but I desire to distinguish between good and evil, truth and error, the solid and the futile ; I desire to do what sceptics require of us, but what they do not practise—*to examine with sincerity, and judge with impartiality.*—I remain, &c.,

J. B.

VII.

Toleration.

MY DEAR FRIEND,—In your last letter you were so
kind as to say that my remarks, although they did not
persuade you to renounce that weakness of mind which
is called scepticism, have nevertheless succeeded in convincing you of what you hitherto considered to be
almost impossible, viz.:—that the Catholic faith is not
incompatible with an indulgent and compassionate
tolerance of those who profess a different religion, or
who have no religion at all.   This announcement, on
your part, has given me great consolation.   It is clear,
however, that, in spite of your Catholic education, you
have allowed yourself to be swayed by the prejudices
of infidels and Protestants, who delight in describing us
as hell-born furies breathing only flames and blood.
You thank me for bearing with patient calmness the
doubts, the uncertainties, and the changes of your mind;
but in this I am only doing my duty in accordance
with the precepts of our holy religion, which holds the
salvation of a single soul to be of such importance,
that any labours, no matter how painful, nay, even the
devotion of an entire life, must be considered as a
trifling price to pay for it.

My own inmost conviction, or, to speak more like a
Christian, the grace of God, holds me fast in my attachment to the Catholic faith; but this does not hinder
me from becoming acquainted with the actual state of

others' ideas, and the different conditions of other men's minds. The sight of a sceptic fills me with lively compassion, because, unhappily there exist at present many causes which may lead to the loss of faith ; and, therefore, whenever I happen to meet any of those unhappy men, I am far from saying, in my pride, *I am not such as this one.* The true believer, who is deeply sensible of the grace he enjoys in being preserved in the Catholic faith, far from exalting himself, should humbly cry out to God in the sincerity of his heart—*O Lord, be merciful to me a sinner.*

I remember when I was studying theology, that I heard the professor explain the doctrine that faith is a gift of God, and to gain it, neither miracles nor prophecies, nor the other proofs of the truth of our religion, are enough, but that in addition to the motives of credibility, we need *the pious stirring of the will: pia motio voluntatis.* I candidly acknowledge that, at the time, I did not comprehend doctrines like these, nor did I thoroughly grasp their meaning, until I had left those abodes where the very air is filled with faith, and found myself in circumstances quite different, and in contact with people of every class. Then it was that I fully realised the depth of God's goodness towards the true believer, and the sad condition of those who rest their faith on the motives of credibility—who confine themselves to science and forget grace. Frequently have I met with men who, in my opinion, saw as well as I the reasons that militate in favour of our religion ; and yet I believed, and they did not. Whence is this ? I asked myself, and I could give myself no other reason, but exclaim:—*Misericordia Domini quia non sumus consumpti.*

From this preamble you will see, my dear friend, your doubts have not taken me by surprise, or produced that shuddering they would naturally cause in me, if I had not had the preceding reflections in view; though *en passant* you will allow me to disapprove of the sharp invective you indulged in against intolerant people. Do you know that in your words you render yourself guilty of intolerance? and that a man is never perfectly tolerant until he tolerates intolerance itself. For God's sake let us be sincere, and let us not look at things with a spirit of partiality. You do me the favour of telling me that "you considered I had a sufficient knowledge of the world, not to imitate the example of those people who cannot bear the slightest word against their faith, and who, constituting themselves the heralds of divine justice, never cease talking of the hour of death, and of hell; and end by deserting whoever had the imprudence or want of caution to open his mind to them." Then you relate the little story of the good clergyman who previously distinguished you with particular marks of esteem and friendship, and who was so horrified on discovering his acquaintance was an infidel, that he thought fit to break off all communication with you. I think, my dear friend, I discover in your own words the apology of the person you blame so much; and in the eyes of whoever looks at the matter with real impartiality his conduct will not appear so strange.

"He was," you say, "a young man of irreprehensible conduct, of strict habits, of ardent zeal, but he had the misfortune never to have mingled but with devout people, never to have handled other books than those of the seminary, and it scarcely appeared to him possible, that there could be circulated in the world other doctrines than those he had been taught for the space of some years in the college which he had just left. I had the imprudence to reply with a smile of mockery to an observation of his on a delicate point, and from that moment I was irretrievably lost in his opinion." Well, you complain in substance, that this young man had not habits of tolerance; where did you expect he should have learned them? Could such a one's mind be disposed for the attack which his opponent made with the significant smile? Is it not too much to require serenity from a man, who sees, perhaps for the first time, what he considers as most holy and august, combated or despised?

It is a grave mistake, and a great injustice besides, to blame the conduct of one who, guided by a strong conviction and a right heart, conducts himself as he necessarily should, considering the education and instruction he has received, and the circumstances that have surrounded the whole course of his life. Our mind is formed and modified under the influence of a thousand causes, and it is absolutely necessary to attend to them, when we want to form an exact judgment on its state, and the path it will probably follow. To act otherwise is to insist on doing violence to things, and to put them out of joint. Could you expect that a missionary grown grey in his holy career, should look at objects in the same way as when he left college? Would not this be a strange requirement? It certainly would; well it would be no less to expect from him the same conduct in his youth as long years of Apostolic labours in distant and various countries have taught him.

It is little less than impossible without a long experience of the world, to know how to place one's self in another's position, and take note of the reasons that impel him to think or act in this or that manner; and it is much more difficult in religious matters, as they relate to what lies deepest in the soul of man. When we are vividly possessed of an idea, we cannot conceive how others can look with indifference on what we regard as most important in this life and in the next. For this reason there is no subject more calculated to excite the mind; and hence it is that religious wars have always been the most obstinate and bloody. I wish those who talk against intolerance without distinction of any sort, would take these reflections into consideration; for then it would not happen so often that men intolerant in the extreme in everything concerning religion, would refuse to suffer the intolerance with which religious people answer them in turn.

But you will understand, my dear friend, I do not desire to avail myself of these reflections to become intolerant; if I have dwelt on the subject it has been with the view of removing the aversion with which the intolerance of certain persons is viewed by some, thereby causing men, for the most part worthy of esteem, to be depreciated.

You talk of the difficulty of our understanding each other, our ideas being so opposed, and the tenor of our lives having been so different : it is possible such a difficulty may exist ; yet as far as I am concerned I cannot discover it. Would you believe I can even comprehend very well that state of mind in which one fluctuates between truth and error ; in which the mind, greedy of truth, finds itself sunk in despair, on account of its inability to discover it ? Some people imagine that faith is incompatible with a clear knowledge of the difficulties which can occur to the mind against it ; and that it is impossible to believe from the moment the reasons that produce doubt in others effect an entrance ; this is not the case, my dear friend ; there are men who believe in all truth, who humble their understanding in reference to faith, with the same docility as the most simple of the faithful can do, and who nevertheless perfectly comprehend what passes in the soul of the unbeliever, and who attend, if I may say so, at its interior acts, as if they saw them with their own eyes.

It is an illusion to think one cannot have a clear idea of a state without having passed through it, and that no one can comprehend a certain order of ideas and sentiments but one who has experienced them. If this were so, what would become of the creative faculty of literary men ? Many things are felt that are not

consented to ; and, if one does not go so far as to feel,
there is the imagination to supply all deficiencies. We
Christians can fittingly illustrate this from what occurs
in temptation—a subject which, though it may not
appear very philosophical to you, cannot fail to interest
you in the application. We read in the Lives of the
Saints, that God often permitted the devil to assault
them with thoughts and desires so contrary to the
virtues which they practised with greatest ardour, that
they were compelled to call to their aid all their confidence in the divine mercy to avoid believing they
were abandoned by heaven, and culpable of the very
sins they detested most in the bottom of their heart.
When the attack was so violent as to make them
conceive fears of having succumbed ; when the images
with which foul objects were represented to their fancy
were so lively, that in spite of the aversion in which
they held them, they began to regard them as a reality,
it may be easily conceived those holy souls could not
but comprehend the state of a man buried in these
vices. You may learn from this, which in the first
years of your life you must have read in some of those
books that could not have been scarce in the college,
how we, who cannot flatter ourselves, even in thought,
with being saints, have often felt the innumerable
intellectual and moral ills poor humanity is heir to
spring up in our souls; and as one of these is scepticism,
it would be very strange if it had not presented itself,
an unwelcome visitor, at the gates of our interior. The
true believer keeps them closed, and, aided by grace,

defies all the powers of hell to break them if they can ; but then occurs what the Apostle St Peter tells us :— " The devil goes about like a roaring lion seeking whom he may devour." Believe me, my esteemed friend, if we *resist him strong in faith,* he cannot harm us; but we are well acquainted with his roar.

Above all, in the age in which we live, it is little less than impossible that this should not happen to those who, from one cause or another, are in contact with it. At one time, a book full of plausible reasons and piquant remarks falls into one's hands ; at another he hears in conversation observations, apparently very judicious and prudent, which at first sight shake the foundations on which truth rests ; perhaps the mind becomes fatigued, and feels itself seized by a weariness, and sinks for some moments in the continual struggle it finds itself compelled to sustain against infinite errors ; perhaps, on casting a glance at the want of faith so patent in the world ; at the multitude of religions ; at the secrets of nature ; at the nothingness of man ; at the darkness of the past, and the obscurity of the future, terrible thoughts flit through his mind. Moments of anguish, in which the heart is inundated with cruel bitterness ; in which a black veil appears to be spread over everything that surrounds us ; in which the spirit weighed down by the torturing fancy that presses on it, knows not whither to turn itself, and has no other resource but to lift his eyes to heaven, and exclaim :— *Domine, salva nos, perimus*—" Lord, save us, we perish."

Thus does the Lord permit His own to be tried, and

renders the faith of His disciples more meritorious; thus
does He teach them that to believe it is not enough to
have studied Religion, but that the grace of the Holy
Ghost is necessary. It were much to be desired that
those who imagine it is a mere question of science, and
the goodness of the Almighty does not enter into it,
would become convinced of this truth. Do you know,
my dear friend, the first thing a Catholic should do
when he meets with an unbeliever for whose conversion
he intends to labour? No doubt you will say he should
look over the apologists of Religion, examine quotations
on the more serious questions, consult learned men of
the first order; in a word, supply himself with arguments as a soldier with arms. It is right, indeed, not
to neglect preparing for every phase of the discussion;
but above all, before commencing to reason with the
unbeliever, what he should do is to pray for him. Tell
me, which class made more conversions, the learned or
the holy? St Francis of Sales composed no work which,
under the polemical aspect, can vie with "Bossuet's
History of the Variations;" and yet I doubt whether
the conversions the latter work effected, though they
were many, are to be compared with those which are
due to the angelical unction of the holy Bishop of
Geneva.

From this you may know, my dear friend, you have
not to deal with what is generally called a disputant
or ergotist; and though I appreciate science in its just
value, and particularly ecclesiastical science, I have
deeply engraved in the depths of my soul the salutary

truth, that the ways of God are incomprehensible to man ; that it is vain to confide in science alone, and that something more than it is required to preserve and restore faith.

You ask for tolerance, and tolerance I offer you, the most ample that was ever met with in any man ; you were terrified at the difficulty we might meet with in understanding each other; and I trust such a fear has already vanished before my declarations. Neither do I dread you shall for the future imagine I will meet you with what are called *subtleties of the schools, and arguments of weight with persons already convinced.* If, then, it please you to continue to propose to me the principal difficulties that impede your return to the religion of which you already begin to feel the loss, though it is but a few years since you abandoned it, I will endeavour to answer you as best I can ; but without looking for the palm if you should be satisfied, or considering myself crestfallen if you should continue in your incredulity.

When one contends against the enemies of Religion, who only seek means of attacking it, availing themselves of whatever their craft or malice may suggest, the dispute may assume the character of a regular combat ; but when one has the fortune to reason with men who, though they have had the misfortune to lose the faith, desire nevertheless to return to it, and heartily seek for what may conduct them to it ; to make a show of science then ; to display a captious spirit ; to strive for a conquerer's laurel, would be an insufferable abuse of the gifts of God; a complete forgetfulness of the paths which, as He himself has manifested, the Lord delights to follow; would be to give reins to pride, that is, to the declared enemy of all good, and the most serious obstacle in the way of availing one's self of the best dispositions.

If we make religious disputes a subject of self-love, how can we promise ourselves that the grace of the Lord shall fructify our words? The Apostles converted the world, and they were poor fishermen; but they did not confide in human wisdom, nor in eloquence learned in the schools, but in the Omnipotence of Him who said :—"*Let there be light*, and light was made." However, you will comprehend I do not for all that despise science; on the contrary, the best means of preserving and elevating it is to mark out its limits, and never allow it to put on the haughtiness of pride.

That want of power to believe which you complain of should not be confounded with the *impossibility* of believing; it is a weakness, it is a prostration of the mind, which shall disappear the day the Lord is pleased to say to the *paralytic:* "Arise, and walk along the path of truth."

In the meantime I will pray for you; and though your mind be not very well disposed to it at present, I will yet presume to tell you to pray too; to invoke the God of your forefathers, whose holy name you learned to pronounce in your cradle, and to beseech Him to grant you the grace to come to the knowledge of the truth. Perhaps, oh horrible thought! perhaps you shall say to yourself, how can I call on God, if, in certain moments, prostrated by scepticism, I feel even this, my one sole conviction growing weak, and I am not well sure of His existence—No matter: make an effort to invoke Him; He will come, I assure you: imitate the man who, having fallen into a deep pit, and not knowing that any human being can hear him, nevertheless strains his voice calling for aid.

Count on the warm affection and esteem of your ever fond friend,

J. B.

VIII.

German Philosophy—Kant—Schelling.

I AM very glad, my esteemed friend, you do not require me to bring forward the arguments which the apologists of religion are accustomed to adduce against the defenders of materialism and blind chance; and I cannot do less than congratulate you on "finding yourself now," as you tell me in your welcome letter, "radically cured of your partiality for the books in which the doctrines of Volney and La-Mettrie are taught." To tell the truth, I did not expect less from your clear mind and noble heart; for I cannot conceive how a man possessing those qualities could possibly read a work of this class through. I, for my part, can say I find them as deficient in soundness as abounding in malice; and far from drawing me from my religion, they confirm me in it. The convulsive efforts of impotent error produce a grander idea of the truth. Nevertheless, you will allow me to call your attention to the mistake which you fall into when you bestow pompous eulogies on the new German and French spiritualists; for you regard them as nothing less than the restorers of sound doctrines, by recovering for humanity the titles of which the Voltairian philosophy had despoiled it. Every age has its fashionable opinions and phraseology. At present one could not belong to the school of the eighteenth century, even though he wished it: it is necessary to talk of the spiritualism of Kant, Fichte, Schelling, Hegel, Cousin; and to reject the sensualism of Destutt-Tracy, Cabanis, Condillac, and Locke, if you wish to avoid passing as a slow-coach in philosophical knowledge. A man may profess no religion, very good; but it is indispensable to have ever in his mouth *religious sentiment, destinies of humanity*, and even not to scruple sometimes to pronounce the words *God* and *Providence*. Speaking frankly, when I read in your letter the names I have just mentioned, I could not convince myself that you troubled your head much with the study of deep and abstruse metaphysical questions. I should rather be inclined to believe your ideas on the subject were picked up by chance in the newspapers, without your having taken great pains in clearing them up or analysing them. I do not blame you for this, because your opinions, as those of a simple individual, will not exercise any influence on the public. If we were treating of a writer who should always know what he recommends or censures, then I would take the liberty to warn him to be more cautious in his desire of introducing novelties which might be injurious to us.

Do you know what the German philosophy is? Have you a knowledge of its tendencies, and even of its express doctrines about God and man? Do you believe the abyss to which it leads is much less profound than that of the school of Voltaire? Do you, in fact, believe that Schelling and Hegel are the legitimate successors of their countryman, Leibnitz; of that great man who, according to the expression of Fontanelle, led the vanguard of all sciences; and who, in spite of what may be objected to some of his theories, entertained such elevated ideas about religion, and so many sympathies for the Catholic Church?

The philosophy of Leibnitz has exercised great influence in Germany, and it was partly owing to him that the materialistic doctrines of the French school of the last century were not introduced into that country. Let the conception formed of his systems be what it may, it cannot be denied that at the same time they reveal eminent genius, they contribute to elevate the mind; to give it a lively consciousness of its grandeur, and show it should be by no means confounded with matter. If he be upbraided with his extreme idealism, we shall answer that this has been the failing of the greatest thinkers, from Plato to De Bonald.

Leibnitz did not look on God as the soul of Nature, or Nature itself, as some modern philosophers maintain, but as a Being infinitely wise, powerful, and perfect in every sense. Pantheism, which has so sadly in these latter times led some German thinkers astray, was, in Leibnitz's opinion, an absurd system. Neither did the illustrious philosopher consider the human soul as a species of modification of the great Being that identifies itself with, and absorbs everything, according to the opinion of Pantheists; but he regarded it as a spiritual substance, essentially distinct from matter; as also infinitely distant from the Creator who gave it existence.

It is well known he victoriously refuted the system of Spinosa, and when treating of God and the immortality of the soul, the principles of morality, and the rewards and punishments of the other life, he could not suffer the spirit of error to spread its darkness over objects so sacred. "It cannot be doubted," he wrote to Molanus, "the wise and powerful Ruler of the universe has rewards destined for the good and punishments for the wicked, and this is brought about in the next life, since in the present many bad actions remain unpunished, and many good ones unrewarded." This certainly is not the language of the modern Pantheists, and it may be seen from it the German philosophers in resuscitating the system of Spinosa, have strayed from the footsteps of their illustrious ancestor. I know the German writers to whom I allude still preserve the abstraction and sentimentalism peculiar to their nation, and do not participate in the lightness and trivialness which characterise the unbelievers of the French school; but we must remember that sentiment is not enough when it is not joined to conviction, and the heart exercises her functions very badly, when they are opposed to the impulse of the head.

Besides, if Germany continue in her impious ideas, in the end her character will feel the effects of them ; and the religious sentiment, already very much weakened by Protestantism, will be extinguished by the systems of impiety. Explain the doctrine of Pantheism as you will, it involves the negation of God ; it is pure Atheism, only it takes another name. If all things are God, and God is all things, God is nothing ; the only thing that will exist is nature with its matter, and its laws, and its agents of diverse orders ; all which Atheists admit, and do not think they have thereby abjured their system. If the creature believes he is a part of God, or God himself ; by the very fact he denies the existence of a God superior to himself, who can demand of him an account of his actions ; the Divinity will be to his ears an empty name, and he can adopt the saying of the German, who, on rising from a banquet, exclaimed :—"We are all gods who have dined very well."

The religiousness of Leibnitz was certainly more solid and profound. See how he unfolds his ideas in the place quoted above. " To forget in this life the care of the future, which is inseparably united with the Divine providence, and to content one's self with a certain inferior grade of natural law, which an Atheist may also have, *is to mutilate science in its most beautiful parts*, and destroy many good actions. Who will run the risk of his fortune, dignity, and life for his friends,

K

for his country, for the State, or for justice and virtue ; if, when others are ruined, he can continue to live with honours and opulence ? For would it not be a virtue of false brilliance to prefer the immortality of man or posthumous fame, which is a rumour nothing of which will reach us, to real and substantial advantages ? "

I do not purpose examining all the opinions of the German philosophers, nor marking how far they may be admissible. I will limit myself to pointing out some of their principal errors, giving the name of the author who may have invented or adopted them, without throwing the responsibility on the thinkers of that nation who do not follow the same path.

Kant did not carry his errors with respect to God, man, and the universe, as far as some of his successors have done ; but I must confess, that while intending to promote a species of reaction against the materialists, he left the principal truths so exposed, that real philosophy has nothing to thank him for with respect to their preservation. In fact, a person who says the metaphysical proofs in defence of the immortality of the soul, the liberty of man, and the duration of the world, appear to him of equal weight with those which militate against them, is not very likely to leave those truths well established, without which all religion would be but an empty name. It is all very well to give great importance to feeling and the inspirations of conscience ; to recognise the weakness of our powers of reasoning, and not to exaggerate its capabilities ; but it is right also to take care not to destroy it, not to

murder reason by sheer want of confidence in it, and
extinguish that lamp which the Creator has given us,
and is really a beautiful emanation of the Divinity.

It sometimes happens, my dear friend, that the negation of reason does not come from humility, but from
an excessive pride, from an exaggerated feeling of
superiority which disdains to examine, and believes
that to see a thing thoroughly it is enough to look
at it without any mental exertion. You will not find
me among the number of those who appeal to reason
in everything, and grant nothing to sentiment ; nothing to those sudden inspirations which spring up
in the depths of our soul without our knowing whence
they have come to us. I know, and I have often told
you, our reason is weak in the extreme, and exces-
sively captious, proves everything, refutes everything;
but between this and denying its right to vote on the
questions of metaphysics, rejecting it as incompetent
to effect anything in them ; between truth and error
there is an immense distance. *Est modus in rebus.*

If Kant carried the sobriety of reason to a repre-
hensible extent, assigning it very narrow limits indeed,
there were not wanting others who exaggerated its
powers, and pretended to explain the entire universe with
its sole aid. It is well known that Fichte launched into
an idealism so extravagant that, by giving all to the
soul, he annihilates, if I may say so, all external objects ;
his system leads to the negation of the existence of
everything which is not the *ego* that thinks. Notwithstanding all the hurtful consequences to which such a

doctrine can lead, they are not more dangerous, or more immediately destructive of all religion and morals, than those of Schelling, in spite of all the veils with which he covers his system, comes in the end to the pantheism of Spinosa. It matters little that in the schools of Schelling I am told of intimate qualities that do not perish when I die, but enter into the vast bosom of nature; when at the same time it is added that the individual, that is, the particular being, the soul, is annihilated. It matters little that I am told of spiritualism, and materialism is condemned, if in the end I be not consoled with the thought of immortality; if I be told this immortality is a chimera, and if anything of me remain after the dissolution of the body, it will not be I myself who think and wish, but certain qualities I know not of, and which will be of little use to me when I cease to exist.

Some one has said that Aristotle left certain passages of his works rather obscure, with the view that being open to different interpretations, they might give his disciples an opportunity of defending him against his adversaries. Be this conjecture as it may, we must agree that the German philosophers have left him of Stagira far behind in this; for they have succeeded in involving their ideas in so dense a cloud that not even the initiated in the secret can flatter themselves with penetrating their profundities. In his "Metaphysical Treatises," says Madame de Stael, speaking of Kant, " he takes words as ciphers, and gives them the value he pleases, without considering what they have from use."

The like may be said of the most famous philosophers of the same nation ; no one is ignorant of the mysterious language of Fichte and of Schelling, and, as regards Hegel, he himself has said:—" There is only one man who has comprehended me ; " and fearing without doubt that this was too much, he added, " and not even he has comprehended me."

It may happen that you will become fatigued, if I give you a few samples of this boasted philosophy ; but I think it right to run a slight risk, for I shall thereby prevent you from being easily deceived by eulogists who praise what they do not comprehend. I doubt not you are already convinced the German philosophers march about through an imaginary world, and that whoever seeks to follow them must divest himself of whatever resembles common thoughts ; but I think I can demonstrate more for you—I think I can show it is not enough to divest one's self of common thoughts, but that it is also necessary to forget even common sense. If you consider the word too hard, do not blame me as rash till you have heard me ; in the meantime, do not forget we are treating of men who have manifested a sovereign contempt for everything that was not themselves ; who have presumed to teach humanity as infallible oracles, and who, under mysterious and emphatic expressions, have carried their pride much farther than all ancient and modern philosophers.

Hegel, he whom, as he says, no one comprehended, assures us he has fixed the principles, regulated the system, and determined the limits, of all philosophy.

He has discovered all: after him there is no more to be found out; humanity should do nothing more than uphold the theories of the sublime philosopher, and apply them to all branches of knowledge. This would not be so intolerable if he were treating of objects of little importance; if Hegel did not call to his tribunal humanity, all religions, God himself, and did not issue his decrees on all with indescribable pride. "Hegel," Lerminier has said, "glories in himself; he sits as supreme arbiter between Socrates and Jesus Christ; he takes Christianity under his protection, and it seems he thinks that if God has created the world, Hegel has comprehended it."[1]

You will meet with these proud pretensions in other philosophers; and the French who have drunk from the same springs, and whose names are sometimes quoted with mysterious emphasis, are not free from them. So I believe the time will not be lost that is employed in giving an idea of those ravings, for they deserve no better name, no matter how they may be clothed with the adornments of science. As this letter is becoming rather long, it is not possible for me to give you the proofs of my assertions in it; but I shall do so without fail in those that will follow. I doubt not you shall become profoundly convinced that this new philosophy so much spoken of, is nothing more than the repetition of the dreams into which the human mind has sunk at all times, whenever, in the inebriation of its pride, it has strayed from the principles of eternal truth.

[1] Su de la du Rhin, t. ii.

Fortunately there is in Spain an amount of good sense that does not suffer the introduction, and much less the establishment of those monstrous opinions, which meet with so easy and gracious a reception in other countries; and for this reason it is not so much to be feared that the errors I speak of will cause among us the evils they have produced in other parts. But, on the other hand, we must remember, that as philosophical studies have been neglected in Spain, there being very few who are at the level of the actual state of the science, it would be easy (without men of sound doctrine and right intention perceiving it) for deluded innovators, who would lead incautious youth astray, to seize upon the instruction of the country. I say this, because I fear others might be led to believe, like you, that the modern German and French schools tended to no less than the restoration of a pure spiritualism, such as our ancestors had, and such as true Christians and judicious philosophers profess even yet.

You shall derive another advantage from the other letters I intend to write to you on this subject, and it is, that you will be able to form clearer ideas than you now have about an important question which agitates France at present, and attracts the attention of Europe; I speak of the disagreements that have arisen between the French clergy and the University. Let the judgment you may form about the greater or less moderation with which the question has been discussed by this or that paper, and about the measures which some bishops have thought proper to adopt, be what it may, you will at least be convinced that the Catholics of the neighbouring kingdom are not alarmed without reason; that there is something more in it than certain parties would wish us to know; that at bottom the question is not simply one of ambition in the clergy, but involves most serious points of doctrine.

And here I have an excellent opportunity of telling you what little regard should be paid to those magisterial decrees which we frequently read on subjects of the greatest importance; and with how much injustice some people accuse the clergy of intolerance, when it is they themselves who are truly intolerant. There are men who, in treating of matters of religion, either drink at certain fountains, or do not consult more than their own deeply-rooted prejudices. If I cannot expect from you much religious zeal, I promise myself at least, impartiality.

In the meantime, be sure of the undying friendship of yours, &c.,

J. B.

IX.

German Philosophy—Hegel.

MY ESTEEMED FRIEND,—In my last letter I gave you my opinion about the modern German philosophy, and ventured to qualify it with a severity that perhaps appeared to you excessive. This boldness when treating of men who have acquired much celebrity, and whose

words are listened to by some as if they came from the
mouths of infallible oracles, imposes on me the duty of
proving what I there said, and of doing so in a way that
can admit of no reply. You recollect my complaints
about the doctrine of these philosophers, with respect to
Pantheism ; I accused them of resuscitating the errors
of Spinosa, though wrapped up in the mysterious forms
of symbolic language. This is the charge I am going
to justify with respect to Hegel.

According to this philosopher, religion is the " production of the feeling, or of the consciousness which the
mind has of its origin, of its divine nature, of its identity
with the universal mind." We might doubt of the real
sense of that expression, *its divine nature*, if it stood
alone, because as our soul is created after the image
and likeness of God, and is distinguished by its elevation above all corporeal beings, it might be thought that
Hegel only wanted to remind us of the nobleness and
dignity of our mind, by founding religious sentiment on
the consciousness which we have that our origin, our
nature and destiny, are much superior to the piece of
clay which encompasses our soul, and embarrasses and
obstructs it. But the German philosopher took care to
explain his ideas by adding that our mind was identical
with the universal mind. What can that universal mind
be that absorbs and identifies itself with all particular
minds ? Is this not the pure and simple enunciation of
a spiritualistic Pantheism ? Is this not to affirm that
God is all minds, and that all minds are God ? That
the thought, the soul of every man, is no more than a

modification of the only Being in whom all others are confounded and identified? But let us hear the German philosopher again, lest we may not have well comprehended the meaning of his words. "This consciousness," continues Hegel, "is at first involved in a mere sentiment, the expression of which is worship; soon the consciousness is unfolded; God becomes an object, and from this arise the mythologies, and all that is called the positive part of religion; but to detain one's self in this second stage in which the God of the universe is adored in the marble of Phidias, in which Jesus Christ is no more than an historical personage, would be treason to the mind."

"In religion people rest their ideas on the essence of the world, and the relations humanity has with it. The absolute being is here the object of their consciousness; there is another further off, which they represent to themselves, now with the attributes of goodness, now with those of terror. This opposition does not exist in prayerful recollection or in worship, and man is elevated to a union with the divine Being. *But this divine Being is reason in itself and for itself, the universal concrete substance; religion is the work of reason which is revealed.*" Perhaps you will wonder why the German philosopher takes so many turns to tell us that religion is no more than an ulterior manifestation of reason, that the divine Being, the Being that is the object of religion and worship, that is, God, is no more than reason itself, but *in itself and for itself,* or the universal concrete substance. I do not know if you be well enough versed in these matters to comprehend the jargon of a being that is *in itself and for itself,* that is human reason, and that in addition is the universal concrete substance. Be this as it may, I will endeavour to give you some explanation of the meaning involved in the enigmatical words of our metaphysician.

To understand this you should know that according to Hegel, the entire world is no more than the evolution of the idea, and according to the degree of this evolution it is said beings are *in themselves ;* and when it has attained its greatest progress, it is said beings are *for themselves.* You will ask me, what is the idea? According to Hegel it is nothing else but "the harmonious unity of this universal aggregate which is eternally unfolding itself;" "all that exists," he adds, "contains no truth but inasmuch as it is the idea that has passed to the state of existence, because the idea is the true and absolute reality." And do not imagine that with this definition he wishes to express the divine intelligence, or otherwise the infinite essence of the Creator, in which is represented from all eternity all that exists, and all that is possible; nothing of the kind. When Hegel speaks of the harmonious unity he refers to this universal aggregate which has an eternal development, that is, to the world itself which receives different forms, and is modified in various ways. "To comprehend," he says, "what this evolution is by which the idea is produced and ends, it is necessary to distinguish two states; the first is known by the name of disposition, virtuality, power, and I call it *being in itself ;* the second is the actuality, the reality, or what I call *being for itself*. The child when it is born has reason virtually, in germ, but it does not yet possess the real possibility of reason. It is reasonable *in itself*, but it does not become so *for itself*, until it is developed. Every effort to understand and know, every action, has no other object than to bring to light what is hidden, to realise or actualise what exists virtually, to make objective what is in itself, to unfold what exists in germ."

"To come to existence is to suffer a change, and yet remain the same; see, for example, how the oak comes of the acorn; the things produced are very different, but the whole was enclosed in the germ, though invisibly and ideally."

I shall pass over the many and serious considerations that could be suggested by the strange signification the German philosopher gives to the word *idea*. It had occurred to the authors of systems of ideology to give various explanations of the mystery of thought, and also different acceptations to the word *idea ;* but to say it is the "harmonious unity of the universal aggregate which is eternally unfolding itself," or in clearer terms, to call nature itself the idea, could only enter into the mind of one who, wanting to confound everything in a monstrous Pantheism, begins by giving to his words a signification unheard-of and extravagant. I would wish to have it explained what necessity there is for so many circumlocutions to tell us that in the world there is but one being, or one substance, that it suffers different modifications, and that everything that exists

is no more than one of the accidents of the universal
aggregate which is being incessantly transformed. This
is certainly Hegel's thought; the child has the use of
reason in *posse*, the adult in *esse:* nay more, and, to
speak with greater precision, the adult himself when he
thinks has the actuality, when asleep, the potentiality of
thought.

Hegel says that every effort to understand and know,
and even every action, has for its object to bring to
light what is hidden, to realise or actualise what exists
virtually; this requires explanation. It is true that
the effort to understand and to know, tends to make
bright and clear what was obscure or entirely hidden
from us; but it is not true that no action has any other
object than to realise or actualise what exists virtually.
It cannot be denied that in the order of nature there is
a continual unfolding, in which some beings spring from
others, as the *oak from the acorn;* but there are some,
too, whose essence is opposed to their having emanated
from any other whatever.

"To come to existence," says Hegel, "is to suffer a
change, and yet remain the same." This proposition
established in general terms destroys all idea of creation, for creation can have no place without a passage
from nonentity to being. If to come to existence is
nothing more than to suffer a change and to remain the
same, when the universe commenced to exist, it was not
because it had been created by God, but because a
transformation in the pre-existent matter taking place,
this aggregate which astonishes us by its immensity,

and enchants us with its beauty and harmony, was the
result.   Such a supposition brings us straight to the
eternity of the world, to the chaos of the ancients, to
all the absurdities about the origin of things, which the
light of Christianity had banished from the earth.

It is strange that philosophers who boast of being
exceedingly spiritualistic, and manifest contempt for the
French materialism of the last century, should establish
it so roundly and fully by combating the spirituality,
the immortality, and the divine origin of our soul.   If
when it commences to exist there be nothing more
than a change of being, as the oak is contained in the
acorn, developed indeed and transformed, we can infer
that the soul springs from the fruitful bosom of nature
just as do material germs; it may be a production
more subtile, more active, more refined, but it will be
nothing more than the being that already existed, than
the plant which had sprung from the seed.   This doctrine is essentially materialistic, and all the mysteries
and enigmas of the new philosophical language are not
sufficient to screen it from this charge.   What is simple,
what is indivisible, cannot be the result of the transformation of another being; what passes from one state
to another, acquiring a new form, a new existence, like
the vegetables that spring from the germ, is composed;
because it is not possible to conceive successive change
without the idea of parts accompanying it.   We can
very well admit that a substance entirely simple may
exercise very different acts, and receive various impressions, since all these modifications may be realised

without altering its nature, as in fact we are constantly
witnessing with respect to our mind ; but to affirm
that the substance itself is no more than another transformed and developed, is to establish that this substance
is composed of parts which can be combined in different
ways.

The difficulty of attacking these ravings arises from
the fact, that those new philosophers have had the
humour to adopt a language so strange and enigmatical,
that one is ever in doubt whether he has caught the
true meaning of the author. Thus, in the present case,
if Hegel had simply said that in the world there is no
more than one being, one substance which comprehends
in itself the whole aggregate of whatever exists, adding,
that what appear to us to be particular beings or
substances, are nothing but modifications of the only
substance that absorbs everything, we should know we
had before us a professor of Pantheism ; and when
about refuting him we should not hesitate about which
would be the best arguments to demonstrate the falsity
of the monstrous system.

But what can you do with a man who begins by
talking of idea ; of harmonious unity; of the aggregate
which is eternally unfolding itself; of the idea which is
reality itself; of evolutions; of being *in itself and for
itself ;* of transitions from virtuality to actuality ; and all
for the purpose of telling us that the entire universe is
nothing more than a successive development ; coming
out in the end with the stupendous discovery that a
child when born has reason virtually, but does not

possess it actualised, and that the oak comes from the acorn.

The branches, Hegel says, the leaves, the flowers, the fruit of one and the same plant, proceed each for itself, whilst the interior idea determines this succession. Could you tell me what can be the meaning of the branches, the leaves, the flowers, the fruits proceeding for themselves ; or what may be the signification of the interior idea applied to plants ? Does Hegel suppose that within nature there is an intelligent and provident being that sees everything, that regulates everything, and call this being's thought idea, while distinguishing it however from matter ?   In that case he would come to the idea of God, for we also say that God is in all beings, in all places, seeing everything, ordaining everything, preserving everything, presiding over that magnificent development which is continually taking place in nature, in conformity with the laws established by the Creator.   But we affirm that the Author of all these wonders existed from all eternity, before anything else existed, and now preserves, moves, vivifies the world, not as the soul does the body, but in a free and independent way, without being bound to the creature, but acting by means of his omnipotent will, repeating every instant what Moses described to us with so sub-lime a touch :—"*Let light be made, and there was light.*" But to give to nature an interior idea, bound, if we may say so, to corporeal things, is to affirm that the world is an animated being, that it performs its functions in the same way as our body does, vivified by the soul ; if this be accompanied by the confusion of mind with matter; if the existence of spiritual and corporeal beings be supposed to be no more than a simultaneous development of the admirable aggregate, it forms pure Pantheism, such as Spinosa conceived it.

Perhaps you did not believe, my dear friend, that the modern philosophy of the unworthy successors of Leibnitz went to such an extreme; but for this very reason I thought it well to give you the very texts of the boasted philosophy, that you might become convinced that its loudly-proclaimed superiority is reduced to resuscitating old errors, though cloaked under extravagant names. This letter would be interminable, and I am sure tiresome to you, if I should endeavour to show you, even briefly, all the paradoxes to which Hegel was led by his enigmatic system. I will say nothing of the development of the idea in the *logical sphere*, of *impersonal reason*, and other things of this kind. I shall limit myself to a few words about the strange hope the philosopher entertained of its being possible by means of his system to determine *a priori* the laws of the physical world. Newton and Leibnitz would certainly laugh at such a strange pretension; all modern physicists would laugh, as they agree that observation is the only means of obtaining a knowledge of the laws of nature; but Hegel would tell them with the greatest gravity, that as the laws of the physical world are nothing more than the laws of our mind, *objectivised*, it is very possible to pass from the knowledge of the latter to that of the former. The

L

German philosopher would certainly find himself somewhat embarrassed, if he were asked for a clear and precise explanation of those laws of our mind, which are at the same time laws of nature. It would be curious to see indicated that law of our mind, which, when applied to the corporeal world, is converted into universal attraction, exercised in direct ratio of the masses and inverse of the square of their distances ; and to what the laws of affinity are reduced when on ceasing to be *objective*, they become simply laws of our soul. Poets, orators, philosophers, had already discovered many analogies between the moral and the physical world—analogies which seized on by genius, and embellished with the colours of a fruitful imagination, serve admirably to compare one with the other, and with different orders of beings, animating, varying, and embellishing the style; but it was reserved to Hegel to be not content with simple comparisons, but to establish complete identity, so that observation ceases to be necessary for penetrating the secrets of nature; it is enough to meditate on the laws of our mind—that is, to make abstraction of everything that surrounds us, and then *objectivise* the laws discovered, thus demonstrating *a priori* all those that direct the heavens and the earth.

You will undoubtedly believe I am jesting without grounds at the expense of the German philosopher, and endeavour to give this turn to the discussion without paying proper regard to the true sense of Hegel, attending only to the fact, that we should relieve in some way

the discussion of subjects so insipid, because so abstruse.
Well, be assured, I am not fighting a giant of my own
creation. Hegel maintains, with all the gravity of a
German, the paradoxes I have just refuted ; and if the
extravagant be mingled with touches of the ridiculous,
it is not my fault. He proposed nothing less than to
establish with the aid of his system all the natural
sciences ; and in his works you will find applications of
it to mechanics, physics, and geology, which he pretends
to found on his metaphysical theories. The heavens,
it is true, paid little attention to the prophecies of the
philosopher, and sometimes sadly confounded him ; foɪ
having had the humour to demonstrate *a priori* that
between *Mars* and *Jupiter* there could be no other
planet, the celebrated astronomer, Piazzi, discovered
for us, in the very same year, *Ceres*, which, as you
know, takes up its position in the very place in which,
according to Hegel's demonstration, no planet could be.

It is not at all wonderful that a man who could presume so much, would go so far as to censure the immortal
Newton in a most shameful manner. In spite of his
pride, it is certain posterity would not allow what is
written on the English astronomer's tomb to be placed
over that of the German metaphysician :—" Sibi gratu-
lenter mortales tale tantumque exstitise humani generis
decus."

Hegel's mania on this point went so far that his
admirer, Link, could not help saying, " It is afflicting to
see how our author talks of objects appertaining to the
natural sciences, astronomy and mathematics ; and yet

he likes to talk of them, and he always does so with a tone so magisterial and bitter, that it would make one laugh, if laugh he could, to see a man like him wandering so sadly. This evil of Hegel's grew worse in the last period of his life, and he even got vexed with those who did not consent to admire him."

I hope you are convinced, my esteemed friend, it was not without reason I was a little severe on modern German philosophy ; for certainly the doctrine we have just examined requires no comments to show its tendency and spirit, as well as its own intrinsic worth. I hope to return to this point some other day, and in the meantime rest secure of the affection of your attached friend,　　　　　　　　　　　　　　　　　　　J. B.

X.

French Philosophical School of M. Cousin.

My Esteemed Friend,—I am now going to pay the remainder of the debt I contracted some days ago, by giving you a brief outline of a certain philosophical school which sprung up in Germany, and spread through France, committing great ravages on religion, and tending to seriously compromise the future of science. You remember what I said in my former letters about the German philosophy, which so openly professes Pantheism, notwithstanding the enigmatical forms with which it sometimes invests itself, and the unintelligible language it employs when speaking of God, of man, and of nature. I endeavoured to support this accusation by

passages from the very philosopher against whom I
brought it ; and I hope you entertain no doubt the
imputation was not calumnious. Perhaps you might
find it hard to persuade yourself that like charges could
be made against the French school which follows the
footsteps of M. Cousin ; for in all probability you will
have imagined, from hearing the frequent invectives of
the partisans of the University against the *intolerance* of
the clergy, that the philosophy of the leader of eclec-
ticism must be innocent in all its parts, and could only
be called impious by men who are alarmed, not at error,
but at the light of reason itself, and condemn the human
mind to eternal inaction and stupid ignorance.

It will cost me little trouble to show you your error,
and to demonstrate to evidence that it was not without
reason the French clergy raised their voice against the
poison offered to youth in golden cups.

In the first place, then, I must tell you that even in
1819, M. Cousin held there was no demonstration,
experimental or other, of the existence of God and His
attributes. It is true he admitted the existence of
God was a truth superior to all others—even to those
principles called axioms. But he does not forget to
add " that no matter what opinion may be held on the
point, it is beyond doubt that neither alone, nor aided
by reason, can experience prove the existence of the
essential attributes of God." What was the use of
saying the existence of God was a truth superior to all
others, when he immediately attacks its foundation, and
declares by implication that the belief which philo-

sophers entertained that they could come to a knowledge of the Creator from His works, was a vain illusion?
Might we not suppose that in 1819 M. Cousin did not
dare to manifest his whole mind, and so paid apparent
homage to the truth that he might continue undermin-
ing it, without alarming too much those who would not
have tolerated the teaching of Pantheism?   You shall
find this conjecture is not totally destitute of foundation.

Let us look at the words of his " Course " of 1818, page
55, and we shall see that the foundation of his philosophy was the same as that of the German school.
" The absolute being," he says, " containing in its bosom
the finite *ego* and *non ego*, and forming, if we may use
the expression, *the unvarying foundation of all things,
one and many at once*—one in substance, many in phenomena, becomes revealed to itself in the human conscience."

" There cannot," he adds, in page 139, " be more than
one substance—the substance of truth, or supreme intelligence. *God is the single and universal being* (page
274) ; God is the universal substance, whose absolute
ideas form the only manifestation accessible to the intelligence of man (page 390) ; God is nothing but the
truth in its essence (128) ; nothing but good itself, *moral
order taken substantially.*"   (Works of Plato, vol. I, argument of the Euthyphron, page 3.)   " We know nothing
of God but that He exists and manifests Himself to us
by absolute truth " (Course of 1818, page 140). " Matter,
as generally defined, does not exist. It is commonly

regarded as an inert mass, without organisation and without rule, when in reality it is penetrated by a spirit that
sustains and regulates it, and consequently is nothing
more than the visible reflection of the invisible spirit:
*the same being that lives in us lives in it—Est Deus in
nobis; est Deus in rebus"* (page 265). "Study nature,
ascend to the laws which govern her and make of her
a living truth—a truth which has become active, sensible
—in a word, *God in matter.* Dive, then, into nature ;
the deeper you penetrate her laws, the nearer you approach the Divine Spirit which animates her. Above
all, study humanity, for it is even more holy than nature,
as it knows the God that animates it equally with her,
while she does not. Embrace the whole aggregate of
the physical and moral sciences ; separate the principles
they contain ; place yourselves in presence of these
truths; refer them to the infinite being who is their
origin and support, and you shall know of God all that
can be known of Him, within the narrow limits of our
finite intelligence" (page 141, 142).

If you reflect on these passages of M. Cousin, or
rather if you merely consider the literal and obvious
meaning of some of his propositions, you must discover
a very thinly-covered Pantheism. According to M.
Cousin there can be but one substance. God is the
single and universal being ; the absolute being is one
in substance and many in phenomena, and man is only
a participation of that absolute being, because the being
which contains in itself the finite *ego* and *non ego*, and
constitutes the unvarying foundation of all things, be-

comes revealed to itself in the human conscience. If
we study nature, if we penetrate her laws, we approach
that Divine Spirit which animates her, for she is really
a *living truth, a truth which has passed to the active,
sensible state,* in a word, we approach *God in matter.*
We acquire all the knowledge we can have of God, by
placing ourselves in presence of the principles of the
physical and moral sciences, and referring them to the
infinite being who is their origin and support. Lest
there might be any doubt that M. Cousin did not understand these words in a sense in which they could be
accepted by people who admit the existence of God as
distinct from nature, our author took good care to explain himself elsewhere, and reveal the whole foundation
of his system. Here are his words :—" God counts His
adorers by the number of men who think ; as it is impossible to think without admitting some truth, even
though it be but one " (*ib.* page 128). Here is the
adoration of God reduced, according to M. Cousin, to
the knowledge of one sole truth. For example, if one
knows a principle of mathematics, no matter what may
be his ignorance or his errors on all other points, natural
or supernatural, such a one is an adorer of God ; and
there can be no Atheists ; for every one will admit his
own existence at least, and thereby he admits a truth,
and consequently adores God. M. Cousin saw that
this was a consequence of his doctrine, and far from
rejecting accepts it in his works. He thus expresses
himself on the point :—" There are no Atheists. The
man who had studied all the laws of physics and

chemistry, even without classifying his knowledge under the denomination of divine truth, or God, would be no less religious, or rather, if you will, would know more of God than another who, after running over two or three principles such as those of *sufficient reason* or *of chance*, would then have formed a whole and called it God. We do not want to adore the name, *God*, but to unite under this appellation the largest possible number of truths, for truth is the manifestation of God " (page 141). "When you have conceived a truth as an idea," he says in another place, "conceive its existence, and you thus unite it to substance. He who conceives truth, conceives substance then, let him be aware of it or not. *If I wanted to know whether a person believed in God, I would ask him if he believed in truth :* whence it follows that natural theology is only ontology, and ontology is in psychology. *True religion is no more than a word added to the idea of truth. She is it*" (page 385).

It is clear M. Cousin's God is not the Christian's God ; for according to him He is nothing but nature herself, the aggregate of the laws which govern her, and it is quite enough to know any truth to escape censure. To believe in God, according to M. Cousin, is to believe in truth ; natural theology is no more than the knowledge of beings in the abstract, and religion but a word added to this truth. In such a theory Pantheism is openly proclaimed. God is all, and all is God ; that is, a being infinitely perfect and essentially distinct from nature, is a chimera, for there is no other being but nature. All that exists are phenomena of the universal substance—that single being which absorbs and identifies all with itself, which is at once spirit and matter, active and inert, which has existed and shall ever exist ; and consequently there is no creation, and all the transformations we see in the universe, are only the various phases of a single being modified in different ways.

Do not imagine, my friend, that these doctrines of M. Cousin were uttered without reflection or connection with other principles to sustain them. On the contrary, they are consequences of Pantheists' fundamental principle about substance. See how he defines it in his " Philosophical Fragments" (lib. I, page 312, 3rd ed.) : —" Substance is that which, relatively to existence, supposes nothing beyond itself." So that substance must be single, as in its very essence it excludes the co-existence of other beings. Therefore all that exists, finite or infinite, can be but one single substance ; and therefore the beings which appear to us distinct, are only modifications of the universal being, which absorbs all. These corollaries do not frighten M. Cousin ; on the contrary, he adopts them as the only rational doctrine. " An absolute substance must be *single* if absolute. Relative substances destroy the very idea of substance ; and finite substances, which suppose beyond themselves another in connection with them, look very like phenomena" (page 63). " The substance of absolute truths," he says in another place, " is necessarily absolute ; and if absolute, *single* also, for if it be not

single, we may seek something else beyond it, and then
it becomes a phenomenon relatively to that new being,
which in its turn would also become a phenomenon if
something else were supposed to exist beyond it. The
circle is infinite, either there is no substance, or there is
no more than one " (page 312).

The fundamental principle of the Pantheists could
not be more clearly professed. It only remained to
know whether M. Cousin admitted the doctrine of
Spinosa's school in all its extension. Unfortunately
we meet a passage in which his mind is most explicitly
expressed. " The God of the conscience is not an abstract God, or solitary king, relegated to periods anterior
to the creation, and seated on the desert throne of a
silent eternity, and an absolute existence which resembles nothingness itself. He is a God at once true and
real, at the same time substance and cause, ever substance and ever cause. He is not substance except
inasmuch as he is cause, nor cause except inasmuch as
he is substance ; that is to say, he is absolute cause,
*one and many, eternity and time, space and number,
essence and life, indivisibility and totality, beginning,
end, and medium, in the perfection of being, and in its
most humble grade, infinite and finite at the same time,*
and lastly being triple, at the same time *God, nature,
and humanity.* In fact if *God is not all he is nothing ;*
if he is absolutely indivisible *in se,* he is incomprehensible ; *and his incomprehensibility is for us his destruction.* Incomprehensible as a scholastic formula, God is
clear in the world, which manifests Him, and to the soul

which possesses and feels him. Though existing in all
things, *he returns to himself in a certain manner in the
conscience of man,* whose mechanism and phenomenal
triplicity he indirectly constitutes by the reflection of
his virtue and substantial triplicity, of which he is the
absolute identity " (lib. 1, preface of 1st ed., page 76).

After so unequivocal a declaration, I think you can
have no doubt about the meaning of the philosopher,
and will agree with us that the professions of Christianity
made by M. Cousin in other pages, are only a species
of compliment to the dominant religion, and not an
expression of faith, nor even of sound philosophical
convictions. For my part, I cannot comprehend how
Pantheism could be more openly proclaimed than by
saying God is one and many, eternity and time, space
and number, essence and life, indivisibility and totality,
beginning, end, and medium, in the perfection of beings,
and in their lowest grade, at the same time infinite and
finite—God, nature, and humanity, and concluding with
these emphatic words, *If God is not all, He is nothing.*

Starting on these principles, we may guess M.
Cousin's moral doctrines will not be very conformable
to the Christian religion, as the profession of Pantheism
carries with it the annihilation of human liberty. For
man being, according to its doctrines, a mere accident of
the one only substance, everything he thinks, wishes,
or does, will be only modifications of the universal substance ; and consequently the liberty of the individual
disappears, as he has no distinct and peculiar existence,
and everything in him belongs to the single being which

absorbs him. And so M. Cousin does not hesitate to say that "man is not absolutely free, because this power he possesses, once brought under the influence of time and space, loses its unlimited and absolute character" (General Introduction to *Course* of 1820, pages 66 and 67). In another place, in explaining liberty, he says:— "*A being is free when it has in itself the principle of its actions—when, in the exercise of its powers, it obeys only its own proper laws*" (*Course* of 1818, page 40.) So that according to the philosopher, to be free, it is not necessary to have the choice between acting and not acting, or between doing this or the other, but it is quite sufficient to have in us the principle of our actions, and to obey only our own proper laws. And the brute which has in itself the principle of its actions—the madman—the imbecile—in a word, all beings which have this principle in them, will be as free as the man of sound sense and judgment!

Revelation, nay, even all religions are reduced to nothing by M. Cousin's theories; and in vain does the philosopher endeavour to show that his doctrines are not opposed to Christianity. After reading the preceding passages you will surely consider M. Cousin's language very strange, when he dares to write the following in the preface to his "Fragments:"—"What can there be between the theological school and me? Am I, indeed, an enemy of Christianity or the Church? In the many Courses I have given, and books I have written, can there be one single word found wanting in the respect due to sacred things? Let a single doubtful or light one be pointed out, and I will withdraw and condemn it as unworthy a philosopher. Could it be that the philosophy I teach causes Christian faith to shake without my knowledge or desire? This would be unfortunate, but not very criminal, because one is not always orthodox, though he desire it. Let me see what dogma my theory endangers. Is it the Incarnation, or the Trinity, or any other whatever? Tell me, prove it, or endeavour to prove it; this at least will be a truly serious theological discussion, and I accept it beforehand, and court it."

You see now, my esteemed friend, that M. Cousin understands the Christian religion in a strange way, as he thinks to pass for a true believer after professing Pantheism, that is, after destroying the fundamental idea of all true religion. You, I am sure, who have no interest in taking a wrong view of things, will find difficulty in conceiving how a man could dare to write such words in his works, after manifesting in previous ones his manner of thinking about these truths to which he now pays such humble homage. Your wonder will vanish when you know that M. Cousin does not admit, as he says, the tyranny of the absolute principle *that it is never lawful to deceive; and in his opinion some deceits are innocent, some useful, and others obligatory* (Trans. of Plato, lib. 4, p. 276, 277.) The unscrupulousness of legitimising a lie is not a great thing after all in one who robs God of His nature and man of his free will; the only thing strange in it is, that he could expect that such a fraud in relation to his doctrine would deceive any one.

One must needs to be blind not to see the contrast, or rather the palpable contradiction between the passages —a contradiction clearer than the light of day.

From this brief sketch you can form a conception of what these philosophical systems are, in which you supposed there were tendencies soundly spiritual—nay even conformable with the teaching of Christianity. You can also rectify, or rather alter, the opinion you had formed of the Catholic clergy of France, when you thought their clamours against the poison of some of the heads of the University were fanatical declamations, which sprung from a pure spirit of intolerance, and the desire to imprison the human intellect within the limits prescribed by the will of the priests. I take the liberty of warning you, now and for ever, when you read in any of our literary and scientific publications, magisterial decrees on this class of questions, not to be deceived by the tone of assurance with which the writer expresses himself, for often, instead of properly reading up the matter, he contents himself with literally translating the words of a trans-Pyreneean newspaper. And as some of those most in vogue are not much addicted to Catholic doctrine, it so happens that the decree pronounced with an air of impartiality and full knowledge of the case, is but a literal copy of the pleas of one side, without noticing the answers of the other. But enough of the philosophy of Schelling, Hegel, and Cousin ; for, if I am not mistaken, you should be rather tired of the *universal substance*, and *the transformations*, and *the phenomena, and the single being which reveals itself to itself in the human conscience,* and the other abstractions of those wonderful philosophers, who rise to such a height above the rest of humanity, but forget to take with them, in their daring flight, the notions of common sense. We, who cannot reach so high, will take care not to wander so far from the beaten tracks of sound judgment, and will feel no pain if upbraided with receiving our inspiration from a *pedestrian muse.* In the meanwhile I am at your service, and remain yours, &c., &c.,

J. B.

XI.

Self-Love.

MY ESTEEMED FRIEND,—I am sincerely pleased your last letter exempts me for ever from dealing farther with the German philosophy, or the French, which is an imitation of it. I knew your naturally clear judgment, thirsting for truth and opposed to abstractions, would not tolerate the symbolic language and the phantastic ideas with which the good Germans have adorned philosophy, in the leisure moments abundantly afforded them by their climate of fogs and frosts. You wonder, and not without reason, that this philosophy could have spread in France, where men's minds lean to the opposite extreme of sensual and materialistic positivism. I believe it was by a kind of necessity, in the supposition that the Voltairian philosophy was completely discredited, and those who wished to be regarded as philosophers must put on a grave and majestic air ; and as they had no desire to follow the sound writers who preceded them in their native country, they had to cast their eye beyond the Rhine, and with great pomp import into the midst of a capricious and novelty-loving people the systems of Schelling and Hegel, as portentous inventions, capable of making the human mind progress indefinitely. For the rest, if I must frankly say what I think, I believe the French genius will not put up with the German philosophy, but will discover there is Pantheism in it at bottom ; and without waiting to subtilise or cavil about the *universal and only substance*, will jump at its last consequence, which is Atheism, without the ambiguity of mysterious words. In arriving at this result, it will observe it is taught nothing new beyond what it learned from its own philosophers of the last century. It will then despise this philosophy, said to be new, as a plagiarism of another worn out and effete ; and then it will be requisite to seek new springs of illusion to supply food, even for a short time, to the curiosity of the schools and the vanity of the professors. This is the history of the human mind, my dear friend. Examine its pages, and you shall at once discover that the phenomenon we witness is the reproduction of what has occurred in all ages. The advantage derived from it by religious men is not small, for when they contemplate the versatility of the human mind, they more easily comprehend the necessity of a guide in the midst of illusions and extravagances.

I have been almost surprised by the argument you

M

use against the truth of our religion, founded on the
fact that with our doctrines we contradict one of the
most indelible and at the same time most innocent
sentiments of the human breast—self-love. I was
amused by the terms in which you develop your ideas.
The reasons on which you ground them would certainly
be strong, only they rest on a false supposition, and
consequently are like edifices void of foundation. " I
know not," you say in your last, " what misanthropic
spirit reigns among Catholics, and covers everything
with gloomy sadness. You don't want anything earthly
to be named, nor permit people to think on the affairs
of this world ; you annihilate, as it were, the entire
universe, and when all is sacrificed to your tetrical
system ; when you have succeeded in isolating man in
frightful solitude, want him to turn against himself, to
deny himself, to annihilate himself also, to despoil himself of his most intimate sentiments, to abhor himself,
and make a cruel effort against the most lively instincts
of his nature. But what ! Is God the Creator opposed
to God the Saviour ? Will God, who has communicated
to us the love of ourselves, who has imprinted it in
indelible characters on our soul,—will that same God,
when working in the order of grace, delight in contradicting himself as the author of nature ? These are things
I could never understand, and I think you shall have
trouble in dissipating the mists that prevent me from
seeing the truth. I know you will utter an eloquent
sermon about the misery and iniquity of man, the just
motives we have for professing a holy hatred of our-

selves, but I now warn you I cannot desire such sanctity; weak and vain and evil as I know I am, I cannot do less than love myself, and when I compare my nothingness with the elevation of the cherubim, I feel more affection, more love for my insignificant being, than for those sublime intelligences which are said to hold a high place in the celestial hierarchy." The tone of security you employ tells me there is here something more than doubts—something approaching true conviction; and no wonder, in the supposition that you build on a false principle and consequently arrive at false conclusions. You have found some expressions in certain mystic works and have taken them literally, and hence your ascribing to our religion doctrines she does not hold.

Who told you Christianity condemns self-love, understanding this condemnation in a rigorous sense? This is the vacuum left by you in your reasoning. You were not careful enough to make sure of the principle on which you founded it, and so whilst you believed you were building on a solid base, you were only raising castles in the air. This is not the first time such a thing has happened to religion, for often and often, for the sake of combating it, phantasms are conjured up, and people make war on them as if they were its offspring, whereas they are only the creations of her opponent's brain. I do not accuse you of acting perversely; I am sure you suffer from misapprehension, which you will correct immediately I point it out; and I flatter myself I can do so notwithstanding your assertion that it is difficult to dissipate the mists that impede your knowledge of the truth. As to the eloquent sermon on the misery and wickedness of man, I think you may make your mind easy, as I have given you sufficient proofs I am not inclined to declamations of any sort. But let us come to the difficulty.

It is false that religion prohibits us from loving ourselves; and so false, that on the contrary one of its fundamental precepts is this same self-love. I need nothing but the Catechism to convince you of this. I hope you have not forgotten we are told in it to love our neighbours as ourselves, in which the precept of love which each one should entertain for himself is most expressly recorded. This love is presented to us as the model of that we should have for our neighbour; and the precept would clearly be contradictory if we were prohibited from entertaining this love which is to serve as the rule and standard of that which we should have for others.

Are you aware the principle so common in the world, that charity should begin at home, is expressly recorded in all the theological tracts that have been written on charity? They all clearly mark out the order charity should observe, according to its different relations with the objects to which it extends, the first and principal being God, the second we ourselves.

You now see all your arguments are upset when I roundly deny the principle on which they rested, and adduce in favour of my negation proofs so clear and simple that you cannot reject them; nevertheless, I will amplify my ideas on the point, and make applications of them which shall satisfy you completely.

We will go back again to the Catechism. In it we are told that man was created to love and serve God in this life, and to enjoy Him in eternal bliss. Now then, all our actions have God and eternal bliss for their end. Does he who desires to be eternally happy not love himself? And is he who is bound to labour all his life to attain this felicity, not also obliged to love himself exceedingly? Or rather, do these two obligations not coalesce in one? The Christian holds it as a dogma of faith that this life is a transit to another. If he despises the terrestrial, if he makes no account of the vanities of the world, it is because all is passing, because all is nothing compared with the happiness he is promised after death, if he endeavour to merit it by his good works —his property, his health, his life, his honour—he should be willing to lose all sooner than stain his conscience with one sole act which might close the gates of heaven against him. But in that abnegation, in that abandonment of self, well-ordered self-love rides safely at anchor, for he despises the insignificant to attain the important, he abandons the terrestrial to obtain the celestial, he leaves the temporal to secure the eternal. When we examine the Christian doctrines, we find they wonderfully harmonise the love of God, the love of ourselves, and the love of our neighbour, and consequently it is totally false that the natural inclination which leads us to love ourselves is destroyed by religion; it is rectified, regulated, purified from the stains which deform it, preserved from ruin, and directed to the supreme end, infinitely holy and good, which is God.

How are we to understand, then, that destruction of self-love of which mystic writers speak? We must understand by it the extirpation of vice, the restraint of the passions, victory over pride, in a word, a solicitude to prevent the love of the sensual from injuring the moral man. To make the superior prevail over the inferior parts of man, is not to destroy his love for himself, but to cause it to act in conformity with the eternal law and advantageously to him. If a man abstains from a banquet for the sake of avoiding injury it might cause him, can it be said he does not love but hate himself? He will be truly said to deprive himself of a gratification, but that privation springs from the regard he has for his health, and consequently flows from his self-love, which induces him to sacrifice the less to the greater, and will not allow him to injure his health for a momentary appetite. This simple example, which we daily witness without any wonder, fairly explains the relations of the Christian doctrines with self-love, as we have only to extend the principle to higher objects, and consider the rule which guides a particular action is the same that regulates the whole conduct of the Christian.

"But how then are we told to abhor ourselves?" This abhorrence does not, and cannot, refer to anything but what is evil in us, whether it be wicked acts or certain inclinations which tend to draw us from the path of the law of God; but we should not, and cannot by

any means, abhor our nature as far as it is good and the
work of God. On the contrary, we should love it, and
the proof is in the fact that we should abhor what is
evil in it, and to abhor the evil of anything is to desire
its good and love it.

You are aware, my esteemed friend, that some of the
rules laid down for the conduct of Christians are precepts, others counsels. The observance of the former is
necessary for eternal life. The observance of the latter
contributes to our perfection in this life, and merits
a higher degree of glory in the next ; but it does not
so oblige that its omission would be culpable. The
same holds in our conduct with regard to self-love. By
the precepts we are obliged to abstain from all infraction of the law of God, no matter how our disordered
appetites may impel us, as also to sacrifice the pleasure
that might result from the satisfaction of our passions
when there is question of doing something expressly
commanded by the law of God ; in this way we are all
obliged to suffocate our self-love, and if we do not, we
hold it as a dogma of faith we can never gain eternal life,
but shall receive a punishment without end. But there
are certain abstinences, certain mortifications of the
senses, which belong not to the precepts, but only to
the counsels. We see these mortifications practised
more or less rigorously by persons who aim at perfection, and in some of the saints we find austerity carried
to a degree that astonishes and bewilders us. But in
these very saints self-love, properly understood, was
not smothered. They gave themselves up unreservedly

to penance, either to purify themselves from their faults, or to render themselves more agreeable to the Lord, by offering him in holocaust their senses, their body, all they had and all they were ; but in the meantime did these extraordinary men forget themselves? No doubt they forgot the sensual man, or rather they declared war to the death on him, and attacked and tormented him whenever possible; but they did so, because they regarded him as an enemy of the spiritual man—a terrible, fearfully dangerous enemy, whom they could not trust for a minute, and from whose neck the chain could not be removed without imminent risk of rebellion against his ruler, the spirit, whom he might reduce to slavery. But those illustrious penitents never forgot the salvation of their soul, and the eternal felicity of the other life, but on the contrary incessantly sighed after it, anxiously longed for God to free them from this body which oppressed them, and their strongest desire was to be dissolved and be with Christ. The vision of God, the union with God in bonds of ineffable love, was the object of their hopes, their desires, and their continued sighs; and so they cannot with propriety be said to abhor themselves, but rather to love themselves with a better love than the rest of men.

I hope the preceding considerations may convince you you built on a false supposition, and if you want to continue your attacks on religion as opposed to self-love, must look out for other principles. In fact to do so, now that your error on the point is removed, and it was proved to evidence that religion not only does not prohibit self-love, but commands us to entertain it, there is only one course open to you, and that is to show that she has a wrong idea of this love, and whilst proposing to direct and purify, suffocates and smothers it. But do you know on what ground the question will then be placed ? Do you know that, considered under this aspect, it has nothing to do with what we have hitherto discussed, but becomes an inquiry whether the precepts and counsels of the Gospel are just, holy, and prudent ? I do not believe you will dare dispute a truth generally admitted even by the most violent enemies of Christianity. They deny its dogmas; they mock its creed ; they laugh at its hierarchy ; they despise its authority ; they consider it as a mere philosophical system, and despoil it of all supernatural and divine character; but when they come to our moral code, they all agree it is admirable, sublime, superior to that of all ancient and modern legislators ; is in intimate harmony with the light of reason ; with the most noble and beautiful sentiments that find shelter in our breast, and is the only one worthy of ruling humanity and directing the destinies of the world. So that when, given up to their vain desires, they idealise new Christianities and totally new religions, they all adopt the morality of the Gospel for their model ; and even when perhaps they profess in the depth of their heart doctrines morally degrading and highly obnoxious, they do not dare to express them publicly, but eulogise the sweetness, the sanctity and sublimity of the maxims uttered by the lips of Jesus Christ.

If then you direct your attacks against this point, you shall meet with serious opposition; and hence I will venture to give you an advice, which most of those who attack religion would do well to take, and it is, that when you come to judge our doctrines or maxims you do not allow yourself to be carried away by that giddiness which decides on things of the utmost importance, without taking the trouble to examine them with proper attention; but reflect that what so many men eminent in talent and wisdom have believed and taught and practised, must undoubtedly be well founded, and not to be overturned by a few observations, which though ingenious, are extremely futile. Believe me when you find arguments of this sort which appear to easily upset any religious truth, you should suspend your judgment, and not be precipitate, but meditate or read and consult; and you shall soon discover the invincible Achilles has no more strength than what is supplied by a false supposition or defective reasoning. I have no doubt you are convinced that if in time you resolve on returning to the bosom of religion, you may love yourself. In the meantime be assured of the affection of your attached friend,

J. B.

XII.

Moral Code of the Gospel.

MY ESTEEMED FRIEND,—The method you employ in our discussion proves, or rather, as I had already known it, convinces me of one thing, and that is, your want of firmness and moral exactness, of which those who build not on the solid foundations of religion are totally devoid. It has been said, with much truth, that morality without dogmas, was justice without tribunals. We hear you incredulists praise and enthusiastically proclaim the sublimity of the doctrine of Jesus Christ in everything appertaining to the regulation of the conduct of man ; you confess there is nothing superior or equal in the precepts of ancient or modern philosophers ; you acknowledge there is nothing to add or retrench ; and you do all this with such a tone of sincerity, and such apparent *bona fide*, as to leave no doubt that if you reject the dogmas of the Christian religion, you at least embrace its code of morality as a philosophical conviction. But then, behold ! you immediately launch into the exposition of some doctrine totally at variance with the morality of the Gospel. You, yourself, have done this in your last letter ; for, after resigning yourself to the abandonment of the trench in which you had fortified yourself concerning *self-love*, you change the argument, but not the object.

You say you agree with me that religion does not destroy, but only rectifies self-love ; and you have no hesitation in acknowledging the objections of your former letter hinged on a false supposition. Nevertheless, you are unwilling to abandon your ground, and insist that the manner in which religion rectifies self-love is too severe, and opposed besides to the instincts of nature. Here we have the application of what I told you a short time ago, viz., that men without religion frequently fall into a manifest contradiction, by praising in one place the moral code of Jesus Christ, and attacking it in another without consideration or respect. You are one of those who recognise the sanctity of the Gospel morality, and yet you do not hesitate to condemn it for what it prescribes concerning the passions. But do you know that to declare a moral code bad or useless, or inapplicable in relation to the passions, is little less than to condemn it in its totality? Have you not remarked that the greater part of moral precepts deal with the regulation and repression of the passions? If then, the morality of the Gospel is not suited to them, of what use is it?

You assert the Gospel precepts are much too severe in their opposition to irresistible instincts of nature; and as regards some of its counsels, you venture to say it will be hard to persuade you they are conformable with reason and prudence. You hold that the secret of directing the passions is to leave them a safety-valve to avoid an explosion, and regard the neglect of this maxim as one of the capital defects of the code of the Gospel. You do not object to its declaring culpable acts which introduce disturbance into families, and even those which tend to multiply the population, while the fruit of the incontinence is abandoned to public charity; but you cannot believe its rigour should be carried so far as to prohibit the very thought, and declare him culpable, in the eyes of God, who should admit levity into his heart, though he abstain from everything repugnant to nature, or that could entail injury on the family or society. Avoiding the discussion to which your objection might tend under many aspects, and circumscribing ourselves to the prudential point of view, I maintain the moral code of the Gospel is so profoundly wise and prudent in its so called harshness, that it would be much more harsh if moulded after your doctrines. This assertion may appear to you extravagant, and yet, I flatter myself with being able to support it with such reasons, that you shall find yourself compelled to subscribe to my opinion.

As you appear fond of the study of the heart, I shall venture to ask you, whether, supposing an act to be prohibited, it is more difficult to secure obedience by prohibiting the desire of it also, or allowing it to roam at will ? I hold it as certain, that it is much more easy to make a man avoid what he cannot even desire, than what he cannot do, but the desire of which is not prohibited. It is said there is as little distance between the thought and the execution, as between the head and the arm ; and daily experience tells us that he who has conceived vehement desires of possessing an object, seldom hesitates at employing the means of attaining it.

Precisely in this very matter in which we are engaged reason becomes so blinded, and the passions preponderate to such a degree, that he who allows himself to be hurried away by them becomes degraded and stupified, and disregards his honour, his property, his health, nay, even his very life,—and, in a passion like this, do you think prudence would advise the desire to be permitted but the execution prohibited? You unhesitatingly assert that the prohibition which extends to the desire is cruel, without adverting that true harshness is found in your system alone, for it tantalises a man, and presents to him pure and crystalline waters, but will not allow him to quench his thirst. Reflect maturely on these observations, and you shall find that real harshness is found, not in the Gospel, but in your code ; that in yours, under the appearance of indulgent suavity, a real torture is applied to the heart, while, in that of the Gospel, the peace and tranquillity of virtuous souls is secured by prudent and timely severity. The man who knows it is not lawful to indulge even in a bad thought, firmly rejects it the moment it occurs to him, and does not allow passion to blind him ; the man who believes there is no sin but in the execution, endeavours to gratify the inclinations of nature, and deceives himself with the hope that pleasure in the thought or desire cannot lead him to commit the act ; but the moment reason and the will abdicate their sovereignty, even under the express condition they should not be carried beyond the limits of duty, it is impossible for them to restrain the turbulent passions which, emboldened by the first concession, would demand to be completely satisfied.

Between religion and the philosophers who, under different names, attack her, there is this great difference:—the former establishes as a principle the absolute necessity of nipping the passions in the bud, believing it will be so much the more difficult to subject or direct them by how much the more growth they are allowed to make ; whilst the latter hold the most irregular passions are to be allowed a certain expansion, beyond which they must be restrained. And is it not strange that this course is pursued by men who have no means of subduing the heart but sterile discourses, whose impotence is manifested whenever they have to struggle with a passion more or less vehement, while religion, which has so many means of influencing the understanding and the will, and lording it over the entire man, adopts quite a different course? Religion, founded by God Himself, adheres to a prudent rule, and regards the prevention of the evil as better than its cure, applying the remedy when it is insignificant to avoid doing so when it is great ; but clever mortals, opening the dyke for the waters, allow them to flow freely, determined, when they have reached a certain limit, to cry out to them—" Stay here, farther you shall not go ! "

I know not, my esteemed friend, if you be convinced by the reasons I have assigned in defence of the moral code of the Gospel, and against that of the philosophic system. You cannot, however, deny these considerations are not to be despised, as they are founded in the very nature of man, and on the teaching of daily experience. What we have said of the most turbulent and dangerous passion that afflicts miserable mortals, can be applied to all the rest, though the saying that there is no remedy but in flight is peculiarly verified in it ; a sentence profoundly wise and prudent, warning a man of how much importance it is not to lose dominion over himself, because once he has given rein to them, it is very difficult to restrain the passions.

We can apply to the individual what happens in society. If the supreme power, whose duty it is to govern, begins to yield to the exigencies of those who should obey, their demands will daily increase, and its authority will become degraded in proportion as it loses ground, until in the end an anarchy supervenes, or an appeal is made to a violent reaction to recover what was lost, and establish rights which should never have been abdicated. The laws of order have an analogy even in their application to very dissimilar things—it might be said to be the self-same law without other modification than what is indispensably necessary to suit it to the species of subject to be governed by it.

I remarked that what I had said of the voluptuous passion could be applied to the others, and I shall make you feel it by attacking you in the most sensitive part, which is philanthropy; for you, philosophers, cannot bear to have your ardent love for humanity called in question. You constantly extol the precept of universal fraternity, which, according to the religion of Jesus Christ, makes all men members of the same family. From this Commandment comes the prohibition to injure our neighbour; and, according to our principle, not only we cannot injure him, but we cannot even entertain the desire of doing so, and we look on it as a sin to simply indulge in a thought of vengeance.

Well, now, if we apply your theory to the present

case, we shall have to condemn the Christian code as
unduly harsh, and limit ourselves to declaring it unlaw-
ful to commit an act that may injure our brethren, but
licit to entertain a thought or desire of doing so. And
so your fine fraternity may be expressed thus :—" Fellowmen, injure us not by word or deed, for by doing so
you would break through the rules of sound morality,
and offend the God who created you, not that you
might act to each other's prejudice, but that you might
live together in peace and harmony. Thus far are you
bound by the law; but entering into the sanctuary of
your own interior, you are at perfect liberty to desire
what evil you wish to other men, certain that by so
doing you are guilty of no fault, for God is not so cruel
as to prohibit not only the act but even the thought
and desire." Does not the precept of charity—of universal fraternity—look rather curious and strange, if
explained in this way? And yet it is thus explained
by you, for I have done no more than collect together
different parts of your system to render the contrast
more striking.

The radical vice of such a system consists in its putting the interior at variance with the exterior; in supposing it right to limit moral obligations to external
acts ; in establishing a species of civil morality which, in
ultimate analysis, is nothing more than a purely human
jurisprudence, without other object than to secure public
tranquillity. This is the result of your doctrines.

And it is no way strange ; for what more natural,
when God is exiled from the world, and no religion

N

admitted—when the divine influence on the acts of men is ignored, than that they should be considered in the purely external order, and have no importance in the eyes of the philosopher but inasmuch as they are capable of producing some exterior good, or causing some exterior evil. By removing God, or what is the same, by destroying religion, you destroy the interior man, and reduce all morality to a combination of well-calculated utilities.

These consequences may be disagreeable to you, and I have no doubt you will make an effort to reject them ; but to avoid disputes, I beseech you to turn back and follow the thread of my argument, convinced that if you do so with impartiality, you must acknowledge my words are not false or exaggerated.

In the meantime, to show how palpable are the errors and the inconveniences of the doctrine you hold with such security, I will make an application of this precept of universal fraternity, not considered in its prohibitive but in its preceptive part. Once admitted the evil of actions is in the external act alone, we must also admit their goodness will be in the exterior also ; and so we shall perform a laudable act by doing good to our neighbour, but not by desiring it. But do you know whither this principle leads us ? Would you believe it does nothing less than destroy at one fell swoop that universal fraternity so extolled by the philanthropy of philosophers ? What is the love which is limited to exterior acts ? Is any love true which does not exist in the heart ? Is it not this which language indicates,

when it distinguishes between beneficence and benevolence—the doing good and the desiring it ? Is not the
latter as well as the former a praiseworthy virtue ? If
a person cannot be beneficent, because he lacks the
means, is he not worthy of praise if he be benevolent,
that is, if he has the desire of doing the good which it
is out of his power to accomplish ? If a person does
good, does he not desire it before he does it ? That is
to say, is not the beneficent man benevolent first ? And
is he not beneficent because he is benevolent ? I do
not know whether you will look at things from this
point of view, but I can say for myself I consider the
desire and the act so united, that they appear to me
things of the same order, and as if the one were the
complement of the other. And, as far as beneficence is
concerned, I will go farther : when I represent to myself
a man who does good from any motive whatever, but at
the same time does not entertain in his heart an affectionate desire, which impels him to act; that is, when
I see beneficence without benevolence, either I do not
conceive an act of virtue there, or at least, I find it lame
and devoid of the beautiful adornments that render it
agreeable and enchanting.

Now, my dear friend, you must see the Christian
religion is not so far astray in introducing herself into
internal acts—in extending her commandments and
prohibitions even to the most hidden things we execute
in the lowest depths of our conscience ; and that to
accuse her of harshness in the matter is to upset not
only religious morality, but even that taught by the

light of reason. Thus are things joined which appeared quite distant; thus are virtues united with an intimacy so close, that whoever dares to deny one finds himself obliged to reject many others, which, perhaps, he respects and venerates with all sincerity and reverence. From these considerations I wish you would draw this consequence—that we should not isolate religious questions too much when we come to examine them, for by doing so we run the risk of mutilating the truth, and a mutilated truth is an error. Infidels and sceptics almost always fall into this mistake: they take up a dogma, a moral precept, a practice or ceremony of religion; they separate it from everything else; they analyse it, prescinding from all the relations it has with other dogmas, precepts, practices, or ceremonies; they look at but one side of it, and endeavour to make the ceremony appear ridiculous, the practice irrational, the precept cruel, the dogma absurd. There is no order of truths that will not fall to the ground if examined in this way; because its truths are not considered as they are in themselves, but as the caprice of the philosopher has regulated them in the closet of his mind. In such a case phantasms are created which do not exist; the real enemies are avoided, and war made on imaginary ones with whom it is in no way dangerous to contend.

When one has to deal with the most sweet and seducing sentiments, it is not difficult to deceive the incautious by representing to them as an innocent expansion what is in reality a deadly poison. Thus, for example, in the difficulty you raise in your letter,

what is more conformable to the instincts of nature, to
the softest impulses of the heart, than the doctrine you
hold? "What!" you say, "is it not enough to prohibit the acts which might entail evil results on society,
the family, or the individual; but must you penetrate
into the interior of the soul too, and there take delight in
tormenting the poor heart by obliging it to abstain from
those exhalations, which, rather than crimes, God should
regard as the innocent alleviations of nature. If the evil
be not consummated, whom does the desire injure? Is
it possible the Creator can take umbrage at the most
inoffensive acts of the creature?" These, my friend, are
what are called sentimental strokes, and decisive arguments for candid and ardent souls, anxious to find a
doctrine to excuse their weakness, and tone down the
austerity of the morality they learned from the catechism. But they are really dangerous sophisms, which
do not conduce to the wellbeing and consolation of
those in whose favour they are made, but on the contrary, sadly corrupt and lead them astray. "What!"
one might reply, imitating your tone, "will you be so
cruel as to allow the sweet fresh liquid to approach our
lips, and not allow us to partake of it? Are you so
harsh as to give passion the reins in the interior, and
refuse it a safety-valve in the exterior? Can you be so
pitiless as to unchain the tempests in the depth of the
heart, kept agitated and tormented by you on all sides,
without giving it freedom to alleviate its pains, and, by
extending the storm, to make it less intense and
grievous? Oh! close the door entirely or allow of a

remedy; do not set the interior man at such variance with the exterior—the heart with its works. As you boast of your humanity, endeavour to render your false indulgence less cruel."

As regards the point, whether God can be indignant at the interior acts of the creature, we might say :— "What! if relations exist between God and man—if the Creator has not abandoned His creature—if He regards it yet as an object of care, is it not clear—is it not evident, that the understanding and the will, that is, what is most precious in man—what renders him capable of knowing and loving his Maker—what raises him above the brute—what constitutes him king of creation—is not that, we repeat, what should be regarded as the object of the solicitude of the Supreme Ruler; and should we not feel certain He does not attend to exterior acts, but inasmuch as they come from the sanctuary of the conscience, where He delights to be known, loved, and adored? What is man if we prescind from his interior? What is morality, if not applied to the understanding and will? Is that doctrine well-founded, which mercilessly destroys what is most independent and dignified in man, whilst it boasts of being instinct with the sentiments of morality?"

Be persuaded, my dear friend, that there is no truth or dignity in anything that opposes religion; and what appears at first sight noble and generous, is base and degrading. And *apropos* of philanthropic sentiments, beware of those sudden inspirations, which may appear to you decisive arguments, but which, when examined at the light of religion, or even sound philosophy, are nothing but unfounded reasonings, or conclusions from unsound principles, conducing to establish the dominion of matter over spirit, and let loose the voluptuous passions on the world.

See if any service can be done you by your fond and affectionate friend, J. B.

XIII.

Humility.

MY ESTEEMED FRIEND,—I find it is useless to attempt to confine you to a connected discussion on the dogmas of religion, and the principles on which they rest, for, faithful to your system of observing no system, and inviolably observing the rule of your method, which is to observe none, you skip like a butterfly from flower to flower ; so that when one believes you absorbed in some capital question, and decided on prolonging the attack commenced on some point of the walls of the Holy City, you suddenly raise the siege, sit down in some other quarter, and there threaten to open a new breach, expecting me to fly to the defence of the point menaced, but only to find you directing your steps to some other place, and uselessly fatigue myself without obtaining the result I desired. No ; I made a mistake when I said I was uselessly fatigued ; for though it is true I have not been able, up to the present, to withdraw you from your error, because you have ever refused to subject yourself to the trouble of a discussion sustained with due order and connexion, yet I flatter myself with having succeeded in removing some of the prejudices which obstructed your advance in the road to faith, hoping that some day, with your understanding illuminated by superior inspirations, and your heart moved by the grace of the Lord, you may resolve to seriously pursue it, and burst the bonds that detain you, and so escape from your present unhappy state, in which I hope the hour of death shall not find you.

Apologising for this preamble, which you may regard as inopportune, but which I consider a salutary inopportunity, I come now to answer the difficulties you propose to me on one of the virtues most extolled by the Christian religion. I am very glad we have escaped from the disputes which were the subject of the last letter; for though it treated of a very transcendent and highly important matter, the subject was of a nature so delicate and fragile, that it was necessary to measure one's words, and go in search of expressions, which, while permitting the truth to appear, might closely veil whatever could offend decency and the delicate considerations due to modesty. But humility is a subject on which we can talk without periphrasis, there being no danger of making the blood rise to the cheek by an unmeasured word. You are somewhat Voltairian when speaking of this virtue, and ironically apply to it the epithet *sublime,* which Christians are fond of calling it. You appear to have formed very mistaken notions about the nature of humility, for you go so far as to assure me that no matter how you might desire it you could not possibly be humble after the fashion mystic works require, simply because you do not think it possible to deceive one's self, and all the efforts to do so would be in vain. I almost laughed when I found you imagined you had proposed an unanswerable difficulty to me when you said you could never persuade yourself you are the most stupid among men, for you meet many who evidently do not possess the knowledge, be it little or great, which your education and instruction procured for you ; or that you are the most perverse of mortals, for you do not rob, assassinate, nor commit other acts with which some men stain their hands ; and, nevertheless, you say, if we accept the doctrine of mystics, this is the perfection of humility, which the most distinguished saints and those most advanced in this virtue, have attained. I do not wonder you feel no inclination to run out on the streets and feign madness, that you might be despised, and so have an opportunity of practising humility ; but what I do wonder at is, that you should consider such arguments invincible, and, proclaiming your victory beforehand, intimate that one must either swallow the absurdities resulting from these maxims and examples, or condemn the lives of great saints, and cast the works of the most famous mystics into the fire. I think the dilemma is not so perfect as to leave no means of escape. I rather believe it will neither be necessary to devour the absurdities nor engage in the repugnant occupation of Don Quixote's housekeeper and the village priest.

I think you, who are so noble-hearted, cannot be at variance with St Teresa of Jesus, to whom, though you regard her as a visionary, you cannot deny the eulogy so well deserved by her eminent virtues, her pure soul, her good heart, her clear and penetrating talent, and her pen, as amiable as sublime. You know this saint had some experience in the Christian virtues, and from all she had meditated and read, and consulted besides with wise men, should know in what humility consisted, and how this virtue was understood and explained in the bosom of the Catholic Church. And do you believe the saint thought that, to be humble, she should begin by deceiving herself? I would wager anything you could not guess the definition she gives of humility— the admirable definition, which, I might say, appears selected on purpose to answer your difficulty. The saint relates that she did not comprehend why humility was so agreeable to God ; and thinking on the matter one day, she found it was so, because *humility is truth.* You see there is no talk here of deceit, and humility, so far from urging us to it, dissipates it ; for its most solid merit, the very title on which it is agreeable to God, is its truth.

I shall explain in a few words that beautiful sentence of St Teresa of Jesus ; and I shall require no more than this luminous observation of our saint's to make you comprehend what humility is, in its relations with ourselves, with God, and with our neighbour.

Is it opposed to the virtue of humility that we should know the good qualities, natural or supernatural, with

which God has favoured us? No; on the contrary,
read all the works of scholastic and mystic theologians,
and you shall find that they all agree that this virtue is
not opposed to any such knowledge. If a man constantly experiences that he comprehends with great
facility whatever he hears or reads, that it is enough for
him to fix his attention on the most abstruse questions
to make them appear clear and simple, there is no inconvenience in the world in his being inwardly convinced
that God has bestowed this great favour on him ; nay,
more, it is impossible for him not to entertain this conviction which has for its object a fact ever present to
his mind, and of which his conscience assures him, or
rather a series of acts, that continually accompany his
existence, and constitute his intellectual life—that intimate life, of which we are as certain as of the existence
of our body. Can you imagine St Thomas was persuaded he was as ignorant as the lay brothers of his
convent ? Was it possible for St Augustine to believe
he knew as little of the science of religion as the lowest
of the people to whom he was explaining it ? Shall we
say St Jerome, who had such a profound knowledge of
the learned languages, and of all the other things necessary for the correct interpretation of the Sacred Scriptures, believed in his heart he knew Greek and Hebrew
but tolerably, and that the investigations with which he
ascended to the sources of erudition were totally fruit-
less. No ; Christians utter no such absurdities. A
virtue so solid, so beautiful, so agreeable to the eyes of
God, cannot demand from us any such extravagances; it

cannot require us to shut our eyes to what is clearer than the light of day.

Real humility brings with it the clear knowledge of what we are, without adding or subtracting anything. If a person have learning, he can be interiorly aware of it; but he should at the same time confess he has received it from God, and that to Him is due all the honour and glory. He should also acknowledge that this learning, though it raises his understanding above that of the ignorant, or of those less learned than himself, leaves him, nevertheless, very inferior to other learned men, who are far before him in comprehensiveness and profoundness. He should also consider that this learning gives him no right to despise any one; for, as he has it by a special beneficence of God, so might others have possessed it, if the Creator had deigned to bestow it on them. He should remember that this privilege does not exempt him from the weakness and miseries to which humanity is subject, and by how much the more the favours are with which God has distinguished him— by how much the more capable his understanding may be of knowing good and evil; by so much the more strict shall be the account he must render to God, who has so made him the object of His bountiful munificence. If a person have virtues, there is no inconvenience in his knowing it, but he should acknowledge they are due to particular graces from heaven; if he does not commit the evil acts with which other men stain themselves, it is because God holds him by the hand; if he does good and avoids evil by means of grace, this grace has been given by God; if, from his very disposition, he is inclined to certain virtuous acts, and has a horror of the contrary vices, this disposition has also come to him from God : in a word, he has motives to be content, but not to become proud, on the supposition that he would be unjust in attributing to himself what does not belong to him, and defrauding God of the glory that is rightly His.

Listen to that great saint, to the man who soared so high in all Christian virtues, especially in humility— to St Francis de Sales ; and see how he not only agrees that it is lawful to know the perfections we possess, but also permitted, and often salutary, to fix our attention on them, and stop to consider them at leisure :—

" But, Philothea, you will desire me to lead you forward in humility, what I have said on it up to this appearing rather like wisdom than humility. Forward, then, I go. There are many who do not like, or do not presume to think on and consider, the graces and favours God has bestowed on them, fearing they might fall into vain-glory or complacency, but in this they are undoubtedly deceived; for as the great Angelical Doctor says, the true means of coming to the love of God is the consideration of His favours, as by how much the more we think on them, by so much the more we shall love Him ; and as particular favours move us more than general ones, so they should be more attentively considered. It is certain nothing can humble us so much before the mercy of God, as the number of His

benefits ; nor can anything humble us so much before
His justice as the multitude of our transgressions.
We should consider what He has done for us, as well
as what we have done against Him ; and as we often
regard our sins, so let us often consider His graces.
There is no fear that the knowledge of what He has
given us shall make us vain, so that we attend to this
truth, that whatever good is in us is not ours. Tell
me, do mules cease to be dull and peevish beasts
because they are loaded with the precious wares and
odours of princes ? What good have we that we have
not received ? And if we have received it, why do we
glory ? (1 Cor. iv. 7). On the contrary, the lively reflection on the favours received makes us humble,
because knowledge engenders gratitude ; but if, on
beholding the beneficence God has employed towards
us, any sort of vanity should come to disquiet us, it will
be an infallible remedy to recur to the consideration of
our ingratitude, our imperfections, and our miseries. If
we think of what we did when God was not with us, we
shall see that what we do when He accompanies us
does not spring from our own industry. We shall be
truly glad, and shall rejoice because we have some
good ; but we shall glorify God above as the author of
it. Thus the Blessed Virgin confessed that God did
great things in her ; but this was to humble herself and
exalt God :—'My soul,' she says, 'doth magnify the
Lord, because He hath done great things in me' "
(Luke i. 46, 49).—*St Francis de Sales' Introduction to a
Devout Life*, part 3d, ch. 5.

There could be no more conclusive testimony in favour of the doctrine I was explaining. You see there is no talk of deceiving one's self, but simply of knowing things as they are. "Then," you will object, "how is it great saints say roundly they are the greatest sinners in the world, that they are unworthy the earth should sustain them, and are the most ungrateful among men?" Understand the true sense of these words; recollect they are accompanied by a sentiment of profound compunction; that they are pronounced in moments in which the soul annihilates itself in presence of its Creator; and you shall see they are susceptible of a very rational interpretation. I will simplify it by an example. When St Teresa of Jesus said she was the greatest sinner on earth, can we imagine she believed she was guilty of the crimes of other women, when she knew well the purity of her body and soul, and the ineffable favours with which God had enriched her? Clearly we cannot. Nay more; can we suppose she believed she had one single mortal sin on her soul? Certainly not, for otherwise she would not have dared to receive the august Sacrament of the Altar, which she nevertheless received so frequently, and with such ecstasies of gratitude and love. Well now: the saint was not ignorant that in the world there were many persons guilty of grievous and very grievous sins in the sight of God; for she herself was the first to deplore it, and to pray heaven to look on those wretches with eyes of mercy; and therefore, when she said she was the greatest sinner on earth, she could not understand it in

the rigorous sense in which you appear desirous of in-
terpreting it. What then did it signify? Here it is, very
simply. Let us assist at one of the scenes represented
in her mind, and we shall perfectly comprehend the
sense of the words which are a stumbling-block to you.
Placed in the presence of God, with lively faith, with
ardent charity, with a contrite and humble heart, she
examines the hidden folds of her conscience, and
observes, now and then, some slight imperfections as
yet unconsumed by the fire of divine love; and she also
recollects times past, when, notwithstanding that she
was very virtuous, she had not fully entered on the
sublime path which led her to that height of sanctity
which constituted her an angel on earth. The light
faults into which she had fallen, her want of promptness
in following the inspirations of heaven, occur to her;
and comparing all with the natural and supernatural
favours heaped on her by God, and measuring it with
her lively faith, her ineffable charity, and that intimate
presence of God, which raised her above this mortal life
and placed her in superior regions, she sees, in all its
blackness, the foulness of even venial sins; she considers
the ingratitude of which she was guilty by not attending
at once, with much more ardour than she did, to the
calls of the Lord; and then comparing the sanctity of
her soul with the divine sanctity; her ingratitude with
the favours of God; her love with the love manifested
for her by God; she annihilates herself in presence of
the Most High—she loses sight of all the good she
possesses, and with her eyes fixed on her weakness and

misery alone, she exclaims she is the greatest sinner among women, the most ungrateful·among God's creatures. Do you find anything irrational or false in this? Can you presume to condemn the expansion of an humble heart, which, annihilated in the presence of the Lord, acknowledges its defects, and in its lively consideration of them exclaims they are the greatest sins of the world? Do you not discover in this the expression of an ardent charity rather than words of deceit?

I may tell you, Christian humility is most suited for forming true philosophers, if true philosophy consists in making us see things as they are in themselves, without adding or subtracting anything. Humility does not cramp us, for it does not prohibit the knowledge of the good qualities we may possess: it only obliges us to recollect we have received them from God; and this recollection, far from depressing our mind, encourages it; far from debilitating our strength, increases it; because, by keeping the source from which all good has come to us ever present to our mind, we know that by recurring to the same spring with lively faith and rectitude of intention, copious floods shall flow again to satisfy all our necessities. Humility lets us know the good we possess, but does not allow us to forget our evils, our weaknesses, and our miseries: it allows us to know the grandeur, the dignity of our nature, and the favours of grace; but it does not permit us to exaggerate, nor allow us to attribute to ourselves what we do not possess; nor if we possess it, to forget from whom we have received it. Humility, then, inspires us, with

O

regard to God, with acknowledgment and gratitude, and makes us feel our nothingness in presence of the Infinite Being.

With respect to our neighbours, humility does not allow us to exalt ourselves above them by aiming at any pre-eminence which does not belong to us. It renders us affable in our daily intercourse with them, for it makes us feel our own weaknesses, and, consequently, be tolerant to those of others; and by excluding envy from the heart, which always accompanies pride, it compels us to respect merit wherever we meet it, and frankly acknowledge it by offering it due homage, without dreading its prejudicial effect on our own glory.

As I have just pronounced the word *glory*, I would like to know whether you take it ill that humility does not permit us to take pleasure in the praises of men, but inspires us with sentiments superior to that smoke which turns the heads of so many. If you do—and I have no doubt of it—a single reflection will suffice to convince you of your error. Do you think everything is good which makes man great? I believe you will not hesitate to say yes. Very well; the world regards him as a hero, who, after performing actions worthy of praise, pays no attention to it, despises it, and on feeling the fragrant aroma, passes quietly on, his head full of elevated thoughts, his heart swollen with generous sentiments. The world then does justice to the despisers of human vanity—that is, to those who practise acts of true humility: do not be less just than the world. Do you want a counter-proof of this? Here it is: those

who are not humble seek after praise; and do you
know what they acquire as soon as their eagerness becomes apparent? Ridicule and mockery. When we
wish to appear well in the eyes of the world, if we are
not humble, we pretend to be so, and exteriorly allow it
to be understood we make no account of praise, and if
offered to us, we resist it, and say it is undeserved. See,
my esteemed friend, how wise, how noble, how sublime
is the Christian religion, for in the very virtue which
apparently brings so much debasement with it, is concealed the means of acquiring solid glory even among
men, who offer it willingly to whoever deserves, but does
not seek it, but ridicule and despise him who solicits it.
Such is the state of things, that pride itself, to quench
its thirst of glory, is compelled to deny itself, and
assume the cloak of humility. And thus is verified,
even on earth, that sentence of the Sacred Scripture :—
"He who exalts himself shall be humbled, and he who
humbles himself shall be exalted."

But enough to-day on humility. I think you are now
convinced, that to be truly humble, conformably to the
spirit of the Christian religion, you do not require to run
through the streets as a madman, nor to look on yourself
as deserving imprisonment or the block, nor to think your
acquaintance with the sciences or literature is as contracted as that of those who do not know how to read.
If at any time you meet in the lives of the saints some
fact you cannot explain by the foregoing rules, remember we have no difficulty in saying there are many
things rather to be admired than imitated; and besides,

you should not attempt to judge by mundane considerations what marches by paths unknown to the generality of men. These are what we call mysteries and prodigies of grace, and what you, philosophers, will regard as the excitement and exaggeration of religious feeling.

I remain your ever fond and affectionate friend,

J. B.

XIV.

The Vicious—The Lukewarm—Arguments against Religion.

MY ESTEEMED FRIEND,—I am almost inclined to believe you begin to feel uneasy in your religious scepticism, for you are apparently ashamed of it, and feel, although you do not like to confess it, in quite a different state from many others whom, with good intention no doubt, but yet most unjustly, you accuse of similar ideas. I could scarcely believe that the conduct of many Christians should appear to you so strange as to make you suppose that they either hypocritically pretend to be addicted to religion, or else profess without understanding a single word of it. You say you cannot comprehend how, when religion teaches doctrines so sublime, transcendental, and even terrible, men can be found, who, though convinced of their truth, either practically contradict or make little or no use of them. You can conceive the religion of a St Jerome, of a St Peter of Alcantara, or of a St John of the Cross—men profoundly penetrated with the idea of the nothingness of the world, of the importance of eternity, and, consequently, disengaged from the things of earth, dead to all that surrounds them, and only intent on the glory of God and the salvation of their own and their neighbours' souls ; but you do not comprehend the religion of the vicious—of men convinced of the eternity of the pains of hell, and yet labouring as it were to plunge themselves into them ; or of others, who, though not sunk in vice, allow their days to pass with indifference, regardless of what may occur after death ; nor even of those who, though they may practise virtue, do it with great tepidity, without showing they are continually possessed of the idea that in a short time they must meet either a happiness without end, or torments which shall endure for all eternity. All this appears to scandalise you, and contribute to keep you away from religion ; if we confine ourselves to this view there is no medium between scepticism and the life of an anchorite.

The reflection occurs to me that it is very curious to note the variety and contradiction of the arguments with which Sceptics and Indifferentists attack religion, and how discontented they ever appear when dealing with her. Is there any one truly Christian and very devout, who passes whole days in prayer and penance ; looks on the things of the world as fleeting and worthless ; shows himself profoundly convinced of the nothingness of earth, and by his words and actions clearly proves that God and eternity never depart from his thoughts ? Well, then it is said religion is essentially a cramper, that it compresses the ideas, crushes the heart, makes men misanthropes and inutilises them, and consequently is only fit for monks and nuns. We are even sometimes prudently advised that we should endeavour to display religion under a more affable and jovial aspect, and thereby prevent many from abandoning her who would otherwise feel inclined to follow her but cannot consent to become sad and taciturn, and go about through streets and churches with eyes cast down and bended heads. And if, on the other hand, there be others who, though profoundly religious and penetrated with the terrible truths of faith, and addicted, perhaps, to the practice of austere virtues, yet display a serene and joyful countenance, and converse in the most affable and agreeable manner, without indicating by word or act that the thought of hell ever enters their mind; their conduct is immediately criticised and condemned, and those who a little before were the objects of mockery and contempt for their austerity of manner, are now quoted as examples to be followed; so that whether religion weeps or laughs you complain; and if she be calm and serene, you accuse her of indifference. It is well to note these most unreasonable contradictions, which are incurred either from want of meditation or an inclination to make charges against religion.

But let us come to the principal point of your objection, and see if it can be answered satisfactorily. How is it possible for a man of religious convictions to be vicious? This, if I am not mistaken, is the principal difficulty you present; and you must allow me to tell you

with all frankness, that the man who seriously proposes
such an objection displays very little knowledge of the
human heart. The life of the greater part of men is a
web of those contradictions you are unable to explain.
If we were to allow any importance to this difficulty, we
should require all men to regulate their conduct by
their convictions and live in strict conformity with them.
But when and where has such proceeding existed? Do
we not daily find it verified that man, even prescinding
from religious ideas, sees the good, approves of it, and
yet does evil? *Video meliora, proboque, pejora autem
sequor.* We do not the good we love, but the evil we
abhor :—*Non quod volo bonum hoc ago, sed quod odi malum
illud facio.* We talk with a gambler, and the conversation turns on his ruling vice ; well, a preacher in the
pulpit will not express himself with more energy against
the evils which spring from play. " What a dreadful
passion," you shall hear him say ; " ever restlessness,
ever uneasiness and distress, ever uncertainty and
anxiety. Now swimming in abundance, not knowing
what to do with your money ; a moment after all is lost
and you must borrow from your friends, or mortgage
an estate, or part with a piece of furniture, or have
recourse to some other disastrous expedient to supply
a small sum at least with which to try your fortune
again. If you lose, you feel yourself in a state of desperation ; if you win, you find yourself forced to witness
the desperation of others; to suffocate the sentiments
of compassion that spring up in your breast, and mask
and cover them with smart sayings and jokes. What

cruel moments are yours on emerging from the play-house, when you recollect you have, perhaps, wrought the misfortune of your family, and think you went with the hope of improving your position, but now find your-self sunk in the narrowest poverty. It is impossible to conceive how men abandon themselves to such a detestable vice. The gambler is a madman, who is constantly pursuing an illusion, though convinced it is an illusion and nothing more, proved to him a thousand times by his own experience and what he has witnessed in others. In a young man, on entering the world for the first time, a slip in this direction is perhaps not very culpable ; but in a man of some experience, the vice has no excuse." My dear friend, have you heard that moralist, so judicious, so severe, so inexorable with gamblers ? Well, you may find, he has scarcely con-cluded his pious discourse, perhaps while perorating, he hurriedly pulls out his watch, or asks the bystanders what o'clock it is, and do you know why ? It is because the hour of meeting is at hand, the table is waiting, the cloth is spread, his companions have already taken their respective seats, and are shuffling the cards im-patiently, and cursing the lazy laggard ; and his poor heart jumps with joy when he thinks that in a few moments he will begin operations, and the heaps of money will go whirling rapidly around, now before one, now another, soon a third, until in the end, at a late hour of the night, the game concludes, and the moralist of course is the conqueror in anticipation, and com-pletely revenged for his misfortunes of yesterday. All this he hopes; and as soon as he finishes his sermon, he rises, takes his hat, and goes off, annoyed with himself for his want of punctuality. What do you think of such a contradiction? Oh! I may be told the man is a hypocrite, and said what he did not think. It is false: he spoke with the most profound conviction, and if the bystanders were not gamblers, they were incapable of conceiving all the liveliness with which he felt what he expressed. In proof of this, suppose he has a son, a younger brother, a friend, any person at all in whom he takes an interest : he will advise him not to play, and will do so with all the truth of his heart. If he have authority, he will prohibit it with severity ; if not, he will beseech him with all earnestness, and if he can speak with entire frankness, will exclaim with accents of sorrow : " Believe a man of experience : this vice has made and is making my misfortune, woe to me ! and I always fear it will bring me to perdition !" The unfortunate wretch is not ignorant of the evil he does himself, he is aware of his rashness—his madness; he upbraids himself with it a thousand times, as well in his moments of calm and of sound sense, as in those of fury and desperation ; but he has not sufficient strength of mind to resist the impulse of an inclination rooted and strengthened by habit, and conform his actions to his words and profound convictions.

Do you wish for another example ? It would be easy to quote them *ad infinitum. There* is a man of respectable fortune, and stainless reputation, who enjoys in the bosom of his family all the happiness he can desire.

His enlightenment, his morality, and even his polite and polished education, make him contemplate with grief the disorders he sees in others. He cannot conceive how they can consent to sacrifice their property to an incontinent passion, stain their honour for it, and make themselves the object of the contempt and ridicule of all who know them. However, after some time, an occasion, a frequent conversation, has involved him in a dangerous friendship; and property, character, health, even life itself—he sacrifices all to his idol. Has he lost, for all that, his former convictions? Is his change of conduct the effect of a change of ideas? Nothing of the sort; he thinks as formerly, he has not departed a tittle from his primitive convictions, but has only laid them aside. To his relatives and friends who admonish him, who remind him of his own words, who use the same arguments with him as he used with others, who exhort him to take the counsels which a little while ago he was accustomed to give—to all he answers:—" Yes, true; you are right—immediately—in time—but."——

That is to say, there is no want of light in his understanding, but there is disorder in his heart. He is sure the gilded cup contains poison, but in his feverish ardour he raises it to his lips, with the risk—the certainty of perishing. Go through all the vices, fix your attention on all the passions, and you shall discover this contradiction of which I speak. Few, very few are ignorant of the evil and harm they entail on themselves by their conduct, and yet how difficult the amendment! From this you can see it is no way strange that a person profoundly convinced of the truth of religion may act contrary to what it prescribes, and his want of practical conformity is no proof that he does not believe what he says.

If you had read theological and mystic works, or conversed with men experienced in the direction of consciences, you would know the sad and torturing situation in which many souls often find themselves; and the patience confessors require to suffer with and encourage those who purpose leaving off vice, bitterly bewail their faults, tremble when they think of the eternal punishments they have deserved, and through sheer force of counsels, warnings, remedies, and precautions of all sorts, have strength perhaps to resist their destructive inclination for some time, and yet fall again, and return to the feet of the confessor, and at the end of a short time yield again and suffer mortal anguish, until, better fortified by grace, they are able to stand firm, and enjoy a peaceful and quiet life.

If it is not impossible, but on the contrary, often happens that a member of a pure and severe religious order lives in relaxation, neither is it incomprehensible that others, who are not sunk in such misery, should nevertheless conduct themselves with coldness and tepidity in spite of their strong, solid, and ardent religious convictions. The causes which can produce and perpetuate such a state are so numerous that it would be troublesome to enumerate them. Suffice it to say, that inconsistencies and contradictions are met with at every turn in the life of man ; that the present affects him to such a degree that he generally forgets the past and the future; that though he is gifted with intelligence and will, he yet often suffers from the tyranny of his passions, which hurry him along the road of perdition, although he is perfectly aware of it. The foregoing examples, and the considerations which accompany them, will, I think, be sufficient to show your attack on religion was unfounded, and if your argument had any force it would prove that many men have no moral principles, because they act contrary to them; that others are extremely ignorant in what relates to their health, because by their actions they constantly impair it; that he who eats to excess does not know it will injure him; and that he who drinks intemperately does not suspect that wine is capable of intoxicating; and thus we would be compelled to assert in general terms that men are ignorant of many things with which we know they are perfectly acquainted. Let us hold that man is inconstant and inconsistent; that the things of the present affect him too much to allow him to conciliate the pleasure or interest of the moment with future felicity, and everything is explained most completely and satisfactorily, without supposing him more ignorant than he really is.

You also appear to labour under another important mistake on this matter, when you tell me in your letter that you think religion produces very little effect on the conduct of men, inasmuch as believers as well as unbelievers are accustomed to live as if they had nothing to hope for or to fear after death. "Men," you say, "take care of their affairs; satisfy their passions or

caprices ; are constantly forming great projects ; in a
word, live so distracted, so forgetful of their last hour,
so unmindful of what may come after, that as regards
the morality of the greater number, it might be said the
effect of religion is very insignificant, if any." To convince you of how false the fact is which you state with
such security, it is enough to remind you of the profound
change wrought in public morality by the propagation
of Christianity ; for the sole recollection of it leaves no
doubt that the teaching of religion is not incapable of
modifying the conduct of men, but, on the contrary, is
a very efficacious means of producing the most happy
and abiding results. Now, as well as then, men take
care of their affairs ; and have passions; and amuse
themselves; and live distracted and dissipated; but
what a difference between the morals of the ancients and
moderns ! If the limits of a letter would allow it, I
could adduce a thousand proofs of this, and show with
how much truth it has been said that more crimes were
committed then in one year, than now in half a century. Bring to mind the doctrines of the first philosophers of antiquity on infanticide—doctrines which were
uttered with a serenity inconceivable to us, and which
reveal the dreadful state of the morality of those societies. Recollect the infamous vices so general at that
time, but covered among us by the fear of censure and in-
famy ; remember what woman was among the pagans, and
what she is in the nations formed by the Christian religion ; and then you shall see the infinite benefits Christianity has dispensed on the world in all that relates to

the improvement of morals; then you shall comprehend the mistake you made when you said religion has little influence on the conduct of men.

It often happens that when we sit down to calculate the good produced by an institution, we attend to the positive and palpable results only, prescinding from others which might be called negative, but are not less real or important than the former. We attend to the good which it does and not to the evil which it averts; when in order to calculate its force and character we should consider both.

As the absence of an evil, which without that institution would have existed, is of itself a great benefit, we should be grateful to the institution for having averted it, and reckon this effect as the production of a good. To make the calculation properly it would be well to suppose the institution does not exist, and see what would happen in that case. Thus, if a person denied the utility of the tribunals of justice, or endeavoured to lower their importance, there would be no more suitable means of convincing him than the one I have indicated. If the tribunals, it might be said to him, appear to you of slight utility, suppose them removed, and that the thief, the robber, the assassin, the forger, the incendiary, and the whole host of evil-doers have nothing to fear but the resistance or vengeance of their victims, society will be at once converted into chaos; one will arm against another; criminals will advance much further in their career of iniquity, and multiply their numbers at a fearful rate. What averts all this? The tribunals certainly ; and the absence of such evils is undoubtedly the production of a great good.

Suppose that religion does not exist; that from childhood no one gives us any idea of the other life, or of God, or of our duties, what would happen ? We would all be profoundly immoral ; and the individual as well as society would sink rapidly into the most abject degradation. And yet, according to your argument, it might be objected :—As we take care of our affairs and live distracted, thinking little or nothing of our duties, of the other life, or of God ; what advantage do we derive from having been instructed on these points— from having received an education in which these truths were constantly inculcated ? You see when the question is proposed under this aspect, it is not possible to sustain the solution you wish to give it, and it is clear your method of arguing cannot be very strong in others, if it fail in the present case.

Who told you *that* man so distracted, so dissipated, does not think of the religion he professes ? Do you think he should be constantly revealing to you what passes in the inmost recesses of his heart, when he has before him a bait which stimulates his passions, and places him in the risk of being wanting to his duty ? Do you believe he should tell you how often religious ideas withheld him from committing a crime, or made him commit less than he otherwise would ?

An evident proof of the many effects religious ideas produce on the conduct of men, and how present they are to their mind, even when they appear to have entirely neglected them, is the instantaneous rapidity with which they occur to them when they find themselves in danger of death. It might almost be said the instinct of preservation and religious sentiment present themselves at the same moment.

How does the instinct of preservation work on the general course of the actions of our life? If we consider it we shall find we are incessantly concerned for our preservation without thinking of it; we are continually doing acts tending to this end without adverting to them. What is the cause? It is the fact that everything intimately connected with the life of man is unceasingly before his eyes. He does not look at it but he sees it; he thinks of it without knowing he does so. What is said of material life may be applied to the life of the soul. There is an aggregate of ideas of reason, of justice, of equity, of decorum, which is constantly flitting through our minds, and exercises an incessant influence on all our acts. A lie occurs to us, and conscience says —"This is unworthy of a man;" and the word about being pronounced is detained by this sentiment of morality and decorum. A person with whom we are at enmity is mentioned in our presence; the temptation of lowering his merit, or of revealing some of his faults or perhaps of calumniating him presents itself, and conscience says—"An honest man would not do that; it is a vengeance;" and we are silent. We have an opportunity of defrauding without detection, without risk to our honour, and yet we do not defraud; who prevents us? The voice of conscience. We are tempted to abuse the

confidence of a friend by betraying his secrets, or
employing them to our own advantage ; and nevertheless, the treason is not consummated, even when our
friend, the victim of it, could never suspect it ; who prevents us ? Conscience. These applicatious, which
could be extended indefinitely, clearly show that man,
without adverting to it, often obeys the voice of conscience, and even when he does not think, or does not believe he thinks of it, or of God, those ideas act on his
mind and impel him, and detain him, and make him re-
cede and vary his course, and continually modify his
conduct in all the instants of his life.

If this happens even among unbelievers themselves,
what will be the case with respect to sincerely religious
men ? In the eyes of the world it may appear they
completely forget their convictions ; that faith in great
and terrible truths is of no service to them ; that heaven,
hell, and eternity are regarded by them as abstract
ideas, without anything practical in them ; but *they*
know well that eternity, and heaven, and hell present
themselves to their mind in the act of desiring to commit sin ; that now they separate them from the path of
iniquity ; now detain them from marching with such
precipitation. They know that when they abandon
themselves to the impulse of their passions, they experience frightful remorse, which torments and makes
them repent their departure from the path of virtue.
There is no Christian who does not experience this influence of religion. If he be really a Christian, that is,
if he believe in religious truths, he repeatedly suffers

P

the punishment of his bad works, or enjoys the reward of his good ones. He feels this punishment or this reward in the depths of his conscience; and the recollection of what he has enjoyed in the one case, or suffered in the other, often contributes to the prohibition of disorders contrary to the dictates of duty.

I have no doubt you will be convinced by these reflections, that what you say regarding the slight influence religion has on the conduct of man, is an error opposed to reason, history, and experience. It is true that those who profess it, do not always conduct themselves as they ought; it is true you will meet with men who have faith, and yet are very wicked; but it is no less true that the conduct of religious people is in general incomparably better than that of unbelievers. How many persons have you known, who, though professing no religion, observe a totally irreprehensible conduct? And when I say this I do not refer to the commission of crimes, from which a certain natural horror, the fear of justice, and the desire of preserving our reputation restrain us: I do not speak of a certain filthy and repugnant immorality, from which honour, decorum, and that delicacy of taste, the fruit of good education, recoil. I speak of that severe morality which rules all the acts of the life of man, and does not allow him to wander from the path of duty, even when neither honour nor the regard of society is interested, nor other considerations but those inspired by sound morals are opposed to it. You will tell me you know some men who, although they are unbelievers, are in-

capable of defrauding, or betraying friendship, and
whose conduct, if it be not as strict as I could desire,
is yet far from dissipation or even levity. It is possible
you may know infidels, such as you paint them ; it is
possible that from education, honour, decorum, and that
interior light which God has given us, and which we
cannot extinguish by vain endeavours, they may
adjust their conduct to the law of duty, when no powerful motive impelling them to the contrary is at work ;
but do not put those men to the test of a violent temptation.

Reduce to misery that man who believes in nothing—
not even in God—and whom you suppose so straightforward and incapable of committing a fraud ; consider
him struggling between the pressure of great necessities,
and the temptation of appropriating a sum which does
not belong to him, so that he could do it without injuring his reputation as an honest man; what will he do ?
You may believe what you like : I for my part would
not trust my money to him ; and I would venture to
advise you not to do so either.

You, my dear friend, who are placed in an independent position, without other temptations to do evil but
those suggested by the illusions of youth, do not well
know what that probity is which is not based on religion. You know not how fragile—how brittle is that
honesty presented to the eyes of the world with such
an air of firmness and incorruptibility. You yet require some undeceptions, which you will meet with in a
short time, when, on the rending of that beautiful veil

through which we view the world in the spring-time of life, you begin to see things and men as they are in themselves ; when you enter on the age of business and behold the complication of circumstances which has place in it, and witness that struggle of passions and interests, which often places a man in critical and even torturing situations, in which the compliance with a duty is a sacrifice, nay, even sometimes an act of heroism ; then will you comprehend the necessity of a powerful curb—of a curb which must arise from something more than purely mundane considerations.

In the meantime, I remain your most affectionate friend,   J. B.

XV.

Fate of Children who die without Baptism.

MY ESTEEMED FRIEND,—I confess the difficulty proposed in your last letter, though not so insurmountable as you imagine, is, superficially considered, plausible enough. It has, besides, the peculiar circumstance of being apparently founded on a principle of justice. This makes it the more dangerous ; because the principles and sentiments of justice are so deeply engraven on his soul, that man, when he can depend on them, believes himself authorised in attacking everything.

I admit at once that justice and religion cannot be enemies ; and that any belief whatever opposed to the

eternal principles of justice, should be rejected as false.
Having thus admitted one of the bases on which your
difficulty rests, I cannot admit the force of the difficulty
itself, for the simple reason that it is founded on purely
gratuitous suppositions. I do not know in what catechism you can have read that the Catholic dogma
teaches that children who die without baptism are tormented for ever in the fire of hell. On my part,
I must frankly confess, I had no knowledge of the
existence of such a dogma, and, consequently, it has
not produced in me the horror you experienced. I am
inclined to suppose you suffer, like many others, from a
great confusion of ideas on this important and delicate
subject, and I feel the necessity of arranging them in
some way for you, as far as the hurry of discussion to
which the incessant shifting of my adversary condemns
me, will permit.

It is absolutely false that the Church teaches as an
article of faith that children who die without baptism
are condemned to the punishment of fire, or any other
pain of sense. It is enough to open the works of our theologians to find it acknowledged by them that the pain of
sense applied to such children is no dogma of faith ; no,
on the contrary, the great majority of them defend the
opposite opinion. It would be easy to adduce innumerable texts in support of this assertion; but I consider
it unnecessary, for you can assure yourself of the truth
of the fact by hurriedly running over the index of any
theological work, and examining the opinions there put
forth.

I am aware there have been some respectable authors who opined in favour of the pain of sense; but I repeat they are in a great minority; and above all, I insist that the opinion of those authors is not a dogma of the Church, and I reject the charges directed on this head against the Catholic faith. No matter how wise or holy a doctor of the Church may be, his opinion is not sufficient authority to found a dogma: between the doctrine of an author and the teaching of the Church there is the same distance as between the doctrine of man and the teaching of God.

For Catholics the authority of the Church is infallible, because it has the assistance of the Holy Ghost assured to it. We have recourse to it in all our doubts and difficulties, and in this consists the principal difference between Protestants and us. They appeal to the private spirit, which in the end is nothing but the cavillations of weak reason, or the suggestions of pride; we appeal to the divine spirit, manifested through the channel established by God himself, which is the authority of the Church.

You will ask me what the destiny of those children is who are deprived of glory, and yet not punished with the pain of sense; and perhaps you may find the difficulty renewed, though in a less painful form, from the mere fact of their not attaining eternal happiness. At first sight it appears very hard to think that children incapable of committing actual sin should be excluded from glory, because their original sin was not blotted out by the regenerating waters of baptism; but entering more deeply into the question, we discover in this neither injustice nor harshness, but solely the result of an order of things established by God, and of which no one has a right to complain.

Eternal felicity, which according to the Catholic dogma, consists in the intuitive vision of God, is not natural to man or to any creature. It is a supernatural state, at which we cannot arrive but through supernatural aid. God, without being harsh or unjust, might not have elevated any creature to the beatific vision, but have established rewards of a purely natural order either in this life or in the next. Hence it results that the privation of the beatific vision in a certain number of creatures, does not argue injustice or harshness in the decrees of God ; on the suppositon that it might have occurred with regard to all created beings, and would have occurred if the infinite goodness of the Creator had not desired to raise them to a state superior to their nature.

I foresee you will reply that the state of things is now very different ; and though it is true the beatific vision would not have been a pain to creatures who had no knowledge of it, yet it is a pain now, and a grievous one, to those who feel themselves excluded from it. I admit that this privation is a pain of original sin, but not that it is as grievous as you wish to suppose. To hold this it would be necessary to determine how far those who suffer it are aware of the privation, and the disposition they are in to lament the loss of a good they could have attained through baptism.

St Thomas very seasonably remarks there is a great difference between the effect the loss of the beatific vision must produce on children, and that which the damned experience from it.   The latter had free will, with which, aided by grace, they could merit eternal glory; the former departed this life before they came to the use of reason.   It was possible for those to obtain that of which they feel deprived, but not so for those who, without the concurrence of their will, found themselves translated to another world, in which there are no means of meriting eternal blessedness.   Children who die without baptism are in the same case as those who are born in an inferior station, in which they cannot participate in certain social advantages enjoyed by their more fortunate neighbours.   This difference does not afflict them, and they resign themselves without difficulty to the state in which they were born.

As regards the knowledge unbaptised children have of their situation, it is probable they do not even know there is such a thing as beatific vision, and so cannot be afflicted at their privation of it.   This is the opinion of St Thomas, who holds that these children have a general but not a specific knowledge of felicity, and consequently do not grieve at having lost it :—" Cognoscunt quidem beatitudinem in *generali*, secundum communem rationem, non autem in *speciali*, ideoque de ejus amissione non dolent."

" To be for ever separated from God must be a great affliction to these children ; because, as we cannot suppose them deprived of all knowledge of their Author, they must have a lively desire of seeing Him, and must experience profound pain on finding themselves excluded from that good for all eternity." This argument supposes the very fact denied above, viz., that these children have a knowledge of the supernatural order. St Thomas denies it roundly ; he says they are perpetually separated from God by the loss of glory of which they are ignorant, but not as regards the participation of natural good which they know:—" Pueri in originali peccato decedentes sunt quidem separati à Deo perpetuo, quantum ad amissionem gloriæ quam ignorant ; non tamen quantum ad participationem *naturalium bonorum*, quæ cognoscunt."

Some theologians, among whom Ambrose Catherinus is reckoned, have gone so far as to hold that these children have a sort of natural blessedness, but do not explain in what it consists, for the simple reason that in cases like this, one can argue from conjectures alone. Nevertheless, I will remark that this doctrine has not been condemned by the Church ; and it is worthy of note, that St Thomas himself, so measured in all his words, says that these children are united to God by the participation of natural good ; and so can enjoy Him by a natural knowledge and love :—" Sibi (Deo) conjungentur per participationem naturalium bonorum ; et ita etiam de ipso *gaudere* poterunt *naturali cognitione et dilectione* (2 D. 33, Q. 2 ar. 2 ad. 5).

Now you see the matter is not so terrible as you imagined, and the Church does not delight in representing the children who die without baptism as consigned to fearful torments. St Thomas very appositely compares the pain of these children to that of those who, in their absence, are despoiled of property without their knowledge. In this explanation the reality of the pain is reconciled with the absence of affliction in him who suffers it ; and the dogmas of original sin and of the pain which follows it remain intact, while we are not compelled to imagine an immense number of children tormented for all eternity, when on their own part they were unable to commit any act that could deserve it.

I have thus far confined myself to the defence of the Catholic dogma, and to the exposition of the doctrines of theologians ; and I think I have shown that as the former limits itself to the simple privation of the beatific vision through effect of original sin unremoved by baptism, it is far from contradicting the principles of justice or involving the harshness of which you accused it. Naturally, theologians avail themselves of this latitude to emit various opinions more or less well founded ; and on which it is difficult to form a fair judgment, as we require data revelation alone could supply us with. However, the doctrine of St Thomas, which says that these children can have a knowledge and love of God in the purely natural order, and so rejoice in Him, appears very rational. As they are free and intelligent creatures, we cannot suppose them deprived of the exercise of their faculties ; for then we should be compelled to consider their minds as inert substances, not by nature, but because their intellectual and moral powers were smothered. And as, on the other hand, it is admitted they do not suffer the pain of sense, nor grieve from that of loss, we must necessarily allow them the affections which in every being naturally result from the exercise of its faculties.

I remain your most affectionate friend,

J. B.

XVI.

Fate of those who live outside the pale of the Church.

MY ESTEEMED FRIEND,—I am exceedingly glad my last letter removed the horror with which you heretofore regarded what you considered the Catholic dogma in relation to children who die without baptism, and showed you that you attributed to the Church a doctrine she never recognised as hers. Your evident mistake on this point will render it less difficult to persuade you you are equally mistaken in regard to her doctrine about the fate of those who die outside her bosom. You believe it is a dogma of our religion that all who do not live in the bosom of the Catholic Church will, *for that mere fact*, be condemned to eternal punishment : this is an error we do not profess, and cannot profess, because it is offensive to divine justice. In order to proceed with proper order and clearness, I must briefly explain the Catholic doctrine on this head.

God is just ; and being so, He cannot and will not chastise the innocent : where there is no sin, there is not and cannot be any penalty.

Sin, St Augustine says, is so voluntary, that if it cease to be voluntary, it is no longer sin. The will required to render us culpable in the eyes of God, must be free. To constitute a fault, the will would not be sufficient, if it were not free.

The exercise of liberty cannot be conceived, if it be not accompanied by corresponding deliberation ; and this implies a knowledge of what is done, and of the law which is observed or infringed. An unknown law cannot be obligatory.

Ignorance of the law is culpable in some cases ; that is to say, when he who labours under it could have conquered it, then the infraction of the law is not excusable through ignorance.

The Church, the column and foundation of truth, the depositary of the august teaching of her Divine Master, does not admit the error that all religions are indifferent in the eyes of God, and that a man can be saved in any of them, and so is not obliged to seek the truth in a matter of such consequence. The Church most justly condemns these monstrosities, and cannot do less than condemn them under pain of denying herself. To say that all religions are indifferent in the sight of God, is equivalent to saying that all are true, which, in the end, is no more than to say that all are equally false. A religion which, while teaching dogmas opposed to those of other religions, should regard all as equally true, would be the greatest of absurdities—a living contradiction.

The Catholic Church considers herself the true Church, founded by Jesus Christ, illumined and vivified by the

Holy Ghost, the depositary of dogmas and morals, and charged with the duty of conducting men by the path of virtue to eternal blessedness. On this supposition she proclaims the obligation under which we all stand, of living and dying in her bosom, professing one faith, receiving grace through her sacraments, obeying her legitimate pastors, and particularly the Roman Pontiff, the successor of St Peter, and Vicar of Jesus Christ on earth.

This is the teaching of the Church; and I see nothing solid that can be objected to it, even examining the question within the sphere of philosophy. Of the principles enunciated above, some are known by simple natural reason, others by revelation. To the first class belong those which refer to divine justice and the liberty of man; to the second those which treat of the authority and infallibility of the Church. These latter, considered in themselves, contain nothing contrary to the divine justice and mercy; because it is evident that God, without being wanting to any of these attributes, could have instituted a body as the depositary of the truth, and subjected it to the laws and conditions He should deem fit in the inscrutable secrets of His infinite wisdom.

Up to this we have examined the question of right, or doctrine, if you will; let us descend now to the question of fact, in which your difficulties are founded. We must not lose sight of the difference between these two questions: doctrines are one thing, their application another. The former are clear, explicit, conclusive; the latter partakes of the obscurity to which facts are subject, the exact appreciation of which depends on many and various circumstances.

We hold it as certain that no man shall be condemned solely for not belonging to the Catholic Church, if he have been in invincible ignorance of the truth of religion, and consequently of the law which obliged him to embrace it. This is so certain that the following proposition of Baius was condemned: "Purely negative incredulity is a sin." The doctrine of the Church on this point is founded on very simple principles: there is no sin without liberty; there is no liberty without knowledge.

When, in relation to this question, does the knowledge necessary to constitute a true fault in the eyes of God, exist? Who are invincible, who in invincible ignorance? Among schismatics, among Protestants, among infidels, how far does invincible ignorance go? Who are culpable in the eyes of God for not embracing the true religion, and who innocent? These are questions of fact, to which the teaching of the Church does not descend. She says nothing about these points: she limits herself to establishing the general doctrine, and leaves its application to the justice and mercy of God.

Allow me to call your attention to this difference, which is not always attended to as it should. Infidels shower on us questions about the fate of those who do not belong to the Catholic Church, and, as it were, require us to save them all, under penalty of accusing our dogmas of being offensive to the justice and mercy of God. With this they spread for us a net into which the incautious may easily fall, by running into one of two extremes, either by sending to hell all those who do not belong to the Church, or by opening the gates of heaven to men of all religions. The first can spring from zeal to save our dogma about the necessity of faith for salvation, the second from a spirit of condescension, and the desire of defending the Catholic dogma from the imputation of harshness or injustice. I believe there is no necessity of running into either of these extremes, and that the Catholic's position is much less embarrassing than would appear at first sight. Is he asked about doctrine, or, to use other words, about the question of right? He can present the Catholic dogma with entire security that no one can accuse it of being contrary to reason. Is he asked about the question of fact? He may frankly confess his ignorance, and can involve in it the infidel himself, who certainly knows no more about it than the Catholic whom he attacks.

To convince you of how unembarrassed our position is, so that we know how to take our stand and defend ourselves constantly in it, I shall present you with a dialogue between an infidel and a Catholic :—

Infidel—The Catholic dogma is unjust, because it damns those who do not live in the Church, although there are many who can have no knowledge of the true religion.

Catholic—That is false; when there is invincible ignorance there is no sin, and the Church, far from teaching what you say, rather teaches the contrary. Those who have invincible ignorance of the divine origin of the Catholic Church, are not culpable in the eyes of God for not entering it.

Infidel—But when—in whom is this invincible ignorance found? Mark a limit which can separate these two things, according to the different circumstances in which men and nations may be placed.

Catholic—Will you have the goodness to mark it for me?

Infidel—I do not know it.

Catholic—Nor I, and so we are equal.

Infidel—True; but you speak of damnation, and I do not.

Catholic—Certainly; but recollect that we only speak of damnation with respect to the culpable, and I think no one will dare deny that sin deserves punishment; but when you come to ask me who and how many are culpable, the ignorance is equal on the side of both. I confine myself to the doctrine: as to its application, I limit myself to asking who are the culpable. If you cannot tell, it is unjust of you to require me to do so.

From this short dialogue we see there are here two things: on the one hand, the dogma, which, besides being taught by the Church, is in conformity with sound reason; on the other, the ignorance of men, who are not sufficiently acquainted with the secrets of conscience to be ever able to exactly determine in what individuals, in what people, in what circumstances, does ignorance cease to be invincible, and constitute a grave fault in the eyes of God.

There is nothing more easy than to form conjectures

about infidels : there is nothing more difficult than to lay these conjectures on solid foundations. God, who has revealed to us what is necessary for our sanctification in this life and our happiness in the future, has not thought fit to satisfy our curiosity by making us acquainted with things which would be of no service to us. These shades with which the dogmas of religion are surrounded, are highly advantageous to us, by exercising our submission and humility, by placing our ignorance before our eyes, and by reminding us of the primitive degeneration of the human race. To ask why God has brought the light of truth to some nations, and allowed others to continue in darkness, is equivalent to investigating the reason of the secrets of Providence, and trying to rend the veil which covers the mysteries of the past and future from our eyes. We know God is just, and at the same time merciful : we feel our weakness, and are aware of His omnipotence. In our mode of conceiving, we often meet with serious difficulties in reconciling justice with mercy ; and we can scarcely understand how a being supremely weak is not made the victim of a being infinitely strong. These difficulties are dissipated before the light of an exact, profound reflection, exempt from prejudices with which the inspirations of senti- ment blind us. And if, owing to our weakness, some shadows still remain, let us wait, and they will vanish in the other life, when, freed from this mortal body that weighs down our soul, we shall see God as He is in Himself, and witness the friendly embrace of Mercy and Truth, and the sanctified kiss of Justice and Peace.

I remain your most affectionate, J. B.

XVII.

The Beatific Vision.

MY ESTEEMED FRIEND,—The concluding words of my
last letter have induced you, I see, to ask for some
explanation about the béatific vision, because you have
never been able, you say, to form a clear idea of what
we understand by this sovereign felicity. I am undoubtedly glad to have my attention called to this point,
which does not produce in the mind the painful impressions, with which some of those examined in other letters
afflict us. In a word, felicity is in question, and this
can cause only one unpleasant sensation, viz.: the fear
of not attaining it.

As far as I see, you do not comprehend "how a
simple knowledge can constitute perfect felicity, and
yet the intuitive vision of God can be nothing else. It
cannot be denied the exercise of our intellectual faculties
affords us some enjoyments; but it is also certain that
these require the concurrence of sentiment, without
which they are cold and austere as reason, from which
they spring." You wish "that we, Catholics, would
note this characteristic of our mind, which, though it
comes at objects by means of the understanding, does
not intimately unite itself to them, so as to produce
enjoyment, till sentiment steps in to realise that mysterious expansion of soul, through which we adhere to the
object perceived, and establish an affectionate compenetration between it and us." These words of yours are

true at bottom, inasmuch as they require, for the felicity of an intellectual being, a union of love, besides the intellectual act. Be the object known what it might, it would never make us happy if we contemplated it with indifference. I unhesitatingly admit that the soul would never be happy, if on knowing the object which is to make her so, she did not love it. Without love there is no felicity.

But though your doctrine is true at bottom, it is applied very inexactly and inopportunely, when you try to found on it an argument against the beatific vision, as taught by Catholics. We make eternal blessedness consist in the intuitive vision of God ; but we do not thereby exclude love, but on the contrary hold that this love is necessarily bound up with the intuitive vision. And theologians have gone so far as to dispute whether the essence of blessedness consisted in the vision or the love ; but all agree that the latter is a necessary consequence of the former. It is easily seen it is a long time since you threw away mystic books and treatises on religion, when you think to improve the Christian felicity by that philosophical sentimentalism, which is far from rising to the pure sphere of the love of charity which Catholics admit, imperfect in this life, and perfect in the next.

The *simple knowledge* of which you speak, when treating of the intuitive vision of God, makes me suspect you do not comprehend what we mean by intuitive vision, but confound this act of the soul with the common exercise of the intellectual faculties as experienced in this life.   Allow me, then, to enter on some philosophical considerations about the different ways in which we can know an object.

Our understanding can know in two ways : by intuition, and by conceptions. We have a knowledge of intuition when the object is presented immediately to the perceptive faculty, without necessity for combinations of any sort to complete the knowledge.   In this operation the understanding limits itself to the contemplation of what is before it : it does not compose, nor divide, nor abstract, nor apply, nor do anything but *see* what it has present. The object, as it is in itself, is given to it immediately, is presented to it with all clearness ; and though the operation terminates objectively, and in this sense exercises the activity of the subject, it also influences the latter, mastering and investing it with its intimate presence.

Knowledge by conception is of a different nature. The object is not given immediately to the perceptive faculty : the latter occupies itself with an idea, which, in a certain way, is the work of the understanding itself, which has formed it by combining, dividing, comparing, abstracting, and sometimes running over the long chain of a complicated and troublesome process of reasoning.

Though I am sure the profound difference there is between these two classes of knowledge will not escape your penetration, still I will render it clear by an example within the comprehension of the whole world. Intuitive knowledge can be compared to the *sight* of objects : but the knowledge acquired by conceptions is like the idea we form by means of descriptions. Being a lover of the fine arts, you must have a thousand times admired the treasures of some museums, and read the description of others·which were not within your reach. Do you discover no difference between a picture *seen* and one *described?* Immense, you will tell me. The picture seen displays its beauty to me at a flash ; I do not require to use my productive powers, it is enough for me to look ; I do not combine, I contemplate ; my mind is rather passive than active ; and if it exercises its activity in any way, it is to expand itself constantly under the pleasing impressions it receives, as plants gently open under the soft influence of the vivifying atmosphere. In the description, I require to collect the elements given me, to combine them conformably to the conditions marked out, and so elaborate the aggregate of the picture, but imperfectly and incompletely, suspecting all the time the difference there is between the idea and the reality—a difference which strikes me instantaneously, as soon as an opportunity presents itself of viewing the picture described.

This example, though inexact, gives us an idea of the difference there is between these two classes of knowledge, and shows us the distance between the *knowledge* and the *vision* of God. In the former we have united in one conception the ideas of a being necessary, intelligent, free, all-powerful, infinitely perfect, the cause of all things, and the end of all : in the latter the divine essence will be immediately presented to our minds without comparisons, without combinations, without reasonings of any sort.   Intimately present to our understanding, it will master and invest it ; the eyes of the soul cannot be directed to any other object, and then we shall purely and ineffably experience that *affectionate compenetration*, that intimate union of seraphic love, described with such magnificent touches by some of the saints, who, filled with the divine spirit, felt in this life a presentiment of what they were soon to experience in the mansions of the blessed.

You must allow me to tell you, I wondered to find you did not feel the beauty and sublimity of the Catholic dogma concerning the felicity of the saved.   Prescinding from all religious considerations, what can be imagined more grand or elevated than to constitute supreme happiness in the intuitive vision of the infinite Being ?   If this idea had sprung from some philosophical school, there would not be tongues enough to praise it.   The author of it would be the philosopher *par excellence*, worthy of apotheosis, and of having incense burned to him by all lovers of the sublime.   The vague idealism of the Germans—that confused sentiment of the infinite that breathes in their enigmatical writings—that tendency to confound everything in a monstrous unity, in an obscure and unknown being, which is called absolute ; all these dreams, all these ravings, meet with admirers and enthusiasts, and profoundly move some men's minds, simply because they touch on the grand ideas of unity and infinity ; and can no claim be laid to admiration and enthusiasm by the teaching of the Catholic Church, which, while it represents God as the beginning and end of all existences, displays Him to us in a particular manner as the object of intellectual creatures, like an ocean of light and love in which all those shall be submerged who shall have deserved it by the observance of the laws that have emanated from His infinite wisdom? Is not the august dogma which represents to us all spiritual beings as drawn from nothing by an all-powerful word, and endowed with an intellectual spark, the participation and image of the divine intelligence, through which, while dwelling for a short time on one of the globes of the universe, they can merit being united with the Being that created them, and living afterwards with Him in intimacy of knowledge and love for all eternity, worthy of admiration and enthusiasm, even if regarded as a simple philosophical system?

If this is not grand—if this is not sublime—if this is not worthy of exciting admiration and enthusiasm, I know not in what sublimity and grandeur consist. No philosophical sect—no religion, has conceived such an idea. It may well be said, the first words of the catechism contain infinitely more wisdom than is to be found in the most lofty conceptions of Plato, surnamed the *divine.* It is lamentable that you who boast of being philosophers should treat with levity mysteries so profound. The more one meditates on them the stronger grows the conviction that they could have emanated from infinite intelligence alone. In the midst of the shades which surround them—through the august veils that cover their ineffable depths from our view, we discover rays of purest light suddenly bursting forth and illumining heaven and earth. During the happy moments in which inspiration descends on the brow of mortals, treasures of infinite value are discovered in that which the sceptic disdainfully regards as the miserable pabulum of superstition and fanaticism. Do not allow yourself to be mastered, my dear friend, by those low prejudices which cloud the intellect and clip the wings of the mind ; meditate profoundly on religious truths; they do not fear examination, for the harder the proof is to which they are subjected, the more complete is the victory they are certain to achieve.—I am, &c., &c.,

J. B.

XVIII.

On Purgatory.

MY ESTEEMED FRIEND,—It is almost impossible for us to content sceptics. One of the most powerful proofs of the justice of our cause is the injustice with which we are assailed. If a dogma be severe, we are accused of cruelty; if benign, we are called temporisers. You justify this observation by the difficulties you raise in your last letter against the dogma of Purgatory, with which, you say, you disagree more than with that of Hell. "The eternity of punishment," you say, "though formidable, is, nevertheless, a dogma full of terrible grandeur, and worthy to be counted among those of a religion which seeks greatness though it be terrific. At least I see in it infinite justice exercised on an infinite scale ; and these ideas of infinity incline me to believe that this fearful dogma is not the conception of the understanding of man. But when I come to Purgatory —when I see those poor souls suffer for faults they were unable to expiate during life ; when I see the incessant communication between the living and the dead by means of suffrages ; when I am told these souls are ransomed, one after another, I think I discover in all this the littleness of human invention, and its idea of accommodation between our miseries and the inflexibility of Divine justice. If I were to speak frankly, I would say that Protestants have been more prudent than Catholics on this head, by blotting out the pains of Purgatory from the catalogue of dogmas." If I were to speak frankly, I would say, in reply, that only for the certainty I have of coming off victorious in the dispute, I could not have calmly read so much injustice accumulated in so few words. I was not unaware that Purgatory was often the butt of the mockery and sarcasm of incredulity ; but I could not believe that a person, who boasts of being impartial and judicious, would try to gild the coarse foulness of those sneers and sarcasms with a tint of philosophical observation. I could not believe that the profound reason of justice and equity, contained in the dogma of Purgatory, could escape a clear understanding ; or a sensitive heart not perceive the delicate tenderness of a dogma which extends the links of life beyond the tomb, and sheds ineffable consolation on the melancholy of death.

As I have spoken largely in another letter of the

pains of Hell, I will not dwell on them here; particularly as you appear reconciled to that terrible dogma, for the purpose, I suppose, of combating with more freedom that of the pains of Purgatory. I believe these two truths are not in contradiction, and, far from injuring, aid and strengthen each other mutually. In the dogma of Hell, Divine justice appears in its terrific aspect; in that of Purgatory, mercy shines in its inextinguishable goodness; but far from encroaching on the rights of justice, these are represented as rigorously inflexible, inasmuch as they do not exempt even the just man destined for eternal beatitude from paying what he owes.

I suppose you do not hold the doctrine of those philosophers of antiquity, who did not admit any degrees in faults; and I cannot think you consider a slight motion of indignation deserving of the same punishment as the horrid crime of a son who buries the assassin's dagger in his father's breast. Would you condemn the first fault to eternal punishment, and confound it with the unnatural cruelty of the second crime? I am sure you would not. Here, then, we have Hell and Purgatory; here we have the difference between venial and mortal sins; here we have the Catholic truth supported by reason and common sense.

Sins are blotted out by repentance : the Divine mercy delights in pardoning him who implores it with an humble and contrite heart; this pardon liberates the person who receives it from eternal damnation, but does not exempt him from the expiation claimed by justice.

Even in the human order, when a crime is forgiven, the pardoned criminal is not exempted from all penalty; the claims of justice are tempered, but not invalidated. What difficulty is there then in admitting that God exercises His mercy, and requires at the same time the tribute due to His justice? Here we have another reason in favour of Purgatory. Many men die who had not the will or the time to satisfy for what they owed for their sins already pardoned : some obtain this pardon a few moments before exhaling their last breath. The Divine mercy has freed them from the pains of Hell ; but should we say they have been translated immediately to eternal felicity without suffering some penalty for their former disorders? Is it not reasonable and fair that, as mercy tempers justice, the latter should moderate mercy in its turn?

The incessant communication of the living with the dead, which displeases you so much, is the natural consequence of the bond of charity which unites the faithful of the present life with those who have passed to the future. To condemn this communication, it is first necessary to condemn charity itself, and deny the sublime and consoling dogma of the Communion of Saints. It is strange, when philanthropy and fraternity are so much talked of, that the beauty and tenderness contained in this dogma of the Church should not be properly admired ! We constantly hear of the necessity under which all men are of living as brothers ; and are we to be cut off from that fraternity which is not limited to earth, but embraces all humanity on earth and in

heaven, in felicity and misfortune ? Wherever there is
a good to be communicated, *there* is charity to prevent
it from becoming isolated in an individual, and to extend
it widely over all men ; whenever there is a misfortune
to be succoured, charity hastens to bring aid from those
who can alleviate it.   Whether the misfortune is in this
life or in the other, charity does not forget it.   She who
feeds the hungry, clothes the naked, assists the weak,
relieves the suffering, consoles the prisoner, she it is that
knocks at the heart of the faithful, and tells them to
succour their defunct brethren by imploring the Divine
mercy to shorten the term of expiation to which they
are condemned.   If this were a human invention, it
would certainly be a beautiful and sublime one.   If
Catholic priests had idealised it, it could not be denied
they had the cleverness to harmonise their production
with the most essential principles of the Christian religion.   *Apropos* of inventions, it would be easy for me to
prove to you the dogma of Purgatory is not an offspring
of the ages of ignorance.   We find its constant tradition
even in the midst of the errors of false religions, which
shows that this dogma, as well as others, was primitively
communicated to the human race, and escaped the
shipwreck of truth provoked by error and the passions
of the disordered progeny of Adam.   Plato and Virgil
were not priests of the middle ages, and, nevertheless,
they tell us of a place of expiation.   The Jews and
Mahommedans did not conspire with the Catholic
priesthood to deceive the people ; and, nevertheless,
they too acknowledge the existence of Purgatory.   As

regards Protestants, it is not exact that all have denied it ; but if they *will* appropriate to themselves this sad glory, we will not dispute it with them. Let them, with all our heart, admit none but the pains of Hell ; let them remove all hope from him who is not sufficiently pure to enter immediately into the mansions of the just ; let them cut all the bonds that unite the living with the dead, and adorn with this formidable gem their doctrines of fatality and desperation. We prefer the benignity of our dogma to the inexorableness of their error. We confess that God is just, and man culpable ; but we also acknowledge the frailty of mortals, and recognise the infinite mercy of the Creator.—I remain yours, &c.,

J. B.

XIX.

The Good and the Bad—A Difficulty.

MY ESTEEMED FRIEND,—The discussion on the pains of Purgatory has reminded you of the sufferings of the just, and you discover a difficulty in the doctrine, that those who pass through so many trying expiations in this life, should be subjected to others in the life to come. " Virtue," you say, " is so well proved on earth, it is unnecessary it should pass through a new crucible in the pains of the other world. On this earth of injustice and iniquities, everything appears topsy-turvy ; and while felicity is reserved for the wicked, all kinds of calamities and misfortunes are the lot of the virtuous.

Certainly, if I had not made a firm resolution of not doubting of Providence, in order that I might not lose all key to the things of the other life, a thousand times would I have vacillated on this point, when I beheld the misfortune of virtue and the insolent success of the wicked. I wish you would answer this difficulty without contenting yourself ·by placing before me original sin and its deplorable results ; because, though it may be, perhaps, a satisfactory solution, it is not so to me, who doubt of all the dogmas of religion, including that of original sin itself."

Do not fear that I shall forget the disposition of mind of my opponent, or argue from principles you do not yet admit. No doubt, the dogma of original sin gives occasion to very important considerations, in the question on which we are occupied; but I will absolutely prescind from them, and confine myself to principles you cannot reject.

In the present question, I think you suppose a fact which, if not entirely false, is at least very doubtful. It matters little that your opinion agrees with the common one ; for I believe that there is here an unfounded prejudice, which, though pretty general, is yet contrary to reason and experience. Like many, you suppose that felicity is so distributed in this life, that the greater share falls to the lot of the wicked, and the less to that of the virtuous, embittered, moreover, by abundant disgusts and misfortunes. I repeat, I consider this belief an unfounded prejudice, incapable of resisting the examination of sound sense.

It has been already observed that the virtuous cannot exempt themselves from the evils that affect humanity in general, if we would not have God perform continual miracles. If many people be travelling by railway, and among them two or three of marked virtue, and an accident occur, it is clear that God is not bound to send an angel to save the virtuous travellers by some extraordinary means. If two men be walking along the street, the one good, the other wicked, and a house fall on their heads, the two will be crushed : the walls, beams, and roof will not form an arch over the head of the virtuous man. If a flood inundate a country-side, and destroy the crops, amongst which are those of a virtuous farmer, no one will require Providence, when the waters reach the farm of this just man, to form a wall of them, as on another occasion in the Red Sea. If an epidemic decimate the population of a country, death is not bound to respect the virtuous families there may be in it. If a city suffer the horrors of an assault, the unbridled soldiery will not respect the house of the just any more than that of the wicked man. The world is subject to certain general laws, which Providence does not suspend, except now and then ; and they commonly affect all those whose circumstances are such as to make them experience their results. Undoubtedly, besides evidently miraculous exemptions, Providence has at hand special means of liberating the just from a general calamity, or at least of attenuating their misfortune ; but I will prescind from these considerations, which would bring me to the examination of facts which it is always difficult to investigate, still more so to establish with precision. I admit, then, that all men, just and unjust, are equally subject to the general evils of humanity, whether they come from natural causes, or spring from unpropitious social, political, or domestic circumstances. I do not think you will make a charge against Providence for this; for I consider you too reasonable to require continual miracles that would incessantly disturb the regular order of the universe.

Leaving aside then the general misfortunes which affect the good as well as the wicked, according to the circumstances in which they are placed; let us see now whether it be true that felicity is so distributed that the greater portion becomes the patrimony of vice. I believe, on the contrary, that, even prescinding from the special benefits of Providence, the physical and moral laws of the world are of such a nature, that of themselves, abandoned to their natural and ordinary action, they distribute felicity and misfortune in such a way that virtuous men are incomparably more happy, even on earth, than the vicious and wicked.

You will agree with me that our judgment about the degrees of felicity or misfortune should not be founded on particular cases, but on the general order, as it results, and must necessarily result, from the very nature of things.

The world is so wisely regulated that punishment, more or less evident, always follows on the heel of crime. If a man abuse his faculties in seeking pleasure, he meets with pain; if he wander from the eternal principles of sound morality to supply himself with a felicity calculated on his egotism, he commonly works out his misfortune and ruin.

I need not speak of the fate that befalls great delinquents, who commit crimes which the action of the law can reach. Perpetual imprisonment, hard labour, public shame, an ignominious scaffold, these are what they meet with at the end of a hazardous career, filled with danger, terror, fits of rage and desperation, corporeal sufferings, calamities and catastrophes without number. A life and death of this kind possess no felicity. In the inebriation of disorder and crime, those wretches perhaps imagine they have enjoyment; but shall we call that true enjoyment which results from the breach of all laws, physical and moral, and is lost like an imperceptible drop in the cup of torture and agony which they drain to the dregs? I suppose then, when you speak of the felicity of the wicked, you do not refer to those who come under the action of human justice, but solely of those who, whilst wanting in their duty by trampling on the high claims of justice and morality, insult their victims with the security they enjoy, and live perhaps under gilded ceilings in the arms of opulence and pleasure.

I do not deny that on a superficial examination there is something in the felicity of these men which wounds and irritates. I am not unaware that if we attend to appearances, without penetrating into the heart of such happiness, and above all, limit ourselves to particular cases, without extending the view as it

R

should be extended in this class of investigations, we become puzzled, and the mind is assaulted by the terrible thought :—" Where is Providence; where the justice of God?" But as soon as we meditate a little, and grasp the matter in the true point of view, the illusion disappears, and we discover the order and harmony that reign in the world with such admirable constancy.

Let us explain and fix these ideas. You will quote for me a vicious and perhaps perverse man, who apparently enjoys domestic happiness, and receives in society a consideration he is far from deserving : be it so. I will not dispute about whether this felicity is real or apparent, or about the interior happiness which undeserved considerations produce; I will suppose the felicity is real and the enjoyment resulting from the consideration intimate and satisfactory ; but neither can you deny that, by the side of this vicious and perverse man, we meet with honourable and virtuous people, who enjoy an equal domestic felicity, and obtain a consideration no way inferior to that of the other. This observation suffices to establish the equilibrium, and destroys the foundation of your assumption that vice is prosperous and virtue unfortunate. You will show me, perhaps, a man endowed with sound virtues, and oppressed with the weight of great misfortunes ; be it so ; but I can show you the reverse of the medal, and present you with an immoral man afflicted with no less misfortunes; and here again we have the equilibrium established. Virtue is represented as unfortunate, but by its side we hear the groans of vice oppressed with the same crushing weight.

You may remark that I do not avail myself of all the advantages the question gives me, but leave you the most favourable ground; as I suppose equality of suffering in equality of unfortunate circumstances, and prescind from the inequality that should naturally result from the different interior dispositions of those who suffer the misfortune: what to one is consolation, to the other is remorse.

It is easy to see we could never solve the question with these parallels; and no case could be cited in support of one without another similar or equal presenting itself in favour of the other. I will, however, observe that, in spite of the prejudice that exists on this point, and which I have already noticed, the constant experience of the unhappy end of wicked men has produced the conviction that sooner or later Divine justice will overtake them; and the good sense of the people has given expression to this truth in most judicious proverbs. The vulgar incessantly talk of the success of the wicked and the misfortune of the good ; but if you follow up the conversation, you will surprise them at every turn in manifest contradictions, when they relate the malediction of Heaven that has fallen on such and such an individual, on such and such a family, and announce the misfortune that cannot do less than happen to others who now wade in opulence and felicity. What does this prove? It proves that experience is more powerful than prejudice; and the inclination to continually complain and murmur at everything, including Providence itself, disappears, at least for some moments, before the imposing testimony of truth, supported by visible and palpable facts.

Those who try to rise to a great height without considering the means, are not accustomed to find the felicity they desire. If they rush into great crimes against the security of the State, instead of attaining their object they work their own ruin. I might say that for every one that succeeds, there are a hundred wretches who succumb without realising their design: history says so and daily experience proves it true. Those who wish to improve their fortunes by upsetting public order are condemned to incessant emigrations, and many of them end by perishing on a scaffold.

There are ambitions that live on lowness and intrigues, which have not the pluck requisite for crime, and can consequently improve without great personal risk. It is true that sometimes those men who substitute the slow windings of the reptile for the flight of the eagle, advance greatly in fortune without suffering any of the terrible expiations, to which those who fling themselves on the road of violence are exposed; but who can count the slights, the repulses, the shameful humiliations they must have endured, before attaining the satisfaction of their desires? who could paint the terror and dread in which they live, lest they may lose what they have obtained? who can describe the sad alternatives through which they must have passed, and are continually passing, according as the favour of the protector who has raised them inclines towards them or recedes in an opposite direction? And what idea should we form in such a case of the felicity of these men, particularly if we consider how much the recollection of their villanies, and the remorse for the evils which perhaps they have caused to well-deserving men and innocent families, must torment them? Happiness is not in the exterior, but in the interior: the richest, most opulent, most respected, or most powerful man will be unhappy, if his heart is torn by cruel pain.

If a man love riches to excess, even to the degree of forgetting his duties so that he may acquire them, instead of attaining felicity he brings misery on his head. Those who trample on the laws of morality to acquire riches are divided into two classes: one simply labours to store them up, and to feel enjoyment in the possession of its treasure; the other desires to have them that it may enjoy the pleasure of spending them with profusion. The first class is avaricious, the second prodigal. Let us see what felicity is met with in both.

The avaricious man feels a momentary enjoyment in thinking on the riches he possesses, and in contemplating them in cautious solitude, far from the view of other men; but this pleasure is embittered with innumerable sufferings. A habitation narrow, unclean, incommodious in every sense; poor old furniture; a garment thread-bare, dirty, and recalling fashions which passed away many years ago; poor and badly-prepared food; a miserable and cracked table service; dirty linen; cold in winter, heat in summer; abhorred by his friends

and debtors; despised and ridiculed by his servants;
cursed by the poor; without discovering in any quarter
an affectionate glance, or hearing a word of love or an
accent of gratitude:—this is the happiness of the
avaricious man. If you desire to enjoy it, my dear
friend, I envy you not.

The prodigal does not suffer in the same way as the
avaricious man. He has extensive enjoyments while
money and health last; and if the accent of the victims
of his injustice reach his ears, he experiences some
consolation in the expression of gratitude he meets
with from those who receive his favours. But, besides
the remorse that always accompanies ill-acquired goods,
besides the discredit unjust proceedings always bring
with them, besides the maledictions which he who
enriches himself at the cost of others is condemned to
hear, prodigality has characteristic annoyances,—which
in the end make a miserable man of him who had
promised himself happiness in the profusion of his
riches. The pleasures to which prodigality conduces
destroy health, distrub domestic peace, often impress a
stain in the eyes of society, and entail annoyances of
a thousand kinds. In fine, at the heel of these evils
comes another to stare him in the face—poverty.
These are not fictitious pictures; they are realities you
will meet with everywhere; they are positive examples
that want nothing but proper names.

Immorality in the enjoyment of the pleasures of life
is very far from bringing felicity to him who expects
happiness from them. This is a truth so well known

that it is difficult to insist on it without repeating commonplaces, which have become vulgar. The works of medicine and morality are full of advice about the evils of intemperance. All classes of infirmities—premature old age, the abbreviation of life, sufferings above all qualification,—these are the results of disordered conduct.

A rich table in magnificent *salons*, served with luxury and taste, in brilliant society, amid the glee of festive companions, followed by toasts, festivities, music, and pleasures of all sorts, is certainly a seducing spectacle. Is not this, my esteemed friend, an incomparable felicity? Well, wait a little; let the music cease, the candles, lamps, and chandeliers go out, and the guests retire to rest. Whilst the sober man of regular habits is sleeping tranquilly, the servants of the happy man are running through the house in a fright. Some prepare soothing drinks, others make ready the bath, these run in haste in search of the doctor, those knock furiously at the door of the apothecary: what has happened? Nothing; only the felicity of the table has been turned into acute pains. The unhappy man finds no rest in bed, on the sofa, on the settee, or on the floor; a cold sweat bathes his members; his face is ghastly; his eyes protrude from their sockets; his teeth chatter, and he cries that he is dying. These are the effects of his felicity; to know how well such sufferings counterpoise the pleasure of a few hours, it would be well to consult the patient, and ask him whether he would not willingly renounce all the pleasures and festivities of the world, so that he could obtain some alleviation of the sharp pains he is suffering.

I should never end if I were to continue the comparison between the results of vice and virtue; but I do not intend to repeat what has been said a thousand times, and what you know as well as I. Suffice it to observe, that felicity does not exist in appearances, but in the inmost recesses of the soul. Of what service can the magnificence of a palace, or the glare of honours, or the incense of flattery, or the fame of a great name be to a man who suffers acute pains; is oppressed by grief; devoured by profound sadness; or slowly consumed by insupportable weariness? Happiness, I repeat, has its seat in the heart; he who has not felicity in his heart, is unhappy, let the appearances of fortune with which he is surrounded be what they may. Well, now, in the exercise of virtue, all the faculties of man are harmonised in his relations with himself, with other men, and with God, both with respect to the present and the future. Vice destroys this harmony, disturbs the interior man, by making reason and the will the slaves of the passions; debilitates health; shortens life by the pleasures of the senses; alters domestic peace; destroys friendship; and sacrifices the future to the present. Thus man marches by the path of remorse and agitation to the portals of the tomb, where he does not or cannot expect any consolation, and where he fears to meet with the chastisement his disorders deserve. The felicity of a being cannot consist in the perturbation of the laws to which by its nature it is subject. The laws of the order of nature are in accord with those of the moral order : whoever infringes them receives his desert, and instead of felicity he meets with terrible misfortunes.

Now you see, my dear friend, it is not so certain as you imagined, that the felicity of earth is solely for the bad, and its unhappiness for the good alone. I hold it as indubitable that if the degrees of felicity distributed between virtue and vice were placed in a balance, the former would weigh down the latter ; and an incomparably greater amount of suffering falls to the lot of vice than to that of virtue. Yes ; there is justice even on earth. God has been pleased to permit many iniquities : He has allowed the wicked to sometimes enjoy the shadow of felicity ; but He has also been pleased to determine that the terrible law of expiation should be felt in this life, and the means employed by the perverse to procure their happiness contribute to this end.

I remain your most affectionate friend,

J. B.

XX.

Homage due to the Saints.

MY ESTEEMED FRIEND,—Day by day I am more convinced of your deficiency in reading in matters of religion, as I suspected in the beginning. I know it is not *reading* you are deficient in, but *good* reading ; for I discover, at every turn, you have taken care enough to look over the writings of Protestants and infidels, avoiding a glance at the works of Catholics, as if they were prohibited books. Allow me to observe, that a person educated in the Catholic religion, and who practised it in his childhood and youth, cannot exculpate himself at the tribunal of God from the spirit of partiality so manifest in such conduct. To assert continually that one has an ardent desire of embracing the true religion, as soon as discovered, and, nevertheless, to constantly go in search of arguments against Catholicity, and abstain from reading the apologies in which all these difficulties are answered, are extremes that cannot be easily reconciled. This contradiction is by no means new to me ; because I am long profoundly convinced that sceptics do not possess that impartiality of which they boast ; and even though they are distinguished from infidels, because instead of saying, " This is false," they say, " I doubt if this be true," they nevertheless entertain prejudicies, more or less strong, which make them abhor religion, and desire it may not be true.

The sceptic does not always render himself an exact account of this disposition of his mind. Perhaps he often deludes himself into the belief he is sincerely seeking the truth ; but if his conduct and words be attentively observed, he will be found to take a secret pleasure in raising objections, and relating facts that may wound religion ; and no matter how he boasts of his temperance, he does not generally avoid giving his objections a passionate or even a sarcastic tinge.

I do not mean to offend you by these observations; but, at the same time, I wish you would take them into account. You will lose nothing by examining and asking yourself—"Am I seeking the truth with sincerity? Is it true that in the difficulties I raise against Catholicism, there is no mingling of passion? Is it true that nothing of the hatred and aversion which the works I have read breathe against the Catholic religion has stuck to me?" I wish you would now and then ask yourself this, as by doing so you would, besides performing a work becoming a sincere man, remove no few obstacles which impede your coming to the truth in matters of religion.

You will probably tell me you wonder at the preceding observations, as you have conducted this discussion with greater decorum than is generally observed by the adversaries of religion. I do not deny that your letters are distinguished by their moderation and refined tone, and, though you do not hold my convictions, you have had delicacy enough not to wound the susceptibilities of him who professes them; but still I have remarked that, notwithstanding your good qualities, you are not completely exempt from the general rule; for, when disputing about religion, you manifest a desire to view things under the aspect that can wound it most, and whether inadvertently or not, endeavour to avoid contemplating its dogmas in their sublimity, their magnificent aggregate, and their admirable harmony with everything that is beautiful, tender, grand and sublime. I have often had occasion to observe this, and at present

I see no signs of amendment; so I think you will pardon me if I do not except you from the general rule, but consider you more passionate and prejudiced than you imagine.

Precisely in the letter I have just received this sad truth is deplorably apparent. In spite of protestations to the contrary, the trail of Protestant fanaticism and Voltairian levity is manifest in every line of it; and I could scarcely believe that before writing it you did not consult some of the oracles of the misnamed Reformation or the false philosophy. In spite of what you say of *popular belief*, and the enchantment you experience on witnessing the religious fervour of *simple people*, it is evident you contemplate all this with benign disdain, and consider you pay sufficient tribute to the sincerity of believers by abstaining from openly condemning or ridiculing them. We are much obliged for your goodness; but let me tell you, the beliefs and customs of these *simple people* are capable of a better defence than you imagine. Far from the homage and invocation of Saints, and the veneration of their relics and images, being the religious pabulum of simple people only, they can afford matter for consideration of the highest philosophy. It is not the credulous and ignorant alone who hold them, but men of the most eminent genius, like St Jerome, St Augusine, St Bernard, St Thomas of Aquin, Bossuet, and Leibnitz.

On reading this last name you will believe my pen has made a slip, and I have written it by mistake. How is it possible that Leibnitz, a Protestant, could defend the doctrines and practices of Catholicity on this point? Nevertheless, it is written in his works, which are in the hands of the whole world; and it is not my fault if the author of the pre-established harmony, the eminent metaphysician, the famous archæologist, the profound naturalist, the incomparable mathematician, the inventor of the infinitesimal calculus, agrees in this matter with *simple people*, and is something less of the *philosopher* than many who know no more history than compendiums in decimosexto, nor more philosophy than the rudiments of the schools, ill acquired and worse retained, nor more geometry than the definition of the straight line and the circumference.

I have been insensibly led into these general considerations, and the preamble of this letter has grown rather long, though I am far from considering it inopportune. Discussion should be carried on temperately, but the interests of truth should not be neglected. Whenever it is necessary to remind you, sceptics, of your spirit of partiality, it should be done; and we should have no scruple in sometimes telling you, you discuss without having studied, and combat what you have a profound ignorance of.

The homage of Saints does not appear to you very rational, nor even conformable to the sublimity of the Christian religion, which gives us such grand ideas of God and man. How is this devotion to the Saints opposed to these grand ideas? Because "it appears man degrades himself by paying to the creature the worship due to God alone." I see you have been

imbued with the objections of Protestants, a thousand
times answered, and a thousand times repeated. Let
us clear up our ideas.

The homage paid to God, is an acknowledgment of
His supreme dominion over all things, as their creator,
ordainer and preserver. It is an expression of the
gratitude the creature owes the Creator for the benefits
received from Him ; and of the submission, respect and
obedience to which he is obliged, in the exercise of
his understanding, his will, and all his faculties. External homage is the expression of the internal ; and is,
besides, an explicit acknowledgment that we owe all to
God, not only our soul, but also our body, and are
ready to offer Him not only His spiritual but also His
corporal gifts to us. It is evident the homage of which
I speak belongs exclusively to God ; the homage due
to God alone can be rendered to no creature ; to
hold the contrary, would be idolatry—a crime ana-
thematised by natural reason, and the sacred Scriptures,
long before philosophic zeal condemned it.

There are few accusations more unjust, or made for
a more distorted purpose, than that which charges
Catholics with idolatry, on account of their dogma and
practices in the homage of Saints. It is enough to
open, I will not say, the works of theologians, but the
smallest catechism, to see that such an accusation is
highly calumnious. Never, in any Catholic writing,
has the homage of Saints been confounded with that
of God ; if a man fell into such an error, he would be at
once condemned by the Church.

The homage rendered to the saints is a tribute paid to their eminent virtues; but these are expressly acknowledged to be the gifts of God : by honouring the saints, we honour Him who has sanctified them. So that, though the immediate object be the saints, the ultimate end is God himself. In man's sanctity, we venerate the reflection of the infinite sanctity. These are not arbitrary explanations, conjured up on purpose to get rid of the difficulty. Open where you will the *Lives of the Saints*, or a collection of panegyrics; listen to our orators and our catechists—everywhere you shall meet with the doctrine I have just laid down. Another observation : the Church prays on the feast of the saints ; and to whom does she direct her prayers ? To God himself. Mark the beginning of them—*Deus qui—Omnipotens sempiterne Deus—Præsta quæsumus Omnipotens Deus*, &c. And in the end she always refers to one of the persons of the Most Holy Trinity, or to two, or to the three.

I cannot conceive what answer can be made to reasons so decisive, and I do not fear you will continue to accuse us of idolatry : after these explanations it is impossible, if you act with good faith, to insist on such an accusation.

I am now going to consider the question under other aspects, and particularly in relation to the discordance you say exists between the homage of Saints and the sublimity of the Christian ideas about God and man. Religion, by giving us grand ideas about man, does not destroy human nature; if it did so, its ideas would not be grand, but false.

It is a common saying among theologians that grace does not destroy, but elevates and perfects nature. True revelation cannot be in contradiction with the constitutive principles of human nature. Hence it results that the sublimity of the ideas which religion gives us about man, are not opposed to the natural conditions of our being, however insignificant. Our greatness consists in the sublimity of our origin; in the immensity of our destiny; in the intellectual and moral perfections which we owe to the bounty of the Author of nature and grace, and in the aggregate of the means with which He has supplied us to attain the end for which He destined us.

But this greatness does not destroy the fact that our soul is united to a body; that besides being intelligent we are also sensible; that at the side of the intellectual will are found the feelings and the passions; and that, consequently, in our grief, in our desires, and in our actions we are subject to certain laws from which our nature cannot prescind. It were to be desired you would not lose sight of these observations, for they serve to prevent the confusion of ideas, and the vague use of the words *sublimity* and *grandeur*, which can occasion serious mistakes, according to the object to which they are applied.

As the opportunity presents itself, allow me to observe that the ideas of greatness and infinity are employed to ruin the relations of man with God. How is it possible, it is said, that an infinite being could occupy itself with one so insignificant as we? And no one sees that the same argument might be used by one who took it into his head to deny the creation. How is it possible, he might say, that an infinite being could have occupied itself in creating things so insignificant? All this is highly sophistical : the ideas of finiteness and infinity, far from destroying, explain each other reciprocally.

The existence of the finite proves the existence of the infinite ; and in the idea of the infinite is found the sufficient reason of the possibility of the finite and the cause of its existence. The relation of the finite with the infinite constitutes the unity and harmony of the universe : this bond once broken, all is confusion, and the universe a chaos.

After these explanations about the true acceptation of the words *grand* and *sublime*, let us examine whether the dogma of the homage of saints is opposed to the sublimity of the Christian doctrines.

We can love a good thing, though finite ; we can respect a respectable thing, and venerate a venerable thing, without any humiliation unworthy our *sublimity* arising therefrom. Now allow me to ask you, is not an eminent virtue a good, respectable, and venerable thing? And if it be so, and there can be no doubt about it, I think there can be no inconvenience in Christians paying a tribute of love, respect, and veneration to those who have distinguished themselves by their eminent virtues. This observation would be sufficient

S

to justify the homage of saints ; but I shall not confine myself to it, for the question is susceptible of much greater amplitude.

Whilst man lives on earth, subject to all the weaknesses, miseries and dangers which afflict the children of Adam in this valley of tears, no one, no matter how perfect he may be, can be sure of not straying from the path of virtue : daily experience gives sad testimony of human frailty. And this is one of the reasons why the love, respect, and veneration which the virtuous man deserves, even on earth, are offered him with a certain fear and hesitation, in application of the wise saying of not praising a man before his death. But when the just man has passed to a better life, and his virtues, proved like gold in the crucible, have been acceptable to the infinite wisdom, and he has secured the precious crown he merited by them ; then the love, respect, and veneration due to his virtues can be displayed without danger; and this is the motive of the homage so affectionate, so tender, so full of confidence and profound veneration, which Christians render the just, who for their great deserts, occupy a distinguished place in the mansions of glory.

I cannot discover, my dear friend, how there can be a want of dignity in an act so conformable to reason, and even the most natural feelings of the human heart. When we are shown a person of great virtue, we regard him with respectful veneration and esteem ; and can Christian people not do the like, with respect to men, who, besides their eminent virtues, are intimately united with God in eternal blessedness? Imperfect virtue is worthy of veneration, and is the perfect which has been crowned with ineffable felicity not so? When a person honours a virtuous man, far from humiliating, he exalts and honours himself. And can it be possible that what is true with respect to men on earth, is not true with regard to those in heaven? A little more logic, my dear friend; for the contradiction is too manifest. The *simple people*, of whom you speak with *benignity* and *compassion*, have on this point more philosophy than you.

I could scarcely imagine you were so delicate as to be unable to endure the multitude of images and statues of saints with which our Catholic churches are filled. I thought that, if not the interest of religion, at least the *love of Art*, should render you less susceptible. The difference between the coldness and nakedness of Protestant churches, and the splendour and life of Catholic temples, is generally remarked by believers as well as by infidels; and precisely one of the causes of this difference is found in the fact, that Art inspired by Catholicity, has profusely scattered its admirable works, in which it presents to the eye and the imagination the most elevated mysteries, and perpetuates with its prodigies the memory of the virtues of our saints, and the ineffable communications with which, elevating themselves to God, they felt a presentiment in this life of the felicity of the future.

I wish to be indulgent with you : I wish to attribute the difficulty you propose to me to some distraction, or an ill-meditated thought ; for without this indulgence, I would find myself obliged to tell you a harsh truth— that you have no taste, no heart, if you have not perceived the beauty abounding in this Catholic practice.

It is strange, when attacking the customs of Catholicity with respect to the images of the saints, you did not advert to the fact that you were putting yourself in contradiction with one of the most natural feelings of the human heart. How is it possible you have not here discovered the hand of religion, elevating, purifying and directing to a useful and august object, a feeling common to all countries and all times ? Do you know any people that has not endeavoured to perpetuate the memory of its illustrious men in images, statues, and other monuments ? And is there anything more illustrious than virtue in an eminent degree, as the saints possessed it ? Were not many of them great benefactors of humanity ? Will you dare to sustain that the memory of the conquerors who have inundated the earth with blood, is more worthy of perpetuation than that of the heroes who have sacrificed their fortune, their ease, and their very lives to the good of their fellow-men, and transmitted to us their spirit in institutions, which are the alleviation and consolation of all classes of misfortunes ? · Can you regard with more pleasure, the image of a warrior, who has covered himself with laurels, too frequently stained with black crimes, than that of *St Vincent de Paul,* the shield and consolation of all who were in misery whilst on earth, and who yet lives, and is met with in all hospitals, beside the bed of the sick, in his admirable *Sisters of Charity.*

You will tell me all the saints have not done what St Vincent de Paul has done; but you cannot deny that those who have not confined themselves to contemplation are innumerable. Some instruct the ignorant, seeking them out in town and country; others bury themselves in the hospitals, serving the feeble sick with inexhaustible charity; these divide their riches with the poor, and then take on themselves the duty of interesting all beneficent hearts in favour of the unfortunate; those boldly enter the dens of corruption, with the ardent desire of improving the morals of defiled and degraded beings : in fine, you shall scarcely find a saint in whom you will not discover a jet of light, and virtue, and love, spreading in all directions, and to great distances, in benefit of his fellowmen. What is there irrational or unworthy in perpetuating the memory of actions so noble, so grand, and useful? Have not all peoples of all countries and times done the same after their own manner? Do you think the prodigies of Art are badly employed in such a work as this?

Suppose we are treating of a life passed sweetly in the midst of contemplation, in the solitude of the desert, or in the practice of modest virtues in the obscurity of the domestic hearth : even in this case there is no inconvenience in *Art's* consecrating itself to perpetuate their memory. Do we not meet at every turn with profane pictures, descriptive of a family scene, or calling to mind a good action without anything of heroism in it ? Is not virtue, be it what it may, even in its ultimate degree, beautiful and attractive, and an object worthy the contemplation of men ? But remember, common virtues are not objects of homage among Catholics ; to have the tribute of public veneration paid them, they must exist in a heroic degree, and receive, besides, the sanction of the authority of the Church.

I abandon with all confidence these reflections to your sound judgment, and entertain the firm hope they will contribute to dissipate your prejudices, by calling your attention to points of view on which you had not thought before. Being an enthusiastic lover of the philosophical and the beautiful, you cannot do less than admire the beauty and philosophy of the Catholic dogma of the homage of Saints.

I remain, &c.,

J. B.

XXI.

Invocation of Saints—A New Difficulty.

MY ESTEEMED FRIEND,—I am very glad my last letter did not produce an unfavourable impression on you ; and that you do not refuse to acknowledge the beauty and philosophy contained in the Catholic dogma, "presented from that point of view." I do not wish, however, that what belongs to the thing itself should be attributed to the manner of treating it. To take up that point of view, which pleases you, I had not to avoid the reality, but to simply show the objects as

they are in themselves, and merely indicate the considerations to which the proposed difficulties led.

You are inclined to believe I have attacked my
adversary on his weakest flank, but cleverly avoided
presenting the dogma in its whole aggregate. You are
no longer an enemy of the images of the Saints in
churches, which means you have ceased to be an
Iconoclast. Now you have taken refuge in another
trench, and say that though it does not appear to you
wrong to perpetuate the memory of the virtues of the
Saints in pictures and statues, and even to pay them, in
religious solemnities, a homage of respect and veneration,
you do not, however, see the necessity of admitting
that incessant communication between the living and
the dead, in which the latter are made our intercessors
in things which we ourselves can ask for immediately.
You add, that as it is one of the principal characteristics
of Christianity to unite man intimately with God,
imperfectly in this life, and perfectly in the mansions
of glory, it should be considered more proper, more
worthy, and above all, more elevated, for man himself
to direct his prayers to God, without availing himself
of mediators, and translating to the regions of bliss
the customs we have here on earth. It is fortunate it
is you who propose the difficulty founded on such a
principle; for if I, by any chance, had said that man
should communicate immediately with God, you would
have censured me for jumping, without regard to human
nothingness, over the distance there is between the
finite and the infinite. You never fail to see what you

call the unreasonableness of our side; if we rise high, we exaggerate, we lose ourselves; if we lower our flight, we are grovelling, and forget the sublimity of human nature! One requires great calmness to suffer accusations so opposed; but this is a sacrifice we are bound to make in the cause of truth, which has a right to exact it from us.

The dogma that the invocation of Saints is not only lawful but advantageous, can, like all Catholic dogmas, suffer the examination of reason, without danger of coming out rough-handled. To fix our ideas, and avoid confusion, let us place the question on clear ground. Is there any inconvenience in admitting that God hears the prayers of the just, when they pray, not for themselves, but for others? I wish you would tell me whether, in the eyes of sound reason, this is not conformable with all the ideas we have of the goodness and mercy of God, and His predilection for the just. If you admit a God—not a cruel God, who has no care for the work of His hands, and closes His ears to the supplications of the unhappy mortal who implores His aid—you should also admit that the prayer of man directed to God is not a vain thing, but can and does produce salutary effects. Very well: now is there anything more natural, more conformable with reason, or more in accordance with the feelings of our soul, than to pray to God, not only for ourselves, but for the objects of our regard? The mother, with her tender child in her arms, raises her eyes to heaven, and implores the goodness of the Eternal in its favour; the wife prays for her husband; the sister for her brother; the children for their parents; and the patriarch, when dying, collects his descendants about his bed, and extending his tremulous hand over them, gives them his benediction, and prays Heaven to bless them. The prayer of man in favour of his fellow-man is a natural inclination of the heart; it is found in all ages, sexes, and conditions—in all times and countries; it is expressed at every turn in the cry of nature in which we invoke the God of mercy whenever we witness another's danger.

The communication of intellectual creatures in the bosom of the Divinity—the reciprocal aid they can afford each other by their prayers, is a universal tradition of the human race—a tradition bound up with the sweetest and most intimate feelings of the heart, described by all historians, sung by all poets, immortalised on canvas and in marble by innumerable artists, admitted by all religions, and expressed in solemn ceremonies by all worships. Look over the history of the remotest periods, consult the most ancient poets, listen to the popular narratives whose origin is lost in the heroic and fabulous times, examine the monuments, the pride of the most civilised nations; ever, in all parts, you shall meet with this fact. There is a war: the youth of a people is running danger on the field of battle; the wives, the children, the parents of the soldiers implore the Divine aid on their behalf—now in the retirement of the domestic hearth, now in the public temples with solemn sacrifices. There is a traveller

from whom no news has been received for a long time ;
his disconsolate family fears he has fallen a victim of
some unfortunate accident, but yet entertains a hope.
Perhaps he is wandering solitary and lost in foreign
lands; perhaps he has been cast as the plaything of
the waves on some inhospitable shore : what is the
inspiration of that family ?   To raise its eyes and hands
to heaven, to pray and implore the Divine mercy in
favour of its unfortunate member.   History, poetry,
the Fine Arts, are an uninterrupted testimony of the
existence of this feeling, of this firm belief that the
prayers of one man for another are acceptable in the
eyes of the Almighty.

Well, now ; is there any inconvenience in our desiring
the prayers of others, even while they live on earth ?
Clearly not.   If there were, we should have to reject
all religion, and put ourselves in open contradiction
with one of the most tender and purest feelings that
find shelter in the human breast.   I do not believe
your philosophy goes to so deplorable an extreme.
No ; you cannot profess a doctrine which drowns the
cry of nature that sounds soft and tender at the foot
of the cradle, and is exhaled slowly and prophetically
in the portals of death.   No ; you cannot profess a
doctrine which responds with a smile of doubt to the
supplication of the mother who prays for her child, of
the wife who prays for her husband, of the child who
prays for its father, of the old man who prays for his
descendants, of the relieved one who prays for his
benefactor, of the friend who prays for his friend, and

of entire nations who pray for the brave fellows defending the independence of their country, or carrying to remote corners of the earth the name of their fatherland under a victorious flag.

I need scarcely deduce the consequences of what I have said, for you must have already seen them without any trouble. According to our doctrine the Saints are just men, who enjoy in heaven the reward of their virtues. They do not require to pray for themselves, for they are exempt from all evils and dangers, and have attained the fulfilment of their desires ; but they can pray for us. If they could do this on earth, how much more can they do so in heaven ? If mortals pray for other mortals, can not or will not those who have attained an immortal felicity pray for us ? Their prayers are particularly acceptable to God, and are an agreeable incense which incessantly burns before the throne of the Eternal. They lived like us in this land of misfortunes, and do not forget us. The Church tells us :— " Implore the intercession of the Saints ; ask them to pray for you : this is lawful ; this is pleasing in the sight of God ; this will be useful to you in all your necessities." There is the dogma. If your philosophy finds it is not in accordance with natural reason and the feelings of the human heart, I pity you and your philosophy, and am unable to comprehend the principles on which you found it. To tell the truth, I expect you will willingly yield to the light of these reasons, to which I cannot see what solid or even plausible answer can be made. In which case I cannot do less than remind you of the necessity, so often inculcated, of not proceeding with levity in matters so serious, and of reflecting that in the dogmas regarded by Incredulity with indifference and contempt, there are concealed treasures of wisdom, which are found the more profound the more they are examined by the light of philosophy and history.

I remain yours, most affectionately,

J. B.

XXII.

Words of Leibnitz in favour of the Veneration of Relics.

MY DEAR FRIEND,—Your letter, in answer to my last, contains various matters, and among them a request that I should translate, although you do not question the truth of my quotations, the passages of Leibnitz, in which he speaks in favour of the Catholic Dogma about the homage of Saints. I have not the slightest hesitation in doing so. Here they are:—" Prudent and pious people think that the *immense* and *infinite* difference there is between the honour which is due to God, and that which is paid to the Saints, should not only be inculcated on the minds of hearers, but also manifested, as far as possible, by external signs: theologians, since St Augustine's time, call the first, *Latria*, the second, *Dulia*." —(Theological System).

Here you have the difference between the homages of *Latria* and *Dulia* acknowledged by Leibnitz—a difference he calls nothing less than *immense* and *infinite;* and it is worthy of remark, that he confesses he took these terms from the theologians. As regards the wishes of the pious and prudent men of whom he speaks, you can see them complied with in all Catholic writings, from the master-work down to the smallest catechism, from the greatest solemnity to the simplest ceremony of the Church. But the illustrious philosopher does not content himself with what we have just seen; he purposes a complete defence, and he proceeds as follows :— " In general it should be held for certain that the homage of Saints and relics is not approved of, except in as much as it refers to God, and there should be no act of religion that does not resolve and *terminate* in the honour of God Almighty. Thus, when the Saints are honoured, it should be understood, as it is said in Scripture :— *"Thy friends have been honoured, O God; and praise the Lord in His Saints.' "—* (Ibid.)

Further on, refuting those who accuse the homage of the Saints of idolatry, he reminds them of the very ancient custom of the Church of celebrating the feasts of the martyrs, and of the pious meetings held at their tombs from the earliest ages; and continues with the following extremely remarkable observations :—" It is to be feared that those who think thus open the way to the destruction of the Christian religion ; for if they hold that dreadful errors prevailed in the Church from these times, they strengthen the arms of the Arians and Samostanians, who sustain that the mystery of the Trinity and idolatry were introduced at one and the same time. . . . I leave the result to which this should lead to the judgment of the reader. Daring geniuses will carry their suspicions farther, and wonder that Jesus Christ, who promised so much to the Church, should have allowed such range to the enemy of the human race, that one idolatry destroyed, another succeeds it; and that of the sixteen centuries there can scarcely be found one or two in which the true faith was properly preserved among Christians; while we see that the Jewish and Mahomedan religions continued pretty pure for many ages, according to the institution of their founders. What, then, of the counsel of Gamaliel, who said the Christian religion and the will of Providence should be judged by the result? What would we think of Christianity, if it could not suffer the test of that touchstone."

The reflections of Leibnitz should be taken into consideration by all those who would see with concern the extirpation of the relics of Christianity from amongst Protestant sects. Unfortunately, the previsions of this great man have been sadly realised in his own country. Germany, at present, presents a deplorable spectacle: the dissolution of ideas in religious matters has gone to the last extreme, and now is gathered the fruit of the seed sown in other times. It was believed that the Catholic dogmas could be attacked, and Scepticism at the same time avoided, by retaining of the Christian religion whatever appeared well to the false reformers; but time has cruelly frustrated these hopes. An inflexible logic has drawn the consequences of the principles established. At present Protestantism is no more than a mere shadow of what it was. Religious anarchy has reached its culmination : Scepticism is making terrible ravages in all classes of society, and a nebulous and seductive philosophy takes care to give it deeper root, by diffusing its pantheistic doctrines, which, after all, are only a new phase under which Atheism presents itself to excite less repugnance.

You make reference to the veneration of relics, though I see what I said with respect to the homage of saints has greatly impaired, in your mind, the force of that difficulty.

It is a feeling natural to man to extend his love or veneration to the objects which were nearest the person beloved or venerated. We preserve with greatest care the articles which belonged to the person who possessed our affection ; and it often happens that things, in themselves insignificant, acquire an immense value when measured by the feelings of the heart.

The bodies of the dead have always been regarded with a species of religious respect ; and the profanation of a grave excites more horror than the sack of the habitations of the living. Every people has respected the sepulchre, and placed it under the shield of Religion ; and the body of an illustrious man has ever been considered a treasure of great value, and worthy of being disputed for by nations who regarded the fortune of possessing it with happiness and pride. This veneration extends to everything that belongs to him. His dwelling is cautiously preserved from the injuries of time, that future generations may visit it; his dress, his articles of furniture, his most insignificant things, are held as a treasure, and have an estimation above all price. Sanctify that feeling of the human race; purify it of everything that can stain it; raise it to the supernatural order in its object and end, and you have a philosophical explanation of the veneration of relics, and free yourself from the necessity of condemning *simple* and other people who do that through religious motives, which is done by the whole human race, even in things profane. You now see that where you thought you had discovered superstition in our mysteries, you find the most tender and sublime feelings of our soul, purified, elevated, and directed by the Catholic religion.

Finally, I now come to answer the last question you put me about the utility of the homage of Saints, with respect to preserving and promoting religious spirit among the people. You fear that by giving this homage a too sensible direction, the principal object may be lost sight of, and secondary practices substituted for the essential part of Religion. Before everything, it is well to remark, the Catholic Church is not to be blamed for certain abuses into which some of the faithful may fall. When you argue thus, far from weakening the Catholic dogma and the sanctity of the practices of the Church, you supply me with a new reason in defence of those practices and the dogma on which they are founded. The exception confirms the rule: you would not have noticed the abuse if the good

use were not general. Long before you had
thought of it, the Church had taken the necessary
precautions to avoid this kind of abuses, by teaching
the people the true sense of the Catholic doctrines, and
warning them that in these acts they should endeavour
to conform to the spirit of the Church and her venerable
practices, agreeably to the example and teaching of
their legitimate pastors. If you insist that in spite of
this there have been abuses, I shall reply that this is
inevitable, considering the condition of weak humanity
and I will ask you to point out a truth, a custom, an
institution, no matter how pure and holy it may be,
which men have not repeatedly abused. Leaving
aside, then, these exceptions, which prove nothing but
human weakness, which certainly does not require to be
proved anew, let us to the principal difficulty.

I am so far from believing it hurtful to the preservation and fomentation of Religion to offer objects to
sensibility, that, on the contrary, I consider it useful
and even necessary. Your argument is one of those
which, by proving too much, prove nothing; for
deducing the ultimate consequences of the purely
spiritualistic worship you desire, we shall have to
condemn all external worship. We must exile from
our temples all religious insignia, music and singing,
and not only this, but even pull down the temples
themselves, since they are destined to move the soul, by
means of sensibility, with their magnificent and imposing
forms. From this it evidently results your theory cannot
be admitted without condemning all external worship;

T

and, consequently, the only thing that can be insisted on is, that sensibility do not trespass its limits, but submit to laws which may give it the true religious spirit.

It is remarkable that the human mind is constantly subject to action and reaction. When it is penetrated with an idea or a sentiment, it expresses its intimate affection in a sensible form; and, on the contrary, sensible forms exercise on our mind a mysterious reaction, exciting and clearing up our ideas, and enlivening and warming our sentiments. There are here two movements which reciprocally aid each other; the one from within to without, the other from without to within; the natural result of the intimate union of the body with the soul, and the expression of the harmony established by the Creator between two beings so different, intimately united by a mysterious bond.

On these principles is founded the philosophical reason why external worship is so natural and useful— natural, in as much as it is very natural to man to sensibly express his thoughts and feelings; useful, in as much as those sensible expressions have the property of clearing up and fixing his ideas, and exciting and warming his sentiments. Well, now, when we view the question from this point, the immense utility of the homage of saints is discovered at a glance. In it we find the most natural sentiments of the heart, and man puts himself in communication with the Divinity, through beings one day as weak as he, and even yet of the same nature. He speaks to them his own language, he tells them his troubles, he interests them to aid him in his misfortunes ; and in thanking them for some favour obtained, he appears to desire to make them participators in his happiness. This, without ceasing to be very pure and holy, accommodates, in a certain measure, the sublimity of religion to human weakness. The highest mysteries are impressed on the memory with sensible forms, and the Christian finds in the Saints a sweet attractive to devotion, and beautiful models from which he can take sure rules for the direction of his conduct.

These considerations are sufficient to remove the difficulties which the Catholic dogma, examined from a false point of view, presented to you ; from them you must be convinced we do not confound the principal with the accessory, nor the essential with the accidental. God, infinite being, origin of all, end of all, final term of all worship ; Jesus Christ, God and Man, Redeemer of the human race, in whose name we hope to be saved ; the Saints, friends of God, united to us by the bond of charity, and interceding for us ; man, composed of body and soul, sensibly expressing what he feels, and foment-ing his interior affections with sensible objects ; God, Jesus Christ, the object of our worship ; the Saints, the object of our veneration, in as much as they are united to God and Jesus Christ, God and Man—these are the grand ideas of Catholicity with respect to homage and worship. Examine them under whatever aspect you may, and you shall find nothing in them that is not reasonable, just, holy, and worthy of a divine religion.

I remain, your most affectionate,   J. B.

XXIII.

Religious Communities.

MY ESTEEMED FRIEND,—I often wondered very much
that as you gave your imagination such loose rein in
attacking everything connected with the dogmas of
Christianity, not forgetting its morality and worship,
you had neglected to speak of religious communities,
which are a favourite institution of the Catholic Church.
Unbelievers can scarcely mention Catholicity, without
indulging in some attack on religious communities; and,
to tell the truth, I have been greatly surprised to find
you so moderate. I had no doubt you professed principles of tolerance and liberty; but as experience has
shown me that a rigorous application of these principles
is not always made, I was uncertain whether you would
make an exception against religious communities, by
putting them outside the pale of the law. Fortunately,
I have had the pleasure of being mistaken; and it has
been to me a particular satisfaction to hear from your
mouth, that though you do not profess the Catholic
doctrines, nor feel inclined to exchange the bustle of
the world for the silence and solitude of the cloister,
you can comprehend that other men may be of a
different turn of mind, and embrace with sincerity and
fervour a system of life totally opposed to worldly ideas
and customs.

I also see, with much pleasure, that you recognise
the necessity and justice of leaving every one at full

liberty to embrace a religious life in the form and manner he pleases. I have nothing to add to the following words I find in your letter :—" I could never comprehend on what the restrictive systems regarding religious life are founded. Those who have money enjoy ample liberty to spend it as they please, and no one interferes with them, though they lead the gayest life in the world ; those who are fond of pleasure enjoy it without more restriction than the limits of their purse, or their sanitary provisions ; the lovers of feasts celebrate them without interference, though the glee of the toasts and the noise of the orchestra disturb the neighbourhood ; those who like to dwell in splendid mansions, and make magnificent displays, do so without more formality than that of consulting the weight of their pockets, or the patience of their creditors ; nor is there a want of liberty for the corruption of morals; and libertinism under different forms is tolerated by the authorities, so that it do not glaringly outrage public decorum. The prodigal scatters; the miser heaps up ; the restless agitate ; the curious travel ; the erudite study; the philosopher meditates ; everyone lives conformably to his ideas, necessities, or caprices. There is complete liberty for the whole world : commercial companies are formed ; societies of employers or tradesmen ; mining associations; societies of beneficence, of science, of literature, of the fine arts ; and shall we not leave some individuals, who believe they are doing a good work, at full liberty to serve God, be useful to their fellow-men, and obey a vocation from heaven, by uniting under

determined rules, with these or those obligations, for
this or that object? I repeat, I could never comprehend
that strange jurisprudence, which restricts a thing which,
if not good, is certainly inoffensive. I can, without
difficulty, understand the partial violation to their prejudice of the principles of tolerance and liberty, when
the religious communities had not only a great number
of individuals, but also possessed great wealth; but at
the present time, when, between ourselves, the dangers
of monastic domination are no more than party cries to
create confusion, it appears to me not only unjust, but
even impolitic, to exercise an oppressive violence, which
conduces to no good. The spirit of the age is certainly
not favourable to monastic institutions; and I think
the world is more threatened with dissolution through
the love of substantial enjoyments, than with sterility
through sack-cloth and fasting." Thus you have saved
me the trouble of entering into reflections on this point,
and give expression clearly and concisely to the feelings
of all judicious men, who are free from a spirit of ran-
corous partiality. I will, consequently, come to deal
rapidly with the questions you put me, about the relations of religious institutions with religion itself and
with society in general.

You ask me to throw some light on the debated
question of whether religious institutions are a thing so
essential in the Church, that they cannot be attacked
without shaking the foundations of Catholicity; "for
the variety of opinions which history and experience
give us on this point, occasions hot discourses and inter-

minable disputes." There is nothing more easy, my dear friend, than to satisfy your desires on this head, for I believe if we once clear up the ideas connected with it, there can be no more hot discourses, nor interminable disputes, nor questions of any sort.

The unity of faith, the sacraments, the authority of the legitimate pastors, distributed in the proper hierarchy under the primacy of honour and jurisdiction of the successor of St Peter and Vicar of Jesus Christ, the Roman Pontiff, are things essential in the Catholic Church. Among them you do not find religious communities; and if for a moment we suppose they have all been suppressed, without a single one remaining on the face of the earth, the Church exists still; she lives with her dogmas, with her morals, with her sacraments, with her discipline, with her admirable hierarchy, and with her divine authority. This is indubitable; and in this sense it is equally true and indubitable that religious communities are not essential to Catholicity. In this there is neither dispute nor question of any sort. Let us proceed.

In the Catholic Church there is faith which teaches us sublime truths about the destiny of man, some terrible, others consoling; there is hope which raises us on its divine wings, and bears us towards the celestial regions, inspiring us with fortitude in the momentary adversities we suffer on earth, and infusing a holy moderation in the smooth fortune which, perhaps, may smile on us, exhibiting it in all its littleness and evanescence when compared with the eternal and infinite good to which

we should aspire ; there is charity, which makes us love
God above all things, ourselves included, and all men in
God, and consequently inspires us with the desire of
being useful to our fellow-men ; there is the Gospel, in
which, besides the precepts, compliance with which is
necessary to enter into eternal life, are contained
the sublime counsels of selling all and giving it to the
poor ; of divesting oneself completely of self-will ; of
embracing the cross and following Jesus Christ without
looking behind and of leading a life chaste as angels,
in heaven; and there is a vivifying spirit which illumines
understandings, masters wills, softens hearts, transforms
the entire man, and renders him capable of heroic reso-
lutions, which human weakness could not even conceive.
All this is there in the Christian religion ; and what is
the necessary result ?   It is this : some men, not satisfied with limiting themselves to the fulfilment of the
Divine Commandments, desire to take, as the rule
of their conduct, not only the precepts, but also the
counsels of the Gospel.   Recollecting the words of
Jesus Christ in which He recommends prayer in common, and promises to be present in a particular manner
with those who practise it; recollecting the august customs
of the primitive Church, in which the faithful sold their
property and brought its price to the feet of the
Apostles; recollecting how very agreeable the virtue of
chastity is to God, and how very acceptable obedience
is to Jesus Christ, who made Himself obedient even
unto death—they collect together to animate and edify
each other reciprocally ; they promise to God to observe

the virtues of poverty, chastity, and obedience, offering Him thus in holocaust what man holds dearest—his liberty—and guarding themselves at the same time against their own inconstancy. Some abandon themselves to the greatest austerities ; others to incessant contemplation ; others dedicate themselves to the education of children ; others to the instruction of youth ; others consecrate themselves to the ministry of the Divine Word ; others to the ransom of captives ; others to the consolation and care of the sick—and, behold ! you have the religious · institutions. Without them Religion can be conceived ; but they are its natural fruit ; they spring up spontaneously in the garden of faith and hope, under the vivifying breath of the love of God. Wherever Religion is planted, there they appear ; if plucked off, they sprout again ; if broken up their dispersed members serve as fruitful seed, from which they will spring again under new forms, equally beautiful and verdant.

You now see, my esteemed friend, that examining the matter from this height, the questions above mentioned disappear. To ask whether there can be Catholicity without religious communities, is to ask whether where there is a sun that sheds light and heat in all directions, where there is a vivifying air, where there is fruitful earth watered with abundant rain, vegetation can fail ; to ask whether religious communities can die for ever, is to ask whether the transitory hurricanes, which devastate the plains, can prevent vegetation from springing up again, the trees from budding anew and producing fruit, and the fields from groaning under rich harvests. So history teaches, and experience testifies. To wish for a Catholicity that will not inspire some privileged men with the desire of abandoning all for love of Jesus Christ, and consecrating themselves to the meditation of eternal truths and to the good of their ʻfellow-men, is to wish for a Catholicity without the warmth of life, is to imagine a sickly tree whose roots do not penetrate into the heart of the earth, and dies at the first heats of summer, or is easily torn up by the rude blast of the north wind.

You ask me what I think about the social utility of religious communities; and whether I believe that under this aspect a future can be promised them, considering the spirit and tendency of modern civilisation. As a letter does not admit of the extension required by the immense question raised by what you ask, I will limit myself to two points of view, which I hope you shall be able to appreciate.

Under the historic aspect it may be taken as a general rule, that the foundation of the different religious institutions, besides their Christian and mystic object, had another eminently social, and exactly accommodated to the necessities of the age. If the history of the religious communities be studied with this idea in view, it will be found wonderfully realised in all times and countries. The East and the West, ancient and modern, contemplative and active life—all afford abundant historical materials to prove the exactness of this observation : in all parts is it found verified with wonderful regularity.[1]

This is what I think about the history of the religious communities. It is not possible to produce in a letter the reasons and facts on which I found my opinion. If you have leisure to dedicate yourself to this class of studies, I abandon the question with all security to your sound judgment. Now I am going to say a few words relative to the future of these institutions.

As we believe the Church shall never fail, but shall last to the consummation of ages, we are also sure the divine spirit which animates her, will not allow her to become sterile, but will cause her to produce not only the fruits necessary for eternal life, but also those which contribute to increase her verdure and beauty. The religious communities shall exist then under one form or another. We know not what modifications this form may suffer, but we rest tranquil in the shadow of Providence.

Regarding the social utility of the religious communities in the future, the question appears to me very simple. Can grand examples of morality, the sight of heroic virtues, and of abnegation and disinterestedness without limits, be useful to modern civilisation ? Has modern society great necessities to satisfy ? Do not the education of youth, and particularly of the poorer classes, the organisation of labour, the spirit of association on behalf of the great procomunal interests, foundling asylums, penitentiaries, houses of correction, and all sorts of charitable institutions, present extremely

---

[1] See "Protestantism compared with Catholicism," vol. 3.

complicated problems, and grave difficulties, and require the aid of a disinterested, unselfish, and ardent love of humanity? That disinterestedness, that abnegation, that ardent love of humanity can spring from Christian charity alone. This charity can act in a thousand ways; but the secret of making its action better directed, more energetic and more efficacious, is to personify it in some of those institutions, which rise above particular affections, and live for long ages as a great moral being, in which individuals play no more part than the molecules in the human body, constantly succeeding each other in the movement of the organisation.

I repeat, I have a lively hope for the social utility of the religious communities. In the future of modern civilisation, they appear to me to be powerful elements of preservation in the midst of the destruction which threatens us, a lenitive for cruel sufferings, and a remedy for terrible evils. Egotism invades everything; and I know no more efficacious means of neutralising it than Christian charity. Men join together to gain, and also to succour each other through calculation; I desire them to unite together to aid each other with absolute forgetfulness of self-interest, offering themselves in holocaust for the good of their fellow-men. This is what the religious communities do; and for this reason I promise myself much from their influence on the future of the world. They cannot be useless, while there are savages and barbarians to civilise, ignorant men to instruct, corrupt men to correct, sick to alleviate, unhappy mortals to console,—Yours affectionately,   J. B.

XXIV.

Reasons for the Severity of Religious Communities.

MY DEAR FRIEND,—You might have remarked that in my last letter I expressed my ideas with the greatest possible brevity, and this was because I feared the subject might become tiresome to you ; for I took it for certain that religious communities had not been the favourite object of your studies, and, consequently, that you could only bear some rapid indications in which the memory of the cloister might not make you lose the recollection of the world. Now I see your mind is taking a more serious turn ; and you no longer believe that objects whose history occupies long ages, and which are so interwoven with the social development of modern nations, can be known by superficial study, or condemned by sharp sayings. At last, you are becoming convinced of the injustice and frivolity of the Voltairian method, which translates its difficulties into sarcasms, and answers the most solid reasons with a smile of mockery. Error is more tolerable when accompanied with a certain show of reason and the sentiments of equity. My observations on religious communities appear to you worthy of attention ; this is enough for me ; for my object was no other than to make you some day study profoundly those matters with the care they deserve. I could not flatter myself with circumscribing this question to the narrow limits of a letter ; as I am of opinion an interesting work of no small dimensions could be written on the subject. However, as you wish to continue the discussion, I have no inconvenience in satisfying your desires.

You regard religious institutions under the aspect of their severity, and, considering human weakness, it appears to you excessive ; and unnecessary besides for attaining the object their founders had in view. I hold very different convictions on the subject, and I found them, not precisely on the respect due to the wisdom and holiness of those illustrious men, but on reasons which spring from the very nature of the human heart. I shall state them briefly.

The religious life isolates, in a certain sense, the individual professing it from other men. With his vows he breaks the ties that bind him to the world; friendship and family disappear as far as they are opposed to the object of the institution. The religious is a man, who, though dwelling on earth, is entirely consecrated to the things of heaven. Property—that powerful link which unites individuals and families, and makes them cling to a fixed place, as a plant clings to the earth from which it receives its life—does not exist for the religious. He not only has none, but is deprived of the power of having it ; for love of Jesus Christ he has made himself poor for ever, and condemned himself to possess nothing. With the vow of chastity, he is deprived of family ; and with the life in common he cannot have those domestic relations which act as substitutes for those of one's own family. Obedience does not permit him to select the place of his habitation, or dedicate himself to his favourite occupations. He is an exceptional man in everything ; who moves in all things by rules different from those of the generality of men.

This individual, thus isolated, without more contact with the world than that which the prescriptions to which he is subject allow him, does not cease to be man, and is not converted into an angel ; he has his weaknesses, his desires, his caprices ; he possesses a heart which beats, and is subject to the same impressions as those who live in the midst of the world. Full of youth and life, his thoughts fly beyond the monastic precincts ; his heart dilates, and requires to be satisfied with some objects, which, if he do not find them in his institution, he will go to seek elsewhere. Unhappy wretch, if he slackens the severity of religious discipline, and having one foot in the cloister, he places the other in the portals of the world, and desires to live in two elements, like the amphibious animal which buries itself as willingly in the depths of a lake as it breathes the scorching air in the burning desert ! The result cannot but be disastrous ; the unfortunate wretch is subject to the action of two opposing powers ; his soul must divide itself in two, and his heart, subject to violent alternations of expansion and compression, breaks in pieces.

Then there necessarily results a clashing disagreement between the institution and his conduct, between his words and his acts ; the disorder being so much the more monstrous by how much the more lively the

contrast is.   Behold a profound reason for the severity
of the founders ; what at first sight appears extremely
rigorous is nothing more than extremely prudent.   A
man without property, without family, without liberty
in his acts, consecrated by vow to the practice of the
evangelical virtues, who could forget his duty, and
mingle with strange confusion the garb of austerity
with the relaxation of the world, would be a very
repugnant object.

Well, now, in the depths of the human soul there is
a spring of activity which increases with the exercise
of the different faculties :   the understanding, the will,
the imagination, the heart require pabulum to devour ;
whilst man lives, his faculties live with him ;   it would
be vain to endeavour to smother them ;   what should be
done is to moderate and direct them, subordinate the
less to the more noble, and take care the expansion and
energy of the latter do not allow the former to trespass
the limits prescribed by reason and morality.   Indulgence with bad passions and dangerous instincts, far
from producing the *salutary alleviation* you promise
yourself, would raise tempestuous storms in the heart
and extinguish all discipline.   The history of the
Church supplies us with frequent examples that confirm
this truth, and justify the prevision of the founders of
religious institutions.   Human nature is so weak, the
folds of our heart so numerous, the illusions with which
we try to deceive ourselves so various and ingenious,
that experience shows us no precaution is too great
when we want to avoid abuses ; particularly, if we must

extend the view beyond the individual sphere, and occupy ourselves with institutions which are to live for ages. This consideration naturally brings me to the examination of what you call "*small things* which might be despised without prejudice to discipline."

All laws, all institutions applicable to men, require, besides their essential constitutive, strong preservatives against the destructive action of time and human contact. The moral, like the physical world, is subject to a continual ebb and flow of action and reaction. It is not enough for whatever has to last a long time, to contain a powerful principle of life, which drives away corruption and death from the heart and vital parts ; it is necessary that preservatives be placed at a great distance from the centre of life, in all the points of the periphery, as advanced sentinels to exclude corruption and death, and prevent them entering on a destructive struggle in the more delicate points of the organisation.

Cast a glance over the laws without observance ; over the customs which have been corrupted ; over the political or social institutions which have lost their strength ; follow the history of the decay of things once great ; and you shall find that in good as in evil, there is in this world a law by which transitions from one extreme to another are made, not suddenly or abruptly, but by soft and imperceptible gradations.

Why has a useful law fallen into disuse, so that no one hesitates to openly infringe it ? Did some one begin by breaking it without hesitation ? By no means. What was done was this: a beginning was made by

U

neglecting a formality, apparently of little importance ; prescription against the law followed ; what was left unobserved was an insignificant thing, purely reglamentary, which never entered into the legislator's mind, and formed no part of the law. The chink was made, time took on itself the duty of opening it.

The law whilst covered by the *insignificant* formality, was not placed in immediate contact with the resistance it met with in its execution. The formality was a species of tough elastic body, which broke the impetus of collisions, and saved the clauses of the law from injury. The formality has disappeared ; the clauses are exposed and naked. Meeting with resistance, they must now bear the unbroken pressure or stroke, and are easily injured. And all law meets with that resistance more or less strong ; because a law would be useless if its object were not to restrict liberty in some way, and oppose itself to forces which tend to trespass their limits.

What happens in such a case ? Formerly the struggle was with the formality, now it is with the very text of the law ; its letter is conclusive ; but its spirit, a thing in itself always vague, lends itself to favourable interpretations. The legislator said this ; no doubt of it ; but his intention could not be so strict ; circumstances have notably changed ; and besides the case in hands *hic et nunc*, is of such a nature, that if the legislator could be consulted, he would be on the side of the benign interpretation. It should be borne in mind, too, that the clause whose letter is to be infringed, is one of the least important; if it were a fundamental one, the case would be different; then both the spirit and letter of the law should be observed by all means. The business, my esteemed friend, is settled; the clause of the law has been broken, and the chink converted into a wide gap: soon all those who wish to reach their object by the shortest route will enter by it; with the continual passing through, the opening shall become more spacious, and the law, without being derogated, shall be completely annulled. The infraction commenced with an insignificant formality, and the result has been to reduce the law to an insignificant formality. Such are men; when anything stands in the way of our passions or interest, we trample it under foot, first breaking down the forms, and then destroying its intimate essence; but when our interest or passions can act without meeting resistance, then we recollect some inoffensive formality, put it in practice, and with the greatest seriousness in the world, delude ourselves into the belief that we still observe the defunct law.

The history of the infraction of laws is the same as the history of the corruption of morals, the decay of the most robust institutions, and the degeneration of the most holy things. Our heart is profoundly sagacious; we are greater hypocrites with ourselves than with others. The plans we employ to deceive them have no comparison in nature or quality with those we invent and practise to deceive ourselves.

Every law, every institution, should be surrounded with strong safeguards. The ability of the legislator and the founder of institutions is shown in how he occupies the avenues by which his work must receive the attacks of human weakness and passions. A law may be severe—may be accompanied with a terrible sanction, and yet not serve its object, but is immediately broken ; while another, though exceedingly gentle, can be so wisely contrived and surrounded by such opportune safeguards, that it can repel the most impetuous attacks, and possess sufficient strength to triumph over the greatest resistance.

At the light of these observations you will easily comprehend the wise prevision contained in the *minutiæ*, which scandalise you. In general the founders of the religious institutions were distinguished not only for their sanctity, but also for a profound knowledge of the human heart. Many among them would have made excellent legislators. I am so far from regarding as excessive the precautions which appear so to you, that I believe, on the contrary, they could not be blamed, but should rather be praised, if they had taken more. The action of time and the fire of human passions continually exercise a destructive pressure, so that, very often, violent shocks are not necessary to put an end to robust institutions. Imagine what would happen if proper precautions had not been taken in time.

You do not comprehend the reason of the "great amount of obligations with which some religious institutions are loaded ; " this being a general objection can only be answered with general reflections. I have already indicated one of these, and one I consider decisive. Activity, and above all in isolated individuals, requires continual pabulum. The flame of life must consume something; if left shut up idly in our interior it consumes ourselves. Without many occupations, without multiplied practices, how can the life of a solitary be filled up? How can formidable storms be prevented from rising in his heart, or how can he be saved from succumbing under the weight of an insupportable weariness? These considerations should be sufficient to remove your prejudices against what you call the "exaggerated mysticism of some religious institutions;" but as this last point is of the highest importance, I shall submit to your good sense other reflections which appear to me worthy of attention.

It is a fundamental fact, constantly observed, that the activity of our faculties expends from a common fund, and that the increase of strength in one generally entails a diminution in the others. It is not possible to have the same degree of activity in many senses; and hence has sprung the proverb of the schools—"Pluribus intentus, minor est ad singula sensus." When the animal faculties have a great development, the intellectual and moral ones suffer from debility; and, on the contrary, when the superior part of man, the understanding and will, are developed with great energy, the passions grow weak and lose their empire over his conduct. Great thinkers have almost always been distinguished by their neglect of the pleasures of life; and those given to sensuality are rarely distinguished by the elevation of their thoughts. If a man is domineered over by brutal passions, he loses that delicacy of feeling which makes one perceive ineffable beauties in the moral and even in the physical world; and a continued exercise of exquisite and pure sentiments, which, escaping from the sphere of common sensibility, appear to touch on the regions of an ideal world, is opposed to the development of the grosser passions, which defile the soul with their impure mire.

You will have already comprehended the drift of these observations; I purpose nothing less than to defend mysticism on philosophical grounds, and show the utility of its development in religious institutions. The imagination requires spectacles with which to enjoy itself; the heart needs objects to excite its love; if it does not find them within the bounds of virtue it will seek them in those of vice, and the flame undirected towards God will turn towards the creature. Do you think a heart like St Teresa's could live without loving? If it had not been consumed with the purest flames of divine love, it would have been burned with the impure fire of earthly affection. Instead of an angel that excites the admiration of infidels themselves, who have by chance read some of her admirable pages, perhaps we should have to deplore the disorders of a dangerous woman, transferring her passions to paper in characters of fire.

Chateaubriand, speaking of St Jerome, has said with profound truth:—"That soul of fire required Rome or the desert." To how many souls might not the sentiment of the illustrious poet be applied? What would the great heart of St Bernard have done with its sensibility,

if it had not found an immense pabulum in divine things?
On what would that inexhaustible activity, which attended to the various occupations of a religious, and
the counsellor of kings and popes, who stood at the
head of a European movement which raised the west
against the east, have fed, if from his first years it had
not had an infinite object—God.

I make these indications with the rapidity which the
brevity of a letter requires; you can easily extend them
by applying them to various personages and situations
in the history of the Church in all ages. All men are
not like St Jerome and St Bernard; but all require to
be occupied and to love. If not well, they will be badly
occupied; idleness is generally nothing more than the
practice of vice. If good be not loved, evil shall. If
our hearts burn not with the flame which purifies, they
will burn with the flame which defiles.

I remain, &c., J. B.

XXV.

The Sceptic's Objection to the Miraculous.

MY ESTEEMED FRIEND,—The state of mind manifested by your last letter is satisfactory; for though you
still doubt of the truth of the Christian religion, you
would desire it were true; that is, you begin to feel
inclined to the side of religion. When we love an
object, considered even as purely ideal, it is not so
difficult to believe in its existence; just as the hatred
of a troublesome reality produces the desire of denying

it. The believer who abhors religious truth, is on the road to infidelity, and the infidel who loves it is on the way to faith.

It has been said, with profound truth, that our opinions are the offspring of our actions; or, in other words, that our understanding frequently places itself at the service of our heart. ✓Cherish, my dear friend, those benevolent dispositions towards religious truths; and allow yourself to be carried away by that soft inclination " which in the midst of scepticism frequently produces the illusion that you are a true believer." As you have had the fortune not to doubt of Providence, be persuaded it is this Providence that is leading you, in whose all-powerful hand are understandings and hearts. You lost the faith by following the disordered inclinations of your heart; and God wishes to bring you back to the faith through the inspirations of that same heart. Begin by loving religious truths, and soon you shall end by believing in them. They require but to be seen to be regarded without aversion; if they can only come into contact with a sincere soul, they are sure of triumphing. The divine spirit which animates them, communicates to them a holy attraction, which nothing but stony hearts can resist.

At the side of this disposition of mind, which fills me with consolation and hope, I have seen, with some wonder, what, with great serenity, you call a powerful reason which prevents your shaking off scepticism. The regularity of the laws which govern the world, so visible in all the phenomena which come under our experience, inspires you with an aversion to everything extraordinary, and makes you fear that whatever leaves the common order, though it be very beautiful and very sublime, should be limited to the regions of poetry. You are sorry there should be disagreement between the reality and those beautiful creations of prolific fancies and sublime sentiments ; "but no matter how fond of poetry, you would not exchange philosophy for it, though clothed in prosaic garb." Neither would I exchange the reality for any illusion the most beautiful human fancy could conceive ; I, too, love the truth, though dressed in prosaic costume ; but I do not comprehend that this truth should be always found as you indicate "in the ordinary—in the common—in what does not attract attention by its prodigies, or excite our wonder and enthusiasm ; but rather in what is real and substantial, and pursues its course with uniform regularity." I have no objection to your "discovering a cause for nocturnal noises, which poetical or frightened imaginations attribute to mysterious beings, in the wind, the rain, or the chirping of innocent birds, which never dreamed of being taken for malevolent genii ;" but when you stand animated with that *positive* philosophy before believers, and exclaim, "the ordinary, the ordinary, nothing else squares with the philosophical mind ;" I doubted whether the letter I was reading was from a person so enlightened as you, and felt a lively desire of revenge, which I hope to have to my complete satisfaction.

First of all, allow me to remark that the want of belief in extraordinary things, is not always a sure sign of much philosophy ; for this incredulity can spring from ignorance, in which case it is stubborn, tenacious, and little less than invincible. We meet this phenomenon in a striking manner when we converse with ill-instructed and proud people. As the lower orders have often heard that *there are many deceits in the world and big lies are told*, they take that vulgarity for criterion, and mercilessly apply it to everything out of the common order. I need not protest I do not reckon my enlightened adversary in the number of these ignorant people ; but as you insist on harmonising philosophy with the ordinary and the *common*, I could not resist the temptation of calling to mind a fact which repeatedly attracted my attention.

Paschal has said, with much truth, that there are two classes of ignorant people—those who are completely so, and those who, having attained the highest degree of wisdom, have a clear knowledge of their own ignorance. The saying is in some manner applicable to incredulity in extraordinary things. Truly wise men have an incredulity on this head, tempered by reason, and ever subject to the conditions of possibility which observation or the light of science has taught them. In general we might say, these men are incredulists, with some timidity, and not unfrequently incline to believe the extraordinary. When one penetrates into the abysses, as well of the physical as of the intellectual and moral world, the profundities he discovers are such, the mysteries he sees flitting among the shades, pierced by some rays of light, so numerous, that great thinkers —those who have approached the edge of these abysses,

contemplating their unfathomable depths—scarcely meet
with anything of which they presume to say, this has
been, this will not be, this is impossible. Such men do
not start at the word *extraordinary*, because they discover
in what appears the most ordinary phenomena, a multitude of extraordinary things ; or, to speak with more
exactness, a multitude of things the more incomprehensible the more ordinary they are.

The incredulity of ignorant people when extraordinary
things are mentioned, is very curious. If they hear of
an uncommon phenomenon, or of a law of nature which
produces something surprising, they apply their sovereign
criterion :—" In the world there are many deceits ; I'll
not be got to believe that ;" and foolishly shake their
heads with an indescribable satisfaction.

You see I am not very indulgent with the enemies of
the extraordinary ; but as these observations are not
applicable to a person like you, I shall enter on another
class of considerations about the ordinary and the extraordinary, without abandoning the sphere of facts.

You do not admit that God has spoken to men, but
prefer explaining the traditions of the human race by
the ordinary method of illusions, impostures, prevision
of legislators, or social necessities, &c., &c. All this is
very ordinary, and consequently satisfies you. Well
now ; do you believe I can discover in the root of this
itself, a very extraordinary thing, which all the philosophers in the world are not capable of explaining ?
Here it is; and I will give you to the end of the world
to answer my question, if you do not appeal to extra-

ordinary means. I do not require to remind you of the opinion of the most eminent philosophers regarding the impossibility of man's having invented language. The human race then has received this gift—from whom? Not certainly from the mute beings which surround us; behold, then, man communicating with a superior being, and receiving language from him. This does not belong to what you call ordinary and common; but unfortunately for infidels it is absolutely necessary that it should have occurred.

Another extraordinary thing :—Whence has man come? Do you admit the narrative of Moses? If you admit it, what difficulty do you find in the fact that God who created man, who taught him, who spoke to him once, should speak to him again? The extraordinary is found equally in one case as the other. If you do not admit the narrative of Moses, I again ask, whence has man come? From the bowels of the earth, and suddenly? This would be a most extraordinary thing. How, when once existing, has he been able to propagate? This is another thing, no less extraordinary. Has he been formed by successive development, passing through the different grades in the animal world, so that the ancestors of Bossuet, Newton, and Leibnitz were some illustrious monkeys, which in their turn were descended from terrestrial reptiles, or sea monsters, and so on to the lowest grade of living creatures? All these things, I believe, would be pretty extraordinary; and yet it is certain we must admit the extraordinary narrative of Moses, or some one similar, or else appeal to sudden apparitions, or successive transformations, things which are all very extraordinary.

The origin of the world, too, involves something which cannot enter into the channel of ordinary events. Appeal to what system you like—to God or chaos, to history or fable, to reason or to fancy ; it is of little importance to the present question ; we meet in all with the problem of the origin of things ; and neither their existence nor their order can be explained without something extraordinary.

Speaking frankly, I am sorry to have to employ this class of arguments to convince one who has studied the natural sciences. What is all nature but an immense mystery ? Have you ever meditated on life ? Has any philosopher ever comprehended in what that magic power consists, which walks by ways unknown ; which acts by incomprehensible means ; which moves, and agitates, and beautifies ; which produces sweetest pleasures, and causes insupportable torments ; which is within us and without us ; which is not found when sought, and presents itself when unthought of ; which propagates in the midst of corruption ; which incessantly becomes inflamed and extinguished in innumerable individuals ; which flits as an imperceptible flame, in the atmospheric regions, on the face, and in the bowels of the earth, in the currents of rivers, on the surface and in the depths of the ocean ? Is there not a mystery, and an incomprehensible mystery here ? Do you not see here—do you not palpably feel a something which does not come under that *ordinary thing* you would confound with philosophy ?

Electricity, galvanism, magnetism, certainly present extraordinary phenomena. Shall we deny because we do not comprehend them? And shall we delude ourselves into the belief that we comprehend them, simply because some of their effects are visible? When you fix your attention on those secrets of nature, do you not feel possessed by a profound feeling of astonishment? Have you never asked yourself what is there behind that veil with which nature covers her secrets? Have you not felt that small philosophy which cries *the ordinary, the ordinary,* disappear, and discovered the necessity of replacing it with the sublime idea that all is extraordinary? Instead of that little sentiment, which confounds the philosopher with the vulgar, and communicates to him a miserable incredulity with regard to extraordinary things, have you not experienced a secret inclination to see in all parts the stamp of the extraordinary?

On a serene night, when the firmament is displayed to our eyes like a blue mantle set with diamonds, fix your gaze on that sublime spectacle. What is there in those profundities—what are those luminous bodies which have shone during long ages in the university of space, and pursue their majestic course with ineffable regularity? Who has spread that creamy belt, called by astronomers the Milky Way, and which in reality is an immense zone, studded with bodies whose size and distances cannot enter into our imagination? What is there in those infinite spaces where the telescope daily discovers new worlds—in those spaces whose portals are at a distance of which we can form no idea? The nearest stars present to our view, not their present situation, but that which they had many years ago. Light travels at the rate of 55,660 leagues and something more a second ; and, nevertheless, it has been calculated the luminous ray of the nearest star cannot reach us in less than ten years ; what will be the case with the most distant ? Do you think that what is taking place in the *Nebulæ*—the revolutions being verified in those profundities without end—can be perfectly explained with the little formula—*the ordinary ?*

The greatest men have been religious, and no wonder ; in the physical as in the moral world, such grandeur, such august shades, such a source of elevated thoughts and sublime inspirations are met with, that the soul feels profoundly moved, and discovers in all a species of religious solemnity. Clearness is the exception, mystery the rule ; littleness exists in this or that appearance ; but in the essence of things there is a grandeur which exceeds all consideration. We do not feel that grandeur—that mystery—because we do not meditate ; but as soon as man concentrates his thoughts, and reflects on that grand total of beings in whose immensity he is submerged, and meditates on that flame he feels burning within him, and which is in the scale of things as a spark of light in an ocean of fire ; he finds himself seized by a profound feeling in which pride mingles with depression, and pleasure with solemn dread. Oh, then, that philosophy which talks of *the ordinary*—of *the common*—and has a ridiculous horror of everything extraordinary or mysterious, appears little indeed ! What ! is everything that surrounds us, everything that exists, everything we see, everything we are, anything else, forsooth, but a union of dread mysteries?

Pardon me, my dear friend, if my pen has run away with me, and I have almost forgotten I was writing a letter. You cannot, however, accuse me of having run into imaginary worlds, for I have not departed from the reality. You provoked me by inculcating the necessity of adhering to *the ordinary, the common, the plain,* leaving aside extraordinary and mysterious things; and I have found myself compelled to interrogate the universe, not the ideal or the fictitious, but the real one before our eyes; and it is not my fault if that universe, that reality, is so grand and mysterious that it cannot be contemplated without a fit of enthusiasm.

Allow us to believe in extraordinary things; with this we do not contradict true philosophy, but act in accordance with its highest inspirations. Let him who does not believe—who is not satisfied with the motives of credibility—raise what difficulties he likes against the truth of our doctrines; but let him take care not to upbraid us with our belief in incomprehensible mysteries, nor accuse us on that score of want of philosophy, for then he undoubtedly improves our cause; the infidel is confounded with the vulgar, and the most eminent philosophers are on the side of the Catholic.

I remain, your affectionate friend,   J. B.

THE END.

PRINTED BY W. B. KELLY, 8 GRAFTON STREET, DUBLIN.